Critical
Regionalism

**The University of
North Carolina Press**
Chapel Hill

Critical Regionalism

Connecting Politics and Culture
in the American Landscape
Douglas Reichert Powell

Designed by Rebecca Gimenez
Set in Minion by Keystone Typesetting, Inc.
Manufactured in the United States of America

Publication of this work has been supported in
part by Columbia College Chicago.

The paper in this book meets the guidelines for
permanence and durability of the Committee
on Production Guidelines for Book Longevity of
the Council on Library Resources.

Library of Congress Cataloging-in-Publication Data
Reichert Powell, Douglas.
Critical regionalism : connecting politics and culture
in the American landscape / Douglas Reichert Powell.
p. cm.
Includes bibliographical references and index.
ISBN-13: 978-0-8078-3091-8 (cloth: alk. paper)
ISBN-13: 978-0-8078-5794-6 (pbk.: alk. paper)
1. Regionalism—United States—Case studies. 2. Politics and
culture—United States—Case studies. 3. Appalachian
Region, Southern—Politics and government. 4. Appalachian
Region, Southern—Geography. 5. Regionalism—
Appalachian Region, Southern. 6. Regionalism—
Tennessee—Johnson City. 7. Politics and culture—
Appalachian Region, Southern. 8. Politics and culture—
Tennessee—Johnson City. 9. American literature—History
and criticism. 10. Film criticism—United States. I. Title.
E179.5.R45 2007
911'.75—dc22   2006027321

cloth   11 10 09 08 07   5 4 3 2 1
paper   11 10 09 08 07   5 4 3 2 1

For Pegeen, Charlie,
and Elizabeth

Contents

Illustrations and Maps

Illustrations

Maps

Acknowledgments

Critical regionalism requires thinking about texts geographically, discerning the connections they draw among often disparate and far-flung places. That is not hard to do with this book, which has been written and revised as I have changed homes and schools and jobs five times in the last dozen years; completed degrees, presented papers, published articles, and taught courses; and, most important, forged a marriage and raised children. I can read this manuscript and see a map that connects Johnson City, Tennessee, with Boston, Massachusetts, with Oxford, Ohio, with Durham, North Carolina, with Oak Park, Illinois. Along the way I've enjoyed the friendship and support of many good, smart, fun people, too numerous to list completely, but they populate the landscape of this text and have helped fashion all its most appealing features.

Special thanks are due to all my new colleagues at the Department of English, Columbia College, in the region of Chicagoland, for making a "fit" for me and my projects. Chairperson Ken Daley has provided support for the completion of the production of the manuscript. I am particularly grateful for the support of the School of Liberal Arts and Sciences and Dean Cheryl Johnson-Odim. At Duke University in Durham, I learned much about placemaking from Joe Harris and Van Hillard, began an ongoing conversation about Appalachia with Phil Troutman, and enjoyed hanging out with Kurt Hagardorn. A course development grant from the Center for Documentary Studies, Duke University, sponsored the writing course I describe at the end of chapter 5, and summer research grants from the University Writing Program supported additional research as I revised. In Oxford, I benefited from the good nature and critical consciousness of Kevin Mahoney, John Paul Tassoni, and Rich Zumkhawala-Cook, the unstinting aid and assistance of Bob Johnson and Kate Ronald, and the hospitality and chops of Ron Curran. At Northeastern University in Boston, I acquired the analytical tools and the critical distance necessary to formulate the earliest versions of the ideas that are this book and that have continued to shape me as a writer and a teacher. For that I am indebted first and foremost to Wayne Franklin, as well as Michael Brown, Michael Ryan, and Susan Wall. Along the way, colleagues and collaborators from various places have read and responded to and otherwise assisted in my work, including (among so many others!) Tony Harkins, Rich Heyman, Katherine Ledford, Peter Mortensen, and Jerry Williamson. Pat Arnow provided feedback on an early version of chapter 1 that appeared in *Southern Exposure* 24:3 (1986), and editor Steven Hoelscher and anonymous reviewers advised a subsequent revision, which appeared in *Historical Geography* 26 (1998). The staffs of Duke University Archives and Rare Book, Manuscript, and Special Collections Library have been most helpful, especially Elizabeth Dunn and Tom Harkins. Thanks also to the staff of the Archives of Appalachia, East Tennessee State University. I am especially indebted to the anonymous reviewers of this manuscript, whose voluminous and detailed critiques transformed the work entirely. Sian Hunter at the University of North Carolina Press has patiently and persistently seen this project through to its present form.

The concept of this book came into being when I returned to Johnson City in 1990 to live and work for three years. At East Tennessee State University, I learned a lot from folks like Jack Higgs about how to look at my immediate surroundings with generosity and good humor, and I had the great good fortune to work with the Center for Appalachian Studies and Services and Jean Haskell. Though I discuss some of the conflicts ETSU has had with its surroundings later in this book, these people showed me how a university can engage with its neighborhood with a caring, collaborative spirit. Meanwhile, in Johnson City, I fell in with a circle of creative and funny folks who got me to thinking how much potential there is in the offbeat places of American culture, how there is no need to make your local culture feel small by measuring it against other places. Thank you, home folks, especially Ginny Alden, Robert Alfonso, Duncan Anderson, Ashley Bowen, Brian and the Nightmares, George Buck, Rev. Lattie Collins III, Mary Edwards, John Hart, Billy Malone, Scott Pleasant, Julie Yong, and Phil E. Young. It was more than fun, as I hope this book shows. The Cabinboys, Frank Alden, Travis Hardaway, James Moody, and Chris Schmitt, have been invaluable in helping me maintain my creative connections to East Tennessee; our work over the past seven years is the soundtrack for this book, an enactment of its theories, and the cabin where we've done it may be the single most beautiful spot on earth. And speaking of cabins, my mother- and father-in-law, Dick and Sara Reichert, are due special thanks for sharing their cottage in Twin Bridge, Wisconsin, at key moments during the making of this manuscript. They have, through their generosity and care, helped me add northeastern Wisconsin to my map of the world's best landscapes.

As I got in the car to leave Johnson City for Boston, my dad, Harry Powell, said to me, "Don't forget where you came from." And I never have. Harry, Janet, Wade, and Allison Powell taught me what a good place is before I knew I was learning it. Now I am trying to make a good place of my own, and I have the greatest partner I could ever wish for to do it. Pegeen, you make my world better than I could ever have hoped; Charlie and Elizabeth, you show me that this world can be better than I could ever imagine.

Critical
Regionalism

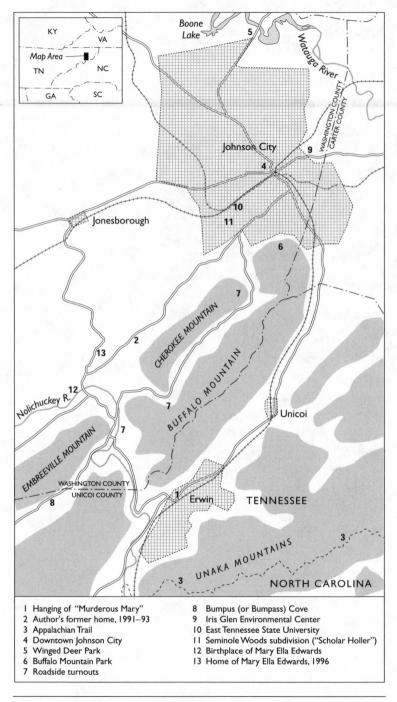

Boone Lake

5

Watauga River

Johnson City

9

WASHINGTON COUNTY
CARTER COUNTY

4

10

11

Jonesborough

6

7

CHEROKEE MOUNTAIN

2

13

BUFFALO MOUNTAIN

7

Nolichuckey R.

12

7

Unicoi

EMBREEVILLE MOUNTAIN

7

WASHINGTON COUNTY
UNICOI COUNTY

8

1   Erwin   TENNESSEE

3

UNAKA MOUNTAINS

3

3

NORTH CAROLINA

1 Hanging of "Murderous Mary"
2 Author's former home, 1991–93
3 Appalachian Trail
4 Downtown Johnson City
5 Winged Deer Park
6 Buffalo Mountain Park
7 Roadside turnouts

8 Bumpus (or Bumpass) Cove
9 Iris Glen Environmental Center
10 East Tennessee State University
11 Seminole Woods subdivision ("Scholar Holler")
12 Birthplace of Mary Ella Edwards
13 Home of Mary Ella Edwards, 1996

Johnson City, Tennessee, and its environs

Introduction: There's Something about Mary
The Practice of Critical Regionalism

The process of preparing this book has been bracketed by two hideous catastrophes: the September 11 attack and the flooding of New Orleans by Hurricane Katrina. Commentators, critics, and historians have already begun the work of drawing out the parallels and the distinctions between these two landmark historical events, a process of debate and discussion that will, I am sure, be ongoing for the foreseeable future. This volume is unlikely to resolve any questions raised by this discussion; I address neither topic directly. But I think the work I present here is relevant to both of these events inasmuch as both highlight the extraordinary difficulty of understanding the relationships of people and places across space. Both of these events have set off soul-searching and reflection about our severely attenuated ability to understand, interpret, and represent the complex skein of political and cultural interconnections between any given point on the landscape, and to make, collectively, effective plans to respond to the exigencies these interactions create.

9/11 not only revealed in the most brutal terms the implication of the United States in global affairs but also reasserted the symbolic and material centrality of the metropolis in American culture: collective grieving over the loss of the Twin Towers was coupled to the total collapse of information and transportation structures around the continent and the world, demonstrating the ways that our cultural relationships to the landscape are intimately tied with our physical (and virtual) negotiation of it. The disaster of New Orleans, the full extent of which is still grimly unfolding as I write, shows us a rich cultural center, constituted but also vexed by its situation at the mouth of a vast, continental watershed. It has become clear quickly that Hurricane Katrina's devastation is not purely a natural disaster but an event fueled by material relations (such as those that produce global warming) and cultural-political ones (those that redline poor, black neighborhoods in southern cities). Each event has become a locus of incredible amounts and varieties of cultural production as well. Just as uncounted images of 9/11 continue to circulate in the United States and around the world, changing meaning as they enter into different spaces and places, images of Katrina and its aftermath now multiply daily, forming a context for mourning, for aid, for political debate, and many other forms of cultural and political work.

Both of these events challenge our understandings of spaces and places at a bewildering variety of scales and in a range of tensions: local and global, marginal and peripheral, interior and exterior, foreign and domestic. People in eastern Kentucky adopt the Twin Towers as a symbol of their commitment to their place. People in Minnesota experience gas shortages because of the closure of ports in the Gulf of Mexico. People from the United Kingdom train in Pakistan to undermine the United States by attacking England. People from the Gulf Coast become residents of megalithic sports stadiums around the nation. A Philadelphia radio show interviews a Chicago musician living in New York about the affect of the Gulf Coast disaster on delta blues. With all these convergences and concatenations of place, filtered, of course, through the economic and geographical complexities of the mass media, all attempts to construct understandings of these events will necessarily be partial, single paths through a vast thicket of discursive relationships. In this volume I argue that regionalism, despite traditionally being used to describe, define, and isolate networks of places and spaces, can provide a rhetorical basis for making claims about how spaces and places are connected to spatially and conceptually broader patterns of meaning. In a time when the breadth of crisis can be so vividly revealed to us, critical regionalism can be a way to assert what the relationships among places should be.

This book is not about a specific region, though I will return to a specific place, Johnson City, Tennessee, and a particular region, the southern Appalachians, throughout the study. It is instead about regionalism, the study of what regions are, how they are made, and what they are for. Postmodern currents across the humanities and social sciences, from literary studies to history to anthropology to geography, have made a scholarly commonplace of the notion that places are the outcome, not the backdrop, of social, cultural, political, and economic activity. This study is in part an attempt to consolidate and connect this line of thinking as it relates specifically to the notion of region in the contemporary United States.

The idea of region is in many ways categorically different from other conceptualizations of place, like home, community, city, state, and nation, in that region must refer not to a specific site but to a larger network of sites; region is always a relational term (even when it appears not to be). The boundaries of a region never have the juridical, insulating force of other kinds of governmental divisions. Regions never have flags: even the identification of the Confederate flag with the contemporary U.S. South traces back to that region's brief experience as a nation-state. Because of its inherent sense of geographical scope, a region can never, ultimately, be an isolated space, withdrawn from larger cultural forces and processes. Even when regional definitions are used to isolate, to idolize, or to stigmatize a network of places, as is often the case with Appalachia, these demarcations are always in relation to broader patterns of history, politics, and culture. The notion of Appalachia as a cultural remnant, for example, at once disconnects the mountain region from the rest of U.S. culture, but also places it (quite contentiously) in a specific relationship. The very idea of a remnant evokes an isolated part and a larger whole. And, of course, no definition of region—whether it is offered by a scholar, a government commission, a novelist, a Hollywood film—exists in a vacuum. At any site on the landscape, multiple definitions of place are continually in play and at work, sometimes convivially and sometimes antagonistically. Ideas of property, of homeland, of natural resource, of infrastructure; of city, county, school district, economic development zone, environmental hazard; of shit-hole, unspoiled paradise, dullsville; of wildness and weirdness and domestication and discipline—all swirl and interconnect and contend and contest in any given space.

When we talk about a region, we are talking not about a stable, boundaried, autonomous place but about a cultural history, the cumulative, generative effect of the interplay among the various, competing definitions of that region. And in so doing, we are, inevitably, contributing to that cultural history, participating in the ongoing creation of regional identities. The term "Appalachia" illustrates this point: "Appalachia" is a container for a tangled and often fractious history that, arguably, began when Spanish map makers in Florida wrote "Appalachee" across their depiction of what is now southern Georgia, and that continues on today perhaps most prominently in the addition and subtraction of counties to the Appalachian Regional Commission's regional map, which sweeps from the Mohawk Valley of upstate New York to counties in western Mississippi. And with each act of definition, each new map of the region, the question of what Appalachia is, exactly, is not resolved but further complicated.

It matters, too, not only how the map is drawn but who is drawing it and why. Generally, regions are evoked unreflectively, reaffirming conventional wisdom about the place—but this, too, is a contribution to those commonplaces. Often, however, when a region is evoked, described, or defined, it is for some particular purpose: to achieve certain changes in the physical or cultural landscape, often changing one by changing the other. The "Piedmont Carolinas" region popularized by James Buchanan Duke in the late nineteenth century was depicted in promotional materials as a capitalist's utopia, populated by "willing labor, unhampered by any artificial restrictions on output; native born of old pioneer stock and not imbued by un-American ideas or ideals" (quoted in Tullos 170). The industrialization of the region these images encouraged, and the deindustrialization that has ensued, have reshaped the culture and the character of the area, drawing its communities into complex, shifting relationships with the nation and the globe.

Regionalism as a scholarly area of interest or an aesthetic school of thought has itself been a remarkably diffuse concept. Regionalism is a term that has currency, but different values, in political science, urban planning, architecture and design, history, literature, and the visual arts. Eighty-seven Library of Congress subject headings contain the words region or regionalism. Like the regional landscapes that are its object of study, regionalism is a loosely and variously defined zone that cuts across the boundaries of the academic landscape.

The core idea of this study, that a region is not a thing so much as a cultural history, an ongoing rhetorical and poetic construction, is not necessarily a new one for any arm of regional studies. In the study of regionalism in the United States, however, the various critical and scholarly endeavors have clustered not only around academic subfields but also around the regions themselves. Both as a scholarly discourse and as a programmatic, curricular, or institutional reality, New England Studies, Appalachian Studies, Southern Studies, Western Studies all engage in often-parallel but less-often collaborative projects. Regional scholarship has, fittingly, tended to develop ideas along separate strands, defined by the area of geographical interest rather than a more cosmopolitan "school of thought." Nevertheless, in U.S. regional studies, geographer Kathleen Morrissey in the Pacific Northwest, historian Patricia Nelson Limerick in the West, literary critic Barbara Ladd in the South, eco-critic Kent Ryden in New England, historian John Alexander Williams in Appalachia, and geographers Frank and Deborah Popper in the Midwest have all called for and enacted scholarship on regional culture that approaches the idea of region as a rich, complicated, and dynamic cultural construct rather than a static, stable geophysical entity.

Given its recurring interest in the Appalachian region, this study might well be seen as a response to assertions by Appalachianists Herb Reid and Betsy Taylor that are typical of this emergent sense of the need for a broader and more synthetic regionalist praxis:

Today, it is more important than ever before to develop . . . regional perspectives and projects in terms of a global regional studies that has as its lodestar a diversified and democratized civic and environmental commons. . . . A regional perspective gives scope and resources to tackle problems that are insoluble at the local level. Against the dislocating forces of globalization, a regional perspective grounds thought and action in the holistic particularity of place and direct accountability to communities of persons and nature. (26–27)

To rise to this challenge requires, I believe, not only a resistance to the disciplinary boundaries that inhibit the kind of "intersectoral, integrated analysis" that Reid and Taylor suggest is central to the practice of critical regionalism (27), but also the geographical boundaries that have balkanized regional studies into relatively self-contained, if not parochial, areas of interest, which nonetheless present strong affinities in their sense of the need for more expansive perspectives and principles.

The common thread through this emerging strand of scholarship is a shifting of emphasis away from the products of regional culture, the definitions of region themselves and all their representative artifacts, to the processes by which ideas about regions come into being and become influential. Instead of asking whether a particular version of region is valid or invalid, authentic or not, this new regional scholarship asks whose interests are served by a given version of region. In short, the emphasis is not on what regions are but why they are that way, on what they do as much as what has been done to them.

To advance that line of inquiry in this study, I hope to create the kind of critical intersection where these coexisting and overlapping revisions of regionalism can find common ground. That is what I am trying to do by putting forward the term "critical regionalism" as a methodological umbrella for this work that recognizes (in ways more cosmopolitan critical and aesthetic communities sometimes do not) that regionalism is not necessarily parochialism. Critical regionalism thus involves tracing a path across the disciplines as well as the dimensions of the place under consideration. It is about being aware that writing about a region creates and sustains a definition of that region and, in so doing, deliberately defines the region to create new, potentially revelatory perspectives on it. It is about being aware of the fact that one's own work participates in that broader constellation of discourse about the region. The path that the practice of critical regionalism draws across this intellectual landscape is designed to lead toward a view of the best possible version of the region from among all the versions that are out there (whether or not it actually gets there).

The precise map that I draw across the intellectual and physical terrain will become clear as the work progresses. What I am creating in this study is not an authoritative map of Appalachia or a definitive statement of what a region is, but a model of region making as a practice of cultural politics. That is why I borrow from urban planner Albert Guttenberg the term "social invention" and use this term throughout the study to describe what critical regionalism does. More deliberate than a passive social construction, but less instrumental than direct forms of social action, critical regionalism self-consciously shapes an understanding of the spatial dimensions of cultural politics in order to support projects of change. The self-consciousness demands an awareness of the fact that critical regionalism is an academic project, and academia's own spatial and political idiosyncrasies must be accounted for. While academia's resources of time, materials, and access to means of cultural production facilitate critical regionalist projects, the impact of the attenuated cosmopolitanism that is such a powerful force in academic placemaking constrains this project in ways significant enough to deal with at some length. Whatever forces act to isolate academia from the local scene, however, colleges and universities offer one very powerful opportunity for social change: access to students, and to the opportunity to teach them ways to invent their own descriptions of the world. So critical regionalism must be, ultimately, a pedagogy, one that teaches students how to draw their own regional maps connecting their experience to that of others near and far, both like and unlike themselves.

The Hanging of Mary, a Circus Elephant

At one point during the writing of this book, I found myself teaching at the Hamilton, Ohio, branch campus of Miami University. As I sat in the faculty lounge preparing my notes for the day's class, I realized that another small group of teachers was discussing a story that I knew well—the strange tale of a circus elephant who, in 1916, was hung for murder in the small town of Erwin, Tennessee, only a few miles from my hometown, Johnson City. The story is so odd and singular that I could not help but take notice, and eventually I sidled over to the group and said, "You know, I'm from the area where that story took place." One of the discussants turned to me and said, "Where are you from, exactly?" When I replied that I grew up in Johnson City, he motioned to the rest of the table. "Oh, we're all from Johnson City."

I should have known. That story, the Tale of Murderous Mary, is a staple of the contemporary oral tradition of that area of upper east Tennessee. Interestingly, the people I overheard telling the story were not

"Execution of 'Murderous Mary' / Sparks Bros. Man-Killing Elephant / at Erwin, Tenn., Sept. 13, 1916." Photographer and date unknown; suspected to be fraudulent. From Appalachian Photographic Archives, courtesy of Archives and Special Collections, East Tennessee State University, Johnson City.

telling it to someone who had never heard it, but to each other, a ritual all the more important because the telling took place far from home. They were, I assert, constructing a region. Regions are not so much places themselves but ways of describing relationships among places. These descriptions serve particular purposes for the people doing the describing. Knowing this might help us develop strategies for devising regions, ways of linking together the experiences and struggles of diverse groups of people and places, that help us confront and respond to the cultural and political conflicts of our times. This deliberate use of region as a way to envision and critique relationships among people and places and envision better alternatives is what I term a "critical regionalism." This book will explain that idea, but I would like to begin that explanation by asking a few questions about "Murderous Mary" and her strange tale.

Mary was a circus elephant, billed in a 12 September 1916 ad in the *Johnson City Staff* as "THE LARGEST LIVING LAND ANIMAL ON EARTH" ("Sparks" 4), performing in Sparks World Famous Shows, a circus that was touring the South in the fall of 1916. As was customary with traveling shows of this period, the Sparks circus lost and gained a fair number of workers as it roamed from town to town on a ten-car train, and when the show reached the small town of St. Paul, Virginia, on 11 September, an itinerant laborer named Walter "Red" Eldridge was hired as an elephant handler. The next day, Eldridge was killed by Mary during a parade through the streets of Kingsport, Tennessee, the show's next stop south. According to most accounts, the elephant paused on the parade route to nab a watermelon rind from the gutter, and when Eldridge struck her on the head to urge her along, she coiled him in her trunk and threw him into a concession stand. Then, as W. H. Coleman, an eyewitness at the age of sixteen, told folklorist Thomas Burton, "when he hit the ground the elephant just walked over and set his [*sic*] foot on [Eldridge's] head . . . and blood and brains and stuff just squirted all over the street" (Burton 2).

The crowd demanded the elephant be killed on the spot, and a local blacksmith apparently shot at Mary several times without inflicting serious harm. Circus proprietor Charlie Sparks, perhaps attempting to protect an investment valued at anywhere from $8,000 to $20,000 (Burton 1), talked the crowd out of killing Mary then and there, claiming there was not a gun in the region that could pierce her hide. And curiously enough, the show went on that night, and Mary played her normal role "without having exhibited the slightest indication of 'bad temper'" according to the *Johnson City Staff* (quoted in Burton 3).

However, the notoriety of the incident, coupled with rumors that Mary had killed trainers and handlers before, spread through the region with the next day's papers. Soon Sparks World Famous Shows was barred from bringing Mary to Johnson City or to nearby Rogersville, two stops due up soon after the Kingsport incident (Price 20). Rumors circulated that an angry mob from Kingsport was bringing a Civil War–vintage cannon to finish off Mary, having failed to do so by electrocuting her with 44,000 volts (Price 21–22). Though the exact details are unclear, some contemporaries recall that the state of Tennessee had begun to seek some official order for the animal's destruction (Burton 3).

So when Sparks reached the show's next stop in the railroad boom-town of Erwin, Tennessee, Mary's fate was sealed. The home of a Clinch-field Railroad repair facility, Erwin had the equipment necessary to ex-ecute a circus elephant in the form of a 100-ton crane car. Surely the value of the spectacle was not lost on Charlie Sparks, who had the elephants paraded out to the rail yard in between the matinee and the evening performances, whereupon Mary was strung up from the crane on a 7/8″ chain.

Five feet off the ground, however, the chain broke, and Mary fell to earth, causing panic amid the crowd of anywhere from several hundred to several thousand (Burton 6–7) who had gathered to witness the execu-tion. Before the elephant could react, however, workers quickly strung a stronger chain around her neck, lifted her off the ground, and hung her until she was dead. Her body was buried in the rail yard, and the circus went on to play Johnson City the next night, and Rogersville after that, before passing out of the local landscape and into public memory.

That is the end of the story, but really just the beginning of The Story, the Tale of Murderous Mary. As Cindy McAfee writes in a contemporary account in *Kingsport Times-News*, "Her story is told by local newspapers every few years and by old codgers in Erwin every few days" (1). A vertical file in the Archives of Appalachia at East Tennessee State University bears out McAfee's assertion about area newspaper coverage: in addition to the original reporting of the hanging in the *Johnson City Staff* on and around 14 September 1916, the file (which is itself only a partial collection) in-cludes articles retelling the story that appear in the *Johnson City Press Chronicle* in 1936, 1968, and 1999; in the *Knoxville Journal* in 1960; in the *Kingsport Times-News* in 1982; and in the *Elizabethton (Tenn.) Star* in 2000. Furthermore, a *Johnson City Press* article in 1993 notes that a local television station, wJHL, created a special program on the incident featur-ing an interview with the last surviving eyewitness, railroad worker Guard Banner, then ninety-three years old (" 'Murderous Mary' " 3).

The incident receives periodic national media attention as well: the vertical file includes write-ups in the *Chicago Saturday Blade* (1919), the

National Enquirer (1979), and the *Atlanta Journal-Constitution* (1999). "Ripley's Believe It or Not" featured the story in its daily cartoon on 29 August 1938, and the *Johnson City Press* reported in 1999 that Dick Cusack, father of actors Joan and John Cusack, was shopping a screenplay based on the incident called "Wrong Turn at County Road F" ("Elephant Hanging" 3). "Murderous Mary" has even found her way into academic culture: not only does material on the hanging form an important part of the Burton-Manning Collection of the aforementioned Archives of Appalachia, a collection that provided the basis for Burton's 1971 journal article on the incident, but the vertical file also includes a 1990 student essay by Wilma Strong titled "Erwin's Claim to Fame," written for a Composition 2 class at East Tennessee State in 1990. And somewhere out there, someone might still know the tune to "The Ballad of Murderous Mary," which musically describes how "five thousand gathered in the gloom / to see her hoisted on a boom."

There's something about the tale of Murderous Mary that speaks to residents of upper east Tennessee in such a way that it demands retelling again and again, in many different genres and forms, even to an audience that already knows the tale. There's something about it that can motivate someone "from there," overhearing the story, to speak up as I did and assert his own proximity to the awful events, to interrupt and say "I'm from there." Knowledge of the incident, manifested in the ability to recount it, helps constitute one's identity as a member of that place (indeed, that is part of the reason I am telling the story to you now). But the relationship of place to people works both ways: telling the story is the practice that sustains the identity of the place it comes out of. The story of Murderous Mary shows how a community, a region, and its constituents can gain definition from something that is singular to the point of being bizarre and even, in this case, rather brutal.

Over time, though, the brutality of this story seems to drop out in the repeated retelling, giving way to a certain bemusement and novelty— believe it or not! as Ripley puts it. This type of local eccentricity is, in my experience, what people often think of when they try to envision what defines a place—especially an out-of-the-way place like Erwin, Tennessee. Sometimes these peculiarities can be a bad thing—think *Bad Day at Black Rock*, the flagship of the "town-with-a-dark-secret" line of films. But they also tend to become an almost endearing eccentricity, which earns a community a place in offbeat guidebooks to kitsch, like *Roadside America*, which includes Mary's story on its Web site in a special section on elephant deaths ("Elephant Graveyard"), connecting the circulatory patterns of the tale to cyberspace.

Introduction

As my encounter in the faculty lounge suggests, however, the story is not just part of the construction of a yokel stereotype, inflicted on the long-suffering locals by out-of-towners, either. The legend enjoys at least enough popularity as a mark of community distinctiveness that a store in downtown Erwin opened a few years ago called "Hanging Elephant Antiques." That it is an antique store that goes by this name is fitting, though. As I argue throughout this study, one of the problems of the "local distinctiveness" approach to defining a regional place is that building community identity around eccentricities and anomalies of legend ties a place inevitably to its pasts, almost as if just one thing of note ever happened there. When you define a place by looking backwards, it's no wonder when communities like Erwin are perceived as "backwards." Often this view is at least ostensibly a "positive" one, invoking rural nostalgia and a longing for bygone days—even when, ironically, those bygone days are, on deeper reflection, disturbing and violent. The elephant hanging itself becomes, in the "Believe It or Not" frame of mind, an event that is disconnected from larger patterns of history, politics, and culture, a perspective that allows us to believe that out-of-the-way places are themselves disconnected from larger patterns of history, politics, and culture, even in their weird, violent outbursts.

Instead of becoming the focus of critical scrutiny, then, the story becomes a matter of a mere referendum, to be believed, or not. This disconnection from the dynamics of culture and history can be viewed from a conservative standpoint as an essentially positive thing, preserving wholesome small-town values against the expansion of a jumbled, postmodern cosmopolitanism, or from a more liberal point of view as a small-minded, parochial resistance to the expansion of postmodern cosmopolitanism: both interpretations stipulate that life outside the cosmopolis is inert, unchanging. Of these versions of place and region, literary critic Roberto Dainotto is quite right to charge, "To claim that culture springs from a place means, after all, to naturalize a process of historical formation, and along with history to negate the historical forces, struggles, and tensions that made a culture what it is" (2). Regionalism, though a somewhat more elaborate mystification, is thus, in Dainotto's terms, "a pastoral sensibility untouched by the evils of history. . . . To put it bluntly, regionalism is the figure of an otherness that is, essentially, otherness *from*, and against, history" (9).

But upper east Tennessee, and southern Appalachia more generally, are not exempt from the larger, historical forces of change that shape life elsewhere. What is needed, and what this study attempts to develop, are the kinds of interpretive tools that can look through and within the cultural constructions that insist on that disconnection. Through the reinvigorated version of "critical regionalism" I discuss in this book, adapted from landscape studies to cultural criticism, we can see the ways that the very practices of place construction that seem to exempt regional spaces from broader cultural conflicts are themselves implicated in the patterns of change they seem to defy. The ahistorical, even antihistorical regionalism Dainotto attacks is only one kind of region, one way of constructing region, and ironically it is a cultural practice with a history of its own. However much the story of Murderous Mary appears to divorce Erwin, east Tennessee, Appalachia, or the South from the rest of American history, the story is itself a growing, changing, conflicted cultural artifact, just like the region it helps define. And looking critically at the story itself provides a crucial starting place for understanding how the identity of the place is rooted in conflict and change as much as in permanence, stability, and continuity.

First of all, the story itself, and its status as a defining narrative of life in upper east Tennessee, is a focus not of universal admiration and assent but of a variety of local interpretations and attitudes. The sort of bemusement that I encountered in and shared with my Ohio colleagues, all of us expatriates of a sort, recalling a favorite local peculiarity, is certainly not shared uniformly by folks back home. Far from relishing the kitsch value of the tale, Hilda Padgett of the Unicoi Historical Society (in Erwin's home county) claims that the story has maligned the local folks: "It made the people from Erwin look like a bunch of bloodthirsty rednecks" (quoted in Brown 1). Ruth Piper, an Erwin resident, also takes the story in a more serious light, as she unsuccessfully proposed to the Erwin Bicentennial Committee that the town erect a statue and fountain memorializing, perhaps even mourning the event (Schroeder 21). While the "local distinctiveness" of the story is unquestionable, the nature of the distinction it imparts, and the way public memory and public space should be shaped as a result, is a matter of dispute, even—perhaps especially—at the local level.

This aspect details one of the cornerstone claims of this study: that "senses" of place and region are not so much essential qualities, imparted by singular events, practices, or topographical features, as they are ongoing debates and discourses that coalesce around particular geographical spaces. Furthermore, it is by looking at those features of a place that seem, at least superficially, to be the permanent stable markers of its identity that we can begin to see the dynamic, evolving, and rhetorical qualities that create and sustain what has often been taken (reductively) to be an ineffable or ethereal, sensory property: the "sense of place."

While that affective description of a place's evocative power underscores each place's singularity, the very factors that lend a place that "sense," for example, the story of Murderous Mary, can be examined for the factors, elements, discourses, and materials that bind the experiences of individual places to each other. Furthermore, the ties that bind the experiences of places together into larger patterns of history, politics, and culture can be discerned through scrutiny of the networks of cultural artifacts, like the trails of articles about and discussions of the meaning of the Murderous Mary story I sketched.

This perspective allows us to see the story of Murderous Mary in a very different light. The story is often, as in much of the press coverage I have examined here, taken to be the unique touchstone (some would say albatross) of the town of Erwin. But we might also see it in more broadly regional terms—a shift in perspective clearly justified by the fact that the story is a part of public memory and public discourse not just in Erwin but in many communities in upper east Tennessee and beyond—at least as far away as the Hamilton, Ohio, campus of Miami University. Although the story itself has become representative in many ways of Erwin, the action of the story moves across the region, from St. Paul, Virginia, where handler Red Eldridge hired on to the Sparks show, to Kingsport, where Mary killed him, to Johnson City and Rogersville, where public pressure mounted against Mary, to Erwin, where the execution took place less because of some particular animus of the people of Erwin toward Mary but because the facilities existed to carry out the task.

Erwin's rail facilities are themselves a kind of metonymy for the connections between that community and the rest of the world: the town and the rail yard lies at the mouth of the formidable Nolichuckey Gorge, a deep and narrow notch in the southern Appalachians through which the railroad passes to this day, on its winding trek through the mountains to points south and east. In this sense the community is a portal, a point of connection rather than disconnection, a status that continues by car and truck today, as Erwin is the first town of any size drivers on Interstate 23 encounter as they head over Sam's Gap out of North Carolina into Tennessee. The railroad points to historical as well as geographical connections: as a railroad town, Erwin is perhaps less a part of the history of small-town stability and continuity in Appalachia as it is a study of succession and change. Like Johnson City ten miles up the line, Erwin is a relatively young town. The coming of the railroad and that rail yard where Mary died gave the community prominence and prosperity sufficient to supplant other, more established communities nearby in Limestone Cove that were part of the earliest networks of white settlements in the area as social and commercial centers (Hsiung 63). That the story itself evinces some concerns or anxieties about the new networks of technology that were spreading across the nation and the globe during this period may be clearest in the (apparently spurious) inclusion of the idea that Kingsport citizens tried to electrocute Mary before sending her to Erwin to be hanged. This detail, which persists from Burton's oral histories from eyewitnesses of the event to Price's 1992 book version of the story, seems very likely to be a conflation of Mary's story with Thomas Edison's more widely known 1903 execution of another female elephant, "Topsy," which was documented in a nationally circulated short film designed to warn Americans about the dangers of alternating current. The evolving intertextuality of Mary's story, manifested in confusions and conflations of this sort, insists on not only the heterogeneous nature of the place itself but its complicated interpenetration by other narratives, concepts, conflicts, and concerns, its status as a site of convergence and conjuncture.

If we can glimpse, through Mary's story, a new sense of Erwin's geographical, economic, and technological interconnectedness with other places, we can also move toward seeing its cultural relationships as well. Indeed, this story would not be possible if it were not for the fact of the circus, a cultural form that relies not only on physical interconnections among communities, making use of that railroad that made Erwin an interface between the mountain region and the broader world as it toured the region, but also rhetorics of connections among cultures (as historian Janet Davis has argued at much greater length). The "Sparks World-Famous Shows" flier that appeared in the *Johnson City Staff* to herald the show's arrival in the region guarantees that the circus provides access to the cultures—both anthropological and aesthetic—of broader geographies as it promises "perfect specimens of the Earth's most curious creatures gathered together into one immense menagerie" as well as "the champions of all countries" who "compete in feats of daring and grace." The poster gives a self-aggrandizing nod to the fact that forms of entertainment are themselves enmeshed in circuits of economic circulation as it boasts that "the princely salaries paid by this mammoth enterprise have robbed all Europe of their most valuable performers." Even if these claims are mere hyperbole, they suggest what its promoters sensed their audiences desired from the spectacle: an imaginary interaction with distant people and places as well as amazing sights and stunts. As we have seen, though, with the example of Red Eldridge, the circus also provided a traveling market for itinerant day laborers, and the circus itself relied on regional networks of communities for its own economic existence.

Many of these kinds of connections have been or could be better examined by scholars with training in geography, history, or economics than a critic like myself whose training and habits of mind are more literary, interpretive, and qualitative. But there are other connections to be discerned here, of a more abstract, thematic, and associative quality, and this line of inquiry is where the work of cultural criticism, especially of the kind informed by politicized critical theories, can discern especially significant links among spaces and places. Clearly, for example, the story of Mary gives us some kind of window on attitudes about the connections and disconnects between human and nonhuman. On the one hand the tale is a clear example of animal cruelty at its most brutal and bizarre; however, there is also the relatively marginal detail in the oral history of the incident of some discussions of justice and due process. Although it does not mitigate the bewildering violence toward the nonhuman here, some ambivalence or at least reflection on the relationship of humans to other species, and on the concept of animal rights, could possibly be detected here.

The story, however, may well tell more, if in a more associative fashion, about attitudes toward and beliefs about other humans. Gender, in particular ideas of femininity and female propriety, is a factor here, for example, in the very formulation of the name "Murderous Mary." Musth, a biological syndrome that causes irrational and irritable behavior in male elephants, was a well-known problem for elephant handlers of the day and caused many attacks, and elephants account for more circus-animal attacks than big cats; yet there appears to be no record of a male elephant mistreated so sensationally and famously as either Mary or Topsy (Gröning and Saller 286). Especially given that the country was still adjusting to the concept of women's suffrage, written into the Constitution only two years before, could it be that part of the monstrosity of Mary's crime, which inflamed the crowd to such violence, was that Mary violated not only the rules of her captivity but also the codes of feminine behavior as well? That her actions touched an exposed nerve about wild, avenging women who refuse to be restrained? Such questions are even more urgent in light of the fact that Mary's victim was male: how might the story have played out differently had Mary's victim been female? Perhaps she would still have faced destruction, but might local outrage have flowed from a different source—one which drew on nostalgic, reactionary narratives of aggrieved womanhood, rather than an embattled fear of transgressive femininity?

The broader historical backdrop of these events allows for further speculation of this sort. Given the circus's associations across its history with empire, with the display (evinced in the rhetoric of the poster) of the exotic, a rhetoric deeply implicated in orientalism and the cosmopolitan racism and classism of colonialism, we might analyze in this case the associations of Mary with kinds of ethnics and exotics—other unusual "specimens"—and the antipathetic and often violent reactions they engender. Mary was, after all, an African elephant. The connection between the hanging of Mary and issues of race in the South is blatant, given that this story is essentially about a lynching, during that abhorrent practice's heyday. Even if it were not, Burton notes that one informant claimed that "Not many people know it, but the elephant's two Negro keepers were also hanged with her" (8), an inclusion Burton attributes to a fusion of Mary's story with that of a contemporaneous Erwin lynching. Others inserted a grim detail from that same lynching into the story when they reported that the body of Mary was burned on a pyre of crossties. Clearly, witnesses' accounts attuned themselves, consciously or not, to the racial resonances of the incident.

Some might take this aspect of the story as confirmation of the region's reputation for xenophobia and deeply entrenched reactionary politics, especially given the bemused pride with which the story is often told. And this interpretation may be valid. However, whatever the political valences that may be interpreted in the community's actions toward and reactions to Mary, the incident can be seen to reveal a place that is not an isolated backwater but a regional network of communities, themselves enmeshed in a broader network of cultural conflicts and interconnections. More important, it is within the very image, the narrative of the Hanging of Murderous Mary, that is so often used in the service of a rhetoric of local distinctiveness and singularity (whether that status is positive or negative), that we can see through critical examination the dense network of interconnections.

Critical Regionalism: Construction, Invention, Action

This book is about how to study this kind of situation, this kind of place, this kind of contradictory moment where something unique and isolated seems to be going on, but something else—something complex and interconnected—is also happening. For me the key to recognizing these affinities, identifications, and associations is to construct a model of place that can incorporate them in a vital way, articulating our "sense" of what is unique about a particular spot on the landscape with a critical awareness of how that spot is part of broader configurations of history, politics, and culture. Simply talking about place—or, more specifically, "the local"—is not enough. As the example of Murderous Mary shows, merely accounting for local history or lore does not necessarily reveal the multiple vectors of race, gender, technology, ecology, or social justice, for starters, that all converge on this historical moment at this geographical site. In fact, in this case, the spread of knowledge of this incident has actually served to obscure those connections in public discourse—the singularity of the incident, coupled unreflectively with the regional stereotypes of peculiarity and xenophobia that provide a ready cultural frame for this narrative, conspires to isolate it from larger forces. Having tried to introduce the practice of this critique first by enacting it, with the case of the Tale of Murderous Mary, in what follows I outline the main theoretical components of the methodology.

The scholarship on regionalism in literary and cultural studies has, I assert, not yet directly addressed the problem of how to disentangle the concept of region from the concept of the local. In the lingua franca of literary criticism, for instance, "regionalism" and "local color" are virtually synonymous (and either term usually connotes a rather narrowly defined body of literature from the United States between 1870 and 1900). What is needed in critical scholarship about incidents in regional culture and the artifacts that are generated around them is a revised and reconfigured idea of region. That model is what I try to develop in this study, along with tactics by which it might be put to good use in progressive cultural criticism. Indeed, it is this very act of forging, through cultural criticism, the broader cultural, political, historical, and geographical connections around a particular text, image, or artifact of local cultural conflict that enacts the new model of region I term "critical regionalism."

Critical regionalism's insistence on places and their cultural artifacts as dense palimpsests of broader forces represents an intentional challenge to the tradition of "regionalism" that informs most literary and cultural criticism. Since the high period of modernism in the 1950s, "regional" has been a pejorative term, or, as Raymond Williams puts it, "a limiting judgment" (*Keywords* 265), to apply to cultural work. The word "regionalism" may denote "local color" but it connotes "provincialism." As art critic Lucy Lippard writes, "Today the term regionalism . . . continues to be used pejoratively, to mean corny backwater art flowing from tributaries that might eventually reach the mainstream but is currently stagnating out there in the boondocks" (36). Elsewhere in the humanities, "New Western" historian Patricia Nelson Limerick observes that, "to many scholars, regional history is where one goes for a nap" (84). In these kinds of critical judgments, assumptions are made, or affirmed and perpetuated, about which kind of people from what kinds of places should be allowed to participate in the production of knowledge, the production of beauty, of cultural value; of public discourse, opinion, and sentiment.

These assumptions persist in literary criticism today, when scholars like Tom Lutz assert that regional literature is by definition a genre that refuses to draw connections between the local and broader cultural circuits (87). For scholars such as Lutz, the antonym of regionalism is cosmopolitanism, and generally, in contemporary United States culture, cosmopolitanism is taken to be a positive virtue just as regionalism assumes a cultural deficit. While cosmopolitanism ostensibly provides a perspective on all places and all things, it has one important blind spot: its own locatedness. Political theorist Craig Calhoun argues that "cosmopolitanism misrecognizes its own social foundations, assuming these to be universal when in fact they are representative of particular social locations. Cosmopolitanism is, too often, the class consciousness of frequent travelers" (2). Too often cosmopolitanism fails to live up to its ideals, instead positing unhelpful juxtapositions between its privileged position and parochial localism. As Calhoun asserts, "Attenuated cosmopolitanism won't ground mutual commitment and responsibility. Some relationship between roots . . . and broader relationships and awareness needs to be found to provide the solidarity on which cosmopolitan democracy must depend" (29). Given university intellectuals' own class positions, and the rootlessness and migration that are structural properties of life in the academy, its not surprising to find that much of the cultural critique is prone to adopt a cosmopolitan point of view, attenuated to various degrees.

On the other hand, the brand of localism that often masquerades as regionalism simply celebrates the veneer of permanence or organic wholeness as a bastion against cosmopolitanism's globe-trotting urbanity. We can see this localist-versus-cosmopolitan binary at work in the controversy over the meaning of Murderous Mary's tale: an impasse between middlebrow embarrassment over the story's confirmation of stereotypes of rural savagery, and parochial bemusement over its idiosyncrasy. Critical regionalism attempts to negotiate between these two poles, and to avoid either the excesses or the limitations of each. Limerick suggests that "region permit[s] one to adjust and train one's vision in a way that uncover[s] connection," serving as a "key transitional category" in recognizing the connections between local circumstances and larger patterns of meaning (84). As a strategy for cultural critique, critical regionalism can, I hope, link individual moments of cultural struggle to larger patterns of history, politics, and culture, by understanding how they are linked not only in time and in the nebulous networks of discourse but also in space, through relationships of power that can be material and cultural.

This geographical turn is intended not to supplant other aspects of identity-driven cultural critique but rather to augment and extend them. To understand the full effects of the impact of injustice, of uneven development, of racism, classism, sexism, and heterosexism, progressive intellectuals and educators must reclaim the supposedly tranquil or quiescent (depending on one's political perspective) spaces of regional culture as vital spaces of cultural strife. And to do this means developing critical strategies capable of recognizing conflict and struggle in forms unique to specific landscapes, and implementing tactics for intervention and action specific to those landscapes. As Murderous Mary's story and its cultural legacy suggests, crucial struggles, matters literally of life and death, are playing out in places occluded by enduring images of city and country, center and margin, metropole and region. Yet despite these disjunctions in the American cultural imagination, multiple linkages bind the experiences of disparate geographical sites.

Region, then, is not a thing in itself, a stable and bounded object of study. My assertion here is that just as "community" is for Raymond Williams "a warmly persuasive word to describe an existing set of relationships, or the warmly persuasive word to describe an alternative set of relationships" (*Keywords* 76), "region" is always at some level an attempt to persuade as much as it is to describe. Because the "set of relationships" intersecting at any one point on the landscape is potentially unsummarizable by any one account, all versions of region are necessarily partial, and hence an attempt to persuade, at the very least, of the validity of their own particular definitions. Attempts at metadescription therefore need to be as much about the representational practices and politics that inform constructions of region as they do about the definitions themselves. Region is a rhetoric to describe these intricate interactions; critical regionalism is a way of harnessing these new tactics of description in cultural work for social change.

The history of the term "critical regionalism" as I understand it is rooted in the theory and practice of architecture, landscape studies, and planning. Architecture scholar Kenneth Frampton, in particular, has espoused the term to describe what he calls "a place-conscious poetic" (27) for the creation of "an architecture of resistance" (16). In some senses this study is an attempt to adapt Frampton's idea to the reading and writing of texts. Architecture represents an apt site for this inquiry inasmuch as its theory is always oriented toward the creation of place representations; just as critical regionalism in architecture or planning is devoted toward the production of new kinds of buildings or landscapes, the practice of critical regionalism terminates not in the production of critique but in the creation of new kinds of texts and images of place.

Frampton asserts that, in building construction, "The bulldozing of an irregular topography into a flat site is clearly a technocratic gesture which aspires to a condition of absolute *placelessness*" (26). Like Frampton's critical regionalist architecture, a critical regionalist cultural studies depends on the development of tactics specific to particular places, so I cannot here recommend or model a specific method for a critical regionalist critique. What follows, then, is more properly thought of as methodology, a matrix for inquiry into the construction and the consequences of regionality.

Region as Social Invention

One key aspect of this methodology is a reclamation in cultural criticism of certain aspects of the language of planning. In *The Practice of Everyday Life*, Michel de Certeau, whose idea of "walking rhetorics" is a central concept for socially constructed ideas about place, describes the planner's vision of place, "the clear text of the planned and readable city," as diametrically opposed to the resistant, elusive practice of place by the person on the street. Against the daemonic wandering of pedestrians and nomads, the planner deploys the rhetoric of a "voyeur-god" who "must disentangle himself from the murky intertwining daily behaviors and make himself alien to them" (93). And, indeed, the scientific, cartographic, objectifying language of planning might seem to be unremittingly panoptical in its centralizing, technocratic authority, disciplining the inhabitants of a landscape by reductively describing and regulating their behavior and movements through policy actions of zoning and regulation.

However, Michel Foucault, whose notion of the "heterotopia" is, with de Certeau's walking rhetorics, another central concept in denaturalizing place, acknowledges that "a society, as its history unfolds, can make an existing heterotopia function in a very different fashion" (25). Regional planning, while often utilized unreflectively as a tool of a purely commercial vision of place, has both its intellectual roots and some of its earliest applications in a problematic but deeply committed, even utopian democratic project. For example, David Whisnant suggests that the Tennessee Valley Authority, though vexed by modernist dogmas of "progress," embraced "a formal rhetoric that was liberal, humane, and progressive" (*Modernizing* 273). The TVA's vision and practice were at least left-wing enough for Red-baiting, evidenced by President Eisenhower's 1954 identification of the TVA as "creeping socialism," to underwrite the dismantling of the agency's social mission (Whisnant, *Modernizing* 49).

This progressive (if not radical) political stance for regional planning is clear in the writings of one of regional planning's intellectually formative figures, Lewis Mumford. Mumford and others who formed the highly interdisciplinary and socially progressive American Institute of Planners in 1917 constituted a "broad social movement" (Guttenberg xvi) that had at the core of its interests a vision of a democratic American cultural landscape and, at the heart of its practice, a transdisciplinary ethic that linked cultural criticism to material social change. Granted, Mumford and his colleagues were often obtuse about their own assumptions on issues of race and gender most especially, and almost wholly unreflective about the undemocratic, technocratic methods by which their visions were to be reified.

What needs to be recalled, retrieved, and reconsidered about these founders of the Regional Planning Association of America (RPAA), whatever their political predilections and shortcomings, is that they offered a version of regionalism that was rhetorical rather than descriptive, which put forward visions and versions of new kinds of regions rather than merely outlining or underlining the defining features of already existing ones. Regions are not specific places for planners like Lewis Mumford and Benton MacKaye but are ways of making arguments about relationships among places, with an eye toward what those relationships should be. In this project, cultural critique and cultural production have a robust role to play in the broader project of political, economic, and physical transformation of regional landscapes into more hospitable, generous, and just places. I do not pretend to have invented the term critical regionalism, or make any proprietary claims to it, but seek rather to reemphasize what I believe to be a dropped thread in the history of the concept as it has traced its way through a broad array of disciplines and fields: that critique of region should sponsor the cultural production of new kinds of regions.

In their earnest, flawed, progressive way, the scholar-planners of the RPAA anticipated the more reflexive brand of contingency that characterizes idea of place in de Certeau or Foucault. In "The Regional Framework of Civilization," Mumford reflects a view of region that is governed by an impulse not to segment and control human activity on the landscape but to allow for the emergence of a more democratic culture that affords collective, productive relationships among different kinds of landscapes: "Regional planning asks not how wide an area can be brought under the aegis of the metropolis, but how the population and civic facilities can be distributed so as to promote and stimulate a vivid, creative life throughout a whole region—a region being any geographical area that possesses a certain unity of climate, soil, vegetation, industry and culture" (207–8). Three things are important in this passage. First, Mumford's definition of region is anything but rigid and intractable. Rather, in that signal phrase "a certain unity," a wide space is left for interpretative agency, for the construction of region at the conjunction of a variety of material, economic, and cultural concerns—a potentially heterotopological model.

Second, Mumford's regionalism is not a description of a single autonomous place with an essential character, but an interconnective model, defining place according to its relationships to larger landscapes. In this respect Mumford's idea of region is like Foucault's heterotopia, which, as a countersite, creates critical insights into larger relationships of discourse and power among places; Mumford's regionalism also reflects de Certeau's walking rhetorics, which not only join moments on the landscape through cultural practices but exist in a dialogical relationship with the panoramic or panoptic perspectives of power. The planner's work is not a purely empiricist and technocratic endeavor, then, but an effort to devise descriptive, interpretive tools that can not only describe but engage with the indeterminacy of this complex and variable network of relationships. For this reason, contemporary planning scholar Albert Guttenberg argues in *The Language of Planning* that the planner's practice is "social invention," an artifice that, unlike the emergent, often collectively subconscious qualities of the social construction, is consciously conceived and applied toward specific social goals and ends (x–xi). The planner's region is thus not an objective description of natural and demographic features of a particular site, but a language of possibility and an argument for work toward that vision of the best (or at least a better) possible version of that place.

If all versions of "region" are to lesser or greater degrees tendentious, then planning can be reconsidered not as an exercise in rational dominion but as a rhetoric, a set of language practices; as Guttenberg writes, "*region* is first of all a word, and . . . words are variables whose precise values are very much a matter of the systems of thought that employ them" (85). Thus, my third and most important point about the legacy of regional planning: though its inheritance is manifest today largely in technoscientific skills and practices, its utopian formulations in Mumford, Benton MacKaye, and certain of their inheritors may be reclaimed and reconceived as a cultural and political critique.

Region as social invention supplies critical regionalism a language of possibility, rooted in the landscapes of particular communities viewed in terms of their vital connectedness to other places, a language that revives a progressive intellectual project and reclaims it for democratic cultural practice. The function of critical regionalist cultural scholarship ideally should be not only to criticize but also to plan, to envision, like the critical regionalist architect, the construction of texts that can envision more just and equitable landscapes. The academic intellectual is in this respect in something of the same position as the professional planner: engaging in projects that could have implications for broader populations, but housed in institutions that often discourage public participation because of the premium placed on expertise. Indeed, in Guttenberg's vision of planning as a rhetorical practice, the planner is reconceived as a public intellectual working by persuasion to facilitate social action, a revision of the profession not unlike the calls circulating in many fields in the humanities today. The planner and the progressive academic are both confronted by what Lewis Hopkins calls a central "question of democracy"—how to reconcile often (seemingly, at least) competing roles of public participation and expertise (quoted in Guttenberg xi).

Individual places—towns, homes, landscapes—come to seem natural to us because their generative processes are so gradual and ongoing, diffuse and disparate. But region, unlike place, is not only constructed but is always deliberately constructed; as Limerick writes, "While geography plays a role in their definition, regions are much more the creations of human thought and behavior than they are the product of nature" (96). Typically, regions are created to try to describe or define the environment and behavior—the landscape—of a group of people within a stable, bounded geographical unit. But the field of planning, especially the lineage traced from the RPAA to advocacy planners and scholars like Kevin Lynch and Delores Hayden, to architectural theorists such as Kenneth Frampton, preserves a sense of regional analysis that rejects organic or essentialized models of place and region in favor of the identification of dynamic, conflicted networks of relationships. At the same time, the emerging thread of critical regionalism in the literature of architecture and planning recognizes, as urbanist Nan Ellin writes, that "architects and planners are interested actors" (54) and that critical regionalist scholarship should "represent and serve, in a critical sense, the limited constituencies in which they are grounded" (68). This sense of the importance of grass roots, of a vigorous, generative understanding of local, material conditions in the formation of ideas about place and region, of regional planning as a basis for social action, in short, of region as social invention, is what I am trying to restore to the practice of regionalism in cultural studies and the humanities. Regionalism typically does, but does not have to, categorically isolate "authentic" or whole spaces. If region is a rhetoric, then critical regionalism can use the construction of region to interconnect more fully, rather than disconnect, local places to broader patterns of politics, history, and culture.

If, like critical regionalist architects and planners, cultural scholars wish to serve not only the expansion of knowledge but also the use of that knowledge to effect or facilitate material change, then a central aspect of critical regionalism as cultural scholarship must be forging greater inter-connection between universities and the communities and regions they are part of, as well as reinvigorating the neglected contacts that already exist. Part of the project of reclaiming the idea of region as social invention to a progressive political critique, as well as investing a socially constructed idea of region with agency and purpose, is to open the intellectual project to local participation, and specifically to be instructed by the voices and experiences of those normally excluded from powerful strands of public discourse for reasons of their race, class, gender, sexuality, and ethnicity. In other words, to make the "social invention" of region an act of radical possibility, it must be broadly social. Recognizing that region is a social construction that can be and indeed continually is shaped by the practices of its inhabitants, and that region can be a social invention used deliber-ately to transform the politics and culture of the landscape, a critical regionalism works in solidarity with the historically disempowered popu-lations of its communities to transform their local material circumstances while linking their particular struggles to larger ones.

Nonetheless, Limerick's cautionary note about the political potential of regionalism is worth repeating: "For all its peculiarity, and despite my continued affection for it, region finally matches most other intellectual antidotes and curatives in the unevenness of its performance. It neither work[s] for everyone, nor work[s] very long" (104). So stipulated—but Limerick also notes that "humans, with all their various techniques of construction and invention, have an endless array of choices in defining and shaping regional identification and loyalty, with an equally endless range of degrees of friction and violence" (103). How much may yet be gained by trying to persuade people to embrace the former and minimize the latter?

The Landscape of This Book: A Map

Recognizing that to represent places and regions is to construct them, the plan of the book is to build the critique "from the ground up," to "culti-

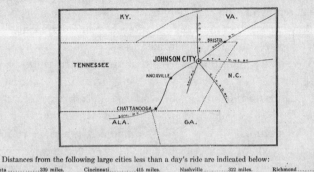

Johnson City, Tennessee

WHERE AND WHAT IT IS

Its Commercial, Financial, Educational and Healthful advantages tersely and truthfully told in pen and picture.

Distances from the following large cities less than a day's ride are indicated below:

Atlanta ....339 miles.	Cincinnati............415 miles.	Nashville ....322 miles.	Richmond............375 miles.
Baltimore ....442 miles.	Columbus............534 miles.	New York............628 miles.	Washington, D. C....492 miles.
Charlotte............298 miles.	Knoxville............122 miles.	Philadelphia ....539 miles.	Wheeling ....668 miles.
Chattanooga ....222 miles.	Louisville ....392 miles.	Pittsburg............724 miles.	

Johnson City is located on the main lines of the Southern and the Carolina, Clinchfield and Ohio Railroads, having ten passenger trains daily—North, East, South and West. All trains meet at one point, near the center of the city.

"Johnson City, Tennessee: Where and What It Is." From 1909 promotional brochure on Johnson City, Tennessee, created by J. O. Lewis of the Commercial Club.

vate the site," as Frampton would say (26). In so doing, I hope both to describe and to enact the kinds of tactics for critical regionalist representation I argue for in this study. The chapters divide according to subject matter, but there is also a landscape-narrative logic to their sequencing, and a persistent connection to a specific place, Johnson City, Tennessee— a place already conflicted in its identity as an Appalachian city, made more complicated, but also more appropriate for this study, as it is my hometown.

Although the persistent use of this community as a site for the experimental staging of this methodology suggests it serves as a "case study," that term may be a bit too clinical for its role here. I am writing not as an anthropologist in the field or an impartial, empirical analyst, but as a stakeholder with both rational and affective investments in the well-being of this area. So while this book uses a specific community and a specific region as its analytical focus, it would be misleading to say that this work is a "community study" per se, or a work about the Appalachian region to the exclusion of other considerations. Indeed, one of the central assertions of the work is that to discuss region is inherently to draw connections, comparisons, articulations, and overlaps with other places, because

Introduction

that is what region is: a rhetoric that connects specific local sites to a variety of other kinds of place constructions of various scales and motives. Critical regionalism is a way of making this inherent connectivity deliberate, conscious, and visible, a methodology for creating a new kind of regional representation that is not only inquisitive about the possibilities for drawing together new configurations of politics and culture, but is always conscious about its own locatedness as a critical practice.

Hence I am, as an author, as a cultural producer, trying to be constantly self-aware and reflective about the geographical, cultural, and political location of this text: as the work of an academic researcher, a college teacher, an Appalachian person (by nativity, if not by current address), a citizen of a nation, and a stakeholder in a planet. And ultimately that is what I hope critical regionalism could be: a way inhabitants of a place, myself included, could create visions of their homes, at their best, freed of the limitations of our damagingly nostalgic or abject cultural vocabulary for life on the American geographical margin. Regionalism as a representational strategy has focused almost to the exclusion of any other concerns on the creation (and supposed re-creation) of a past; critical regionalism is about constructing (and, I suppose, deconstructing) a present out of which could project a better future.

Furthermore, one of my key assertions is that the creation of texts about places—including this text—is actually a part of the larger creation of place itself. Thus I begin the study by considering the dynamics and the consequences of the act of representing a place, surveying a range of representational strategies, particularly academic writing strategies, for defining place and region, making the creation of this very study one central example. Chapter 1 thus provides the broad intellectual context for the work as a whole as it considers the variability and the mutability of the concept of place generally and region in particular. I examine the idea that something as seemingly material as the landscape can be the product of rhetorical and discursive practices by studying the ways ideas about place and region are expressed or implied in a variety of artifacts, including a look at the contradictory modes of and motives for place construction in Abraham Verghese's *My Own Country*, a memoir set in my hometown, Johnson City, Tennessee, and a self-reflexive examination of this study's composition process and circulation. The Appalachian Trail, however, provides an example of the kind of regional representational practices I espouse throughout this book: a politically engaged, generative, public and collective project of place-centered social construction, with its intellectual roots in the regional planning movement. The Appalachian Trail can be seen not only as the locus of a variety of kinds of textual production (much like the hanging of Murderous Mary), but as a text itself, the expression of a kind of literacy, broadly construed, that reshapes the world using a critical regionalist rhetoric connecting places, histories, memories, politics, and cultures.

Chapter 2 builds on the terrain established by chapter 1 by turning attention to the built environment. I examine the ways typical images of place, and in particular regional stereotypes, can occlude important cultural conflicts and political struggles that are taking place, or, more appropriately, making place. I develop at greater length and complexity a reading of the landscape similar to my treatment of Murderous Mary at the beginning of this introduction: interrogating the ways that the very images that delimit and disconnect places, or circumscribe the potential for political action and a vital local public discourse, can be reread to discern the tense and dynamic interconnections that converge in regional spaces. I begin by analyzing "official" landscapes of regional identity, examining the historical trappings of public parks in Johnson City and what they teach park visitors to value about the surrounding community. Examining grass-roots resistance to environmental injustice in the area around my hometown, I consider how dumps and dumping can be conceived of not just as "waste space" but as foci of broadly regional political and cultural conflicts that generate a living culture of representation and contestation. Here I examine the need for a socially inventive rhetoric of region to connect struggles for environmental justice to even more broadly transformative political struggles. The readings of these regional landscapes illustrate the possibilities for critical regionalism to construct a vernacular language of planning, the literate tools for understanding how ideas about place are encoded in and encode local landscapes, and how those landscapes might be interpreted and shaped by a regionalist vision of dynamic, interconnected local cultures.

If one central assertion of this work, then, is that local texts, images, and discourses must be interpreted in light of their relationship to texts from elsewhere, I suggest in chapter 3 that the reverse might also be true: that the interpretation of extrinsic texts, images, and discourses can be approached from a specifically local perspective. Considering the challenge of a critical regionalist analysis of constructions of place in popular culture, I encounter there a particular problem—namely, that in the contemporary United States, the most visible and powerful representational forms and practices are not necessarily local ones. Yet, despite their origins in the very centers of cosmopolitanism, mass media images construct powerful visions of and models of place forms: community, region, and nation. Thus critical regionalism must develop not only critiques of depictions of specific places, but also readings of texts driven by the concerns of specific places. A critical Appalachian regionalism, for example, must be concerned with more than depictions of Appalachia. In chapter 3, then, I deal with the problem of media depictions of the southern Appalachian region, noting how representational practices link ideas of the mountain region, centering pejorative conceptions of literate practices in regional cultures. I then compare the constructions of place in the films *Pulp Fiction* and *Fargo* to the ideas of place that inhere in a series of violent crimes that occurred in the southern Appalachian region, in order to bring into sharper relief the kinds of rational and affective resources place constructions in mass media texts make available to their local and regional audiences. To intervene in the cultural production of regional landscapes requires the creation of literate tactics that can both engage with the representations that delimit or restrict their sociopolitical efficacy, and expand their reach and range of concerns, creating new connections within and configurations of definitions of regional public life.

In chapter 4, I pursue this project of expanding the possibilities for critical regionalism by turning from popular culture to more restricted cultural spheres, as I examine literary models of place in novels both national and more traditionally regional in scope. At the same time I add another layer of discourse and representational practices to my own project of place construction. Scrutiny of assumptions about place and region in John Dos Passos's *U.S.A.* (1933) and John Steinbeck's *The Grapes of Wrath* (1939) illustrate how politically progressive literature, read from a critical regionalist perspective, can be seen to discount the progressive potential of regional places, seeing displacement as a precondition of radical politics. Against this backdrop of both a suspect localism and an attenuated cosmopolitanism, I read James Still's Appalachian novel *River of Earth* (1940) alongside Dos Passos and Steinbeck to demonstrate that commitments to place can nurture a transformative cultural politics. My reading of Still's novel lays the groundwork for an analysis of *Stories I Ain't Told Nobody Yet* (1989) by Johnson City author, performer, and cultural worker Jo Carson, whose genre-bending and genre-blending text represents, I argue, the kind of site-specific and politically engaged literate practices that a critical regionalist literary aesthetic might aspire to. By building upon the keen awareness not only of the site-specific cultural resources but also the way those local means are connected to broader histories, cultures, conflicts, and struggles, Carson updates and extends Still's regionalism in much the same way as I assert that the Progressive

Era of Mumford and his colleagues in the RPAA could be revised and reclaimed.

By linking a critique of representations of place and region to an attempt to discern and advocate for representational practices that enact a critical regionalist sensibility, chapters 3 and 4 both model the movement from a socially constructed view of place to a use of place and region as social inventions. Carson's work, however, because it is both performative and participatory, a cultural form designed for circulation among wider populations and adaptation to new places, suggests how critical regionalism can function as social action.

In chapter 5, I consider how academic writing about place of the kind I am engaged in in this study might function in a similar way, recognizing and responding to the particular location of my own work, of this study, in the culture of United States higher education. In this project the academy, itself a distinctive network of particular places, presents a unique set of both opportunities and obstacles. On the one hand, the university is designed specifically to transmit its tactics for representation to wider audiences; on the other hand, however, academic practice tends to deny its own emplacement, assuming instead the kind of attenuated cosmopolitanism Calhoun describes. By looking at how academic controversies emerge into local public life in the case of Johnson City's East Tennessee State University, I offer perspectives on how the landscape of the academy might be seen in a less discontinuous light. A new emphasis on place in higher education is one necessary goal of critical regionalism—a change in the conception and practice of academic literacies by their constituents. It is also a necessary precursor to the development of a critical regionalist pedagogy, which might in turn change the way university students learn to represent how their localized experiences figure in the broader sweep of history, politics, and culture. This goal demands that both research and pedagogy address cultural conflict, not only in the readily recognizable forms it takes in the urban centers of American culture, but in the myriad shapes that it presents in out-of-the-way places, on the geographical margins of American public life, and it is the goal I pursue throughout this study.

In his meditation on the experience and meaning of place, *Invisible Cities*, Italo Calvino offers a brief parable describing life in the city of Leandra. Calvino explains the relationship of two types of household gods, Lares and Penates, who both lay claim to representing the "true essence of Leandra": the Penates, who attach themselves to specific families, "believe they are the city's soul, . . . and they believe they take Leandra with them when they emigrate." The Lares, whose loyalties are instead to a particular house or lot, "consider the Penates temporary guests . . . ; the real Leandra is theirs, which gives form to all it contains, the Leandra that was there before all these upstarts arrived and that will remain when all have gone away" (79). This chapter centers on a similar debate: does the "true essence" of a place derive from the people and the practices that "take place" in it, or does it come from some special quality about the place itself? Is there, indeed, something we might speak of as the "true essence" of a place?

I bring up these questions not to answer them, or even take sides on them, but to suggest that it is the very asking of questions like these that generates the complex and variable experience of place. Throughout this book I argue for a conflict-driven, evolving, generative, rhetorical model of region, and so this work begins with an inquiry into the concept of place more generally. Calvino's fable is to the point in that it concludes not with the victory of Lares over Penates, or vice versa, but with the quarrel itself: "If you listen carefully, especially at night, you can hear them in the houses of Leandra, murmuring steadily, interrupting one another, huffing, bantering, amid ironic, stifled laughter." It is the bustle of voices that distinguishes Leandra, voices that, importantly, are always critical of the current state of affairs: "The Penates bring out the old people, the great-grandparents, the great-aunts, the family of the past; the Lares talk about the environment before it was ruined." These are also voices, however, that look to the future with both anticipation and concern: "[T]hey daydream of the careers the children will follow when they grow up (the Penates), or what this house in this neighborhood might become (the Lares) if it were in good hands" (79).

What neither party realizes is that it is not either definition, but the interaction of their definitions, that makes Leandra what it is. Calvino's vision of place as a dense and layered network of worries and desires, debates, ambitions, and conflict, all framed by the land and the people who inhabit it, is a vision I wish to bring out of his fiction and insert into another set of debates, in order to suggest a complex, multivalent, generative model for thinking of place, and its articulations in other forms such as "region," in terms which fully engage with its historical, geopolitical, and discursive character.

Region and Cultural Texts

By studying the idea of region, and in particular the ways southern Appalachia has been constructed, this chapter makes the argument that "place" is more complicated than anything about the physical nature of the place, the social practices of its inhabitants, or the qualities of the individual observer, taken singly, will account for. Rather, place is suspended somewhere between the absolutes of objectivity and subjectivity, of geography or sociality, a quality geographer Nicholas Entrikin terms the "betweenness of place." "To understand place," Entrikin asserts, "requires that we have access to both an objective and subjective reality." Viewing place in purely social or purely empirical terms, as either location or social practices, is reductive; rather, "Place is best viewed from points in between" (Entrikin 5).

More important, this very suspension, a tense and dynamic state maintained by the exchange of opinions, ideas, and arguments about the nature of the place in question, gives that place its distinctive character. Place is thus a constantly generative construction in which the physical place, the practices of its inhabitants, and the intellectual observer are factors, but three among many factors. The experience of place is always mediated by preconceived notions, expectations, biases, and attitudes of the observer, and by these same considerations as they intersect from other sources. The idea of place, often described as a "sense" of place, is not so much sensory, as it is textual—taking text in the broad sense of its use in cultural critique, as any configuration of signs, any meaningful, communicative set of objects.

It would be a rash reduction, however, to say that places are "merely" textual creations. Writers are one of the many factors that create places, and they never act alone. At the very least, the physical space of the place the writer is helping to create must exist before that person, and in most instances a writer comes to write about a place because it is well-known in advance, whether popular, notorious, or sacred. Indeed, that renown is often the subject of and motivation for contemporary place writing, the vast majority of which consists of ephemera: guidebooks for travelers, regional interest pieces for tourists, pieces that are designed specifically to precondition the experience of a particular place by underscoring some aspects and omitting or deemphasizing others.

What I am describing here is a kind of layering—an appropriately geological metaphor, I think—of texts, experiences, and interpretations of specific locales that produces, in its ongoing processes, a place. In geological terms, though, the experience of place is more metamorphic than sedimentary: the layers have been bent, folded, broken, and melted into each other; they are transformed and transforming. To know a place, to acquire that "sense" of place, is not to consume an experience, or witness a spectacle, or appreciate a landscape, but to participate, through consumption, through witness, through appreciation, in the ongoing creation of that place, of its different interpretations and articulations, of its different "textual" expressions, as dense and political and historical as culture itself. In this sense, no place exists without its observers, or before it is observed—observation is in itself a creative act (though not a very durable one, until those observations are recorded and circulated in some form). The definition and etymology of "landscape" tells us that landscape without an observer is merely terrain and, indeed, that landscape is more about the representation of the land than the land itself (Jackson 3–8). Geographer Tim Cresswell acknowledges that, "Like a book, the landscape is created by authors, and the end product attempts to create certain meanings. But also, like a book, the people who 'read' the landscape and its places can never be forced to read it only one way" (13). This study proposes not only to read regional landscapes as textual forms, but to reverse the analogy and read texts as landscapes, asking how texts and their makers create versions of places that are more or less tendentious, influencing (intentionally or not) broader understandings of the places they depict.

Acknowledging that acts of writing affect the meanings of places means there is no privileged position for the writer from which to observe this process. All versions of a place and its culture are interested and partial, with political tendencies if not outright allegiances; this chapter discusses the politics of some more or less typical methods of depicting places. However, I claim no apolitical advantage for myself. In fact, one thing I would like for my reader to keep in mind is that this project is itself a deliberate part of the matrix of place. Especially since the place I am about to discuss is my home, east Tennessee, and the broader regional setting of the southern Appalachians of which it is a part, the comments I make here are self-conscious and reflexive, and unapologetically partisan. I want you to witness as you read a moment in the workings of place, not receive a coolly detached analysis of them. Indeed, I am alleging that such an analysis, regardless of its rhetorical invocation of objectivity, is necessarily implicated in the dynamics of place. Thus this study is not only about producing an analysis that can identify the cultural politics of place, but about developing a rhetoric that deliberately intervenes in these ongoing processes to create deliberate visions and versions of place —a project not only of cultural critique but of cultural production.

The Process in Motion: The Case of This Chapter

If the creation of place is like the writing of a text, then perhaps some reflection on the creation of the text before you is in order as well, in order to observe a segment of the larger processes of place formation. By considering how the text before you now has reached its present form, connecting along the way with a range of other visions and versions of place, I want to illustrate a set of related points central to my arguments throughout this book. First, a region is not a stable, finite thing, but a concept that emerges cumulatively from the circulation of texts about the region. Second, this rhetorical and representational character makes the concept of region particularly available for analysis by a transdisciplinary cultural criticism. Regardless of the field, the scholarly practice of regionalism generally takes the existence of the region as an a priori, more or less natural fact; by considering the example of my own work here, I want to suggest that even scholarly texts are partial, tendentious versions of region that circulate in broader discourses. Finally, this example illustrates how practitioners of critical regionalism could recognize and engage with the awareness of the partiality and the rhetorical character of their ideas of region, through a reflexive awareness of one's own locatedness, a deliberate consciousness of where one is writing from and why.

No text leaps full-blown from the head of its author, and this text is no exception. The "boundaries" of this text and its history are just as contingent and unstable as the boundaries of the southern Appalachian region to which our attention will momentarily turn. This chapter has gone through a lengthy process of development, and appeared in various forms, before arriving before you now, and like other authors I hope it will continue to be re-presented, in discussion and debate, in the footnotes of other authors, perhaps in letters, in replies to letters, and so on. The text itself reminds you, through the occasional citation, of its own indebtedness to other texts, by other writers. This chapter alone uses a photograph, and maps, as well as some less traditionally scholarly texts: an imaginary picture (more about that shortly), excursions into the memories of the author, even a bit of a poem; beyond this chapter, the rest of the work invokes philosophy, history, film and popular culture, newspapers, magazines, novels—all manner of traditional texts, and textual readings of the built environment as well. Furthermore, that I have come to write this text at all represents a moment in my academic, intellectual training (which consists mostly of reading and writing texts), but also, more broadly, my biography (a term giving a textual coherence to the labyrinth of experience).

This text, then, has its own geology, strata that both represent its current form and encode the processes of its development. The current version of this chapter is a revision of an article that appeared in the academic journal *Historical Geography*, an article that was itself an expansion of an earlier one, which appeared in a magazine called *Southern Exposure*. This earliest published version was written very much in a different register; its language was designed for a nonacademic audience, and it was accompanied by a number of pictures and graphic enhancements intended to open access to a nonacademic readership. Furthermore, the magazine concerns itself with issues and events in the southern United States as a whole: perhaps its appearance in that venue encourages its readers to mentally annex Appalachia onto the image of the South as a kind of appendage, even though nothing in the article itself does so deliberately, and in fact a passage or two attempts to distinguish the Appalachians from the rest of "the South." Meanwhile, the version that appeared in *Historical Geography* contextualized my discussion less in terms of the problems of a specific place but more as a reflection of a broader, abstract disciplinary problem, with the added complication that, as a humanities scholar publishing in a social science journal, it represented as well the translation between different disciplines, different sites on the intellectual landscape.

There are more layers, however, to be accounted for. That earlier *Southern Exposure* article was an expansion of a talk given at a gathering of people interested specifically in things Appalachian, the annual meeting of the Appalachian Studies Association (where the conflation of Appalachia with the South, or the decontextualization of place as an intellectual or disciplinary concern, is a potentially controversial maneuver). The session was well attended, and furthermore, I distributed some copies of the talk both before and after the session, so previous textual versions of the ideas here have been in circulation since then at least.

The conference presentation had a side effect that produced another line of texts, reproducing, complicating, and engaging with my texts. Douglas Imbrogno, a reporter, covered the meeting for the local newspaper (the *Charlestown Gazette-Mail*) and reproduced in that article some of my remarks. Here, however, they were reconfigured in several important ways. By way of introduction, for example, the article humorously contrasts the academic meeting with the "Eenie Weenie Bikini Contest" taking place that same weekend in a crosstown bar. The opposition of an uninhibited romp in a bar to a weekend of academic banter is frivolous (and telling) enough, but it also creates a context for a general readership in which to "place" academics and their work, a context that assigns academics a certain humorless niche in cultural life.

On the whole, though, the newspaper article does more than poke fun at the uptight reputation of scholars. In giving general coverage to a meeting of this kind, which involves not only a variety of people but also a wide range of forms of presentation—audio, video, and live performance—the article presents to the public readership of the newspaper the energy and range of interests that the meeting, and that the idea of Appalachia, encompasses. Perhaps most important, the article offers a perspective on the meeting that is not only focused on the panels themselves but also on "the discussions . . . the talk and music that often carries on toward dawn in bars and hotel rooms" (E1). In a phrase recalling Calvino's talkative Lares and Penates, the article emphasizes a generative, social aspect to the meeting that a volume of proceedings might well fail to capture.

Most important, Imbrogno's article carries the discussion of region to a broader range of the people of that region, in a forum to which they have at least limited access. One resident, the paper's local history and local affairs columnist, Alice Faye Bragg, took up the issue in her column of 7 April 1995, in seeming response to a line from my talk, which served as a kind of epigraph to Imbrogno's article: "What are we talking about when we talk Appalachia?" "I would never presume to align my simple mind with these intellectual thinkers and learned scholars," she writes. But Bragg's analysis is interesting in its own right, as it commences from a position of absolute certainty—"I know what Appalachia means to me"— through a dictionary definition relying wholly on geography (" 'parts of 11 states, with a population of 15 million' ") to a lengthy, nostalgic catalog of cultural practices, scenic tableaux, and metaphysical intuitions, culminating in the assertion that "Appalachia is that longing in the heart to come home again" (3D). This argument, in its total conviction (despite its internal contradictions), is part of the evolving, variable, larger debate over the region's identity and, far from closing discussion, perpetuates it: indeed, it has just, in this paragraph, been reconfigured and responded to itself.

The process this text before you has undergone, because it is exactly the kind of circulation and modification that the broader cultural text of the idea of "Appalachia" undergoes, with no clear beginning or end point. By the same token, one could follow different moments in the development of this essay by linking events, activities, and works in my life and in others' lives back to my birth, and in that spirit, continue on back through my own family tree. Shifting into a forward gear, we witness the manuscript of this chapter undergoing the debate, scrutiny, and revision of a dissertation defense; a publisher's review process, including the careful critique of outside readers and my responses and reactions to those comments; and, I hope, reviews in scholarly journals, citation and critique in future academic works about place and region, and so forth. But even if nothing further happens to this project, it will have shaped some perceptions, perhaps changed or reinforced some opinions; even if you disagree with what I say here, the statement itself has helped provoke your disagreement, given you an interlocutor to argue against. Perhaps you will underline a phrase, make a remark in a margin. When you do, you inscribe your own text onto this one, altering its intellectual landscape, and the process continues.

The Process Arrested: An Imaginary Picture

Perhaps we can best understand the cultural and political issues at stake in the place-creation process in which the production and circulation of this manuscript are embroiled if we see how they are present at every moment. To do so requires taking one moment and (per the geological metaphor) breaking it to pieces, inspecting its layers, studying its composition—especially since we have just seen, in overview, the sedimentation that has produced it. Imagine a picture: a picture of me, composing the original conference-presentation version of this essay. I am sitting at a desk, wearing a flannel shirt, a baseball cap, facing a computer screen. Behind me is a window framing a view of the Boston skyline, the Prudential and John Hancock towers dominating the landscape. Above me on the wall is another vista, this one provided by a map, or rather a series of maps folded and thumbtacked and taped together to become one map, including the Johnson City, Jonesborough, Unicoi, Erwin, Elizabethton, and Iron Mountain Gap quadrangles of the United States Geographical Survey, U.S. Department of the Interior. I am looking at a black dot in the northeast corner of the Erwin quadrangle that indicates the farmhouse on forty acres where I used to live when I returned to Johnson City after college, in the early 1990s. Where is Appalachia in this picture? Indeed, what are we talking about when we talk about Appalachia? Is it on the map? Or is it in me?

For most of the people I knew around Boston, the latter would have to be the answer. Of course, for most of the people I knew around Boston, I am the only experience of Appalachia any of them had ever been aware of, so I bore the task of representing to them an entire region, people, practices, landscape and all. For these folks, I was a sort of traveling museum exhibit of Appalachia, a display of its traits and practices. Two years after the moment you are now picturing, in 1996, I will move to Ohio, and there I will find that in cities like Cincinnati and Dayton entire neighborhoods are labeled "Appalachian"—a practice that reinforces this model. Ohioans in general, I will discover, are very conscious of this point of geographical origin as lending one a crypto-ethnic identity. Ohioans hold festivals (like "Appalachian Days" at Cincinnati's Coney Island park) that present a stable, autonomous image of Appalachian culture composed of a finite and fairly predictable set of cultural artifacts and practices—fiddles, whittling, quilts, folk dancing, and so forth—a version of my Boston friends' interpretation of me, writ large. At a typical festival you will find little about the historical causes of the migration of populations mostly from the mountains of eastern Kentucky and West Virginia to these urban centers, an intricate pattern of economic, political, and social interconnections that have bound industrial cities to outlying regions.

As that historical aside implies, I am not willing to commit to this idea that Appalachia is somehow "inside" me anymore than I am to the ethereal, metaphysical idea of a "sense" of place. This group affiliation has more to do with a conscious, willful use of cultural commodities, an element of artifice, especially in settings where "Appalachianness" is a foreign, almost exotic trait. In other words, Appalachia seems to be something I can represent—by doing things like wearing a feedstore ball cap or saying "fixin' to" or "you'uns." By putting on my camouflage pants, a flannel shirt, and a cap with a chain saw logo on it (something I might have worn on any given day on that forty-acre farm where I used to live) and billing it as my native dress, I could fulfill my role as a one-man Appalachian exposition. As you will see in the conclusion, however, while this "exhibit" may be persuasive for my Boston audience, it is a spurious gesture at best.

Therefore, one might say that I am not in Appalachia at all: Appalachia is a geographical reality; it is on the map, not with me at all. This position postulates a very different model of regional identity, tying the region to the land exclusively, and suggesting that rumination over what

An informal regional boundary: the Lewis Fork Baptist Church sign beside U.S. Highway 421 between Deep Gap and Wilkesboro, North Carolina. The sign was later removed during road widening. Photograph 1999 by Janet Powell; collection of the author.

region is exactly is futile, because a region is a body of land and either you are in it or not. This model is one that I was raised on: when my family would travel down to eastern North Carolina—the U.S. South "proper"— to visit my grandparents, we would pass by a sign at the bottom of a winding descent from the crest of the Blue Ridge, on U.S. Highway 421, outside of North Wilkesboro, North Carolina. The sign, for Lewis Fork Baptist Church (Jesus Saves), signified, by acclamation of all in the car, that we were officially leaving the mountains and entering the Piedmont, and it represented the border-crossing back into Appalachia on the return trip. While a border of great clarity, however, it is limited to one family's personal geography. And now it is solely a part of my family's personal history and memory as well, since, in the recent widening of U.S. Highway 421, that sign has been removed. For me, driving west to Johnson City from my recent home in Durham, North Carolina, the sign is now conspicuous only in its absence. Like Alice Faye Bragg's sense of certainty about her definition of Appalachia, this one appears, in a broader view, a bit more arbitrary than it seems for its adherents.

Both rhetorics of region that I have outlined here, region as museum and region as map, have their uses, to be sure, but both, when pushed to the logical extreme, show very similar problems, which point toward an

Rhetorics of Place and Region

underlying difficulty with trying to create a unified, fixed, hermetic regional model in the first place.

Regional Disconnections I: Region as Museum

Consider this anecdote, which Stephen Greenblatt offers in his introduction to *Marvelous Possessions*:

> In August, 1986, on a tourist's typical first night in Bali, I walked by moonlight on narrow paths through silent rice paddies glittering with fireflies. . . . I saw a light from the *bale banjar*, the communal pavilion in which I knew—from having read Clifford Geertz and Miguel Covarrubias and Gregory Bateson and Margaret Mead—that the Balinese gathered in the evening. I drew near and discovered that the light came from a television set that the villagers, squatting or sitting cross-legged, were intent on watching. Conquering my disappointment, I accepted the gestured invitation to climb onto the platform and see the show: on the communal VCR, they were watching a tape of an elaborate temple ceremony. (3)

The disappointment Greenblatt registers as an immediate reaction to this situation of cultural hybridity—a scenario highly reminiscent of the stereotype of the tar paper hillbilly shack with the satellite dish out back—is entangled with a problem that vexes the traditional idea of a "region" as a stable and inherited set of beliefs and practices. The problem with this idea is its stability: an inordinate emphasis on preservation of "authentic" ways, the idea that inheritance of practices can or, rather, should ideally occur only along the sanctioned, existing lines. One feels that the Balinese should be watching the ceremony itself, and that the VCR and television are intrusions from another culture, a kind of pollution of the "real" Balinese culture.

Greenblatt recognizes, however, that the material and historical circumstances of this cultural moment are more complicated than this superficial and judgmental analysis admits. He notes that "if the television and the VCR and, for that matter, my presence on the platform suggested the astonishing pervasiveness of capitalist markets and technology . . . the Balinese adaptation of the latest Western and Japanese modes of representation seemed so culturally idiosyncratic and resilient that it was unclear who was assimilating whom." Greenblatt uses this platform to raise a similar set of questions to my own: "Whose ideological triumph is being registered here? Whose possession is disclosed? Representational practices are ideologically significant . . . but I think it is important to resist what we may call an *a priori* ideological determinism, that is, that particular modes of representation are inherently and necessarily bound to a given culture or class or belief system" (4).

Greenblatt's emphasis on avoiding ideological determinisms sounds an appropriately cautionary note for defining cultures, regional or otherwise, as a set of finite practices. To designate a particular practice as the exclusive domain of a people is to engage in an act that is ideologically fraught and, more urgently for the purposes of this study, methodologically unsound. First of all, such a methodology can be easily co-opted into the service of racist or otherwise discriminatory politics: those practices identified as "authentic" can readily become a litmus test against which to measure who belongs and who does not. If we stipulate, for example, that Appalachia is a place of strong familial connections, even if we do so to endorse the powerful networks of mutual support kinship affords folks facing capitalist domination, we risk tacitly endorsing a patriarchal politics that ignores the very real struggles of female and queer (not to mention progressive male) Appalachians within and against patriarchal strictures. If we envision the Appalachian working class as the paragon of this region's experience, we risk ignoring the very real ways the emergence of local elites and social differences have shaped the region's history (Billings et al. 13). Even done with the best of intentions, the argument from authenticity is a dangerous one. For those then designated as legitimate members of the culture in question, it leads to a sense of exclusivity that results in something akin to nationalism, something that can and will be enforced by someone, to someone else's enduring harm.

That Greenblatt's disappointment comes at least in part from his exposure to Geertz and company is intriguing. This points to the ways in which Balinese culture was defined for him not by his own experience but by academic writing. When his experience ran up against the expectations that these academic studies created in him, he felt, at least at first, that it was the culture, not the studies of it, that needed emendation. This disjuncture is, I believe, part of the determinism of which Greenblatt speaks, a force that works to limit possibility for expansion, assimilation, and transformation of a culture even as it attempts or pretends to protect, privilege, or honor it.

The visible manifestation of this external determinism is the museum, which Benedict Anderson notes is one of the ways in which nationalism imagines itself to be written within nation, a historical inevitability (185). The museum is part of the grammar of the metalanguage of colonialism. Anderson points to the ways in which colonialists in Southeast Asia systematically "reconstructed" ancient cultural sites—Angkor Wat in Kampuchea, Borobudur in Indonesia—in the process draining them of their use value to the cultures in question (163–85). These same processes are at work in the preservation through depopulation that has taken place in the Great Smoky Mountains, giving us the meticulously "authentic" but now almost empty Cade's Cove, for example. Historian Durwood Dunn says of the preservation of this mountain community, which suffered "death by eminent domain" when it became part of the national park in the late twenties and early thirties, that "The single guiding principle was that anything which might remotely suggest progress or advancement beyond the most primitive stages should be destroyed. . . . the community's corpse was now to be mutilated beyond recognition. If the history of the cove had any meaning, it was simply that the people followed regional and national patterns of development" (256). Expropriation of farmland for parkland came amid other broad environmental, economic, and cultural changes: logging, for example, and the infamous chestnut blight which destroyed what historian John Alexander Williams describes as "one of the mainstays of the Appalachian forest, a tree whose role in human, animal, and plant ecology was irreplaceable" (298). This turbulence led to a period of out-migration tinged with bitterness. Williams documents residents' responses: " 'When families moved out, their hearts were broken,' a native of the Cattaloochee Valley in North Carolina remembered. 'Most of them left crying,' a Tennesseean recalled." Thus, far from preserving an autonomous mountain culture, the development of Cade's Cove and the Great Smoky Mountains National Park of which it is a part intensified and accelerated changes in Appalachian life.

This is a story seldom told in historic sites, despite the body of work currently being done by public historians urging them to do so. Instead, just as colonial archaeologists subverted first peoples' connections to their heritage by subjecting it to scientific scrutiny, and then reconstructing it in ways that make it seem irretrievably distant in history, heritage parks and preservation efforts sometimes sever contemporary Appalachia from its past. In *The Culture of Nature*, cultural landscape critic Alexander Wilson notes that "historical theme parks are . . . pessimistic affairs. They construct the idealized past of an organic community in harmony with nature, in the belief that this harmony is something we cannot look forward to again" (205). Not only do they sunder us from an imagined organic harmony, however, they also reconstruct it before our eyes in strangely alienating terms. This lost order survives only in commodity form, in a set of things that have replaced the complex dynamic of lived experience. This phenomenon Anderson terms "logoization," the conversion of cultural identities and subjectivities into uncomplicated emblems. Thus postcards of Angkor Wat—devoid of people—that allege to be the entire experience of Kampuchea, find their Appalachian counterparts in the "hillbilly gewgaws" that Alexander Wilson catalogs at Gatlinburg: "carved wood figurines, plastic flowers, Dolly Parton T-shirts, whiskey-still charm bracelets, Christian inspirational plaques, and fake folk medicines" (211). The character of the logo is in this case particularly distinguished by "its emptiness, contextlessness, visual memorableness, and infinite reproducibility" (B. Anderson 185), which is the ultimate destination of the quest for authenticity. When one nails down exactly what artifacts are at the heart of a culture, one is ready for the trip from Cade's Cove to Dollywood, which Wilson cunningly notes "calls into question the piousness of authentic reconstructions" (211) because it is at least upfront about its irony.

This is not to pose spaces like Cade's Cove and Dollywood as "phony" versions of the region against which some imagined, organic, authentic version stands in contrast. The question should not be whether these places are or are not "Appalachia," but instead what kind of Appalachia it is that they are, and how that version of the region interacts with others. In other words, we should view these sites as moments in a larger process of regional definition, no one of which may lay claim to any totalizing authority—whatever claims to such authority may be inherent or explicit in the ways they assemble logos or artifacts of the region. A critical regionalism must see these sites as moments in the composition of a larger rhetorical history, interacting convivially, antagonistically, or indifferently in an evolving process of regional definition and redefinition, not only with each other but also with other tactics and genres of regional definition—cartographic approaches, for example.

Regional Disconnections II: Place as Map

Ultimately, these various museum-like sanctuaries of "authenticity," facilitated by an approach to region centered on authoritatively defining a set of cultural practices, are of the same genus if not the same species as industrial parks, shopping centers, and suburbs inasmuch as, in Alexander Wilson's phrase, "their forms fragment geographies" (195). Wilson's emphasis on the geographical aspect of these parks—the ways in which they balkanize the past, and hence the present—points to the problem with the more commonsensical approach to defining region, like Calvino's Penates, as a land within boundaries. It may seem simpler to say, especially in light of the critique of defining culture in terms of practices, that culture is tied to a place, but when we start examining the implications of that alternative, we see geographies quickly fragment here as well.

"New Regionalist" scholars David Wrobel and Michael Steiner, for example, challenge the geographically monolithic idea of "The West": "The West (almost regardless of one's specific geographical definition) is a vast place, and it is home to many and often very different people, economies, histories, and regions" (17). Thus "The West in this context becomes . . . something rather difficult to map" (11). In Steiner and Wrobel's regionalism, multiple, fragmentary regional maps drawn by manifold social and natural factors play off, refocus, conflict with, and correct each other. What I suggest is that we take one more step in thinking about how these competing definitions map the region. As with the museums and historical reconstructions of the region, instead of seeing each map as a discrete definition of the region, we need to see the historical and contemporary interactions of these definitions—convivial or agonistic—as constituting the definition of the region.

Maps themselves are only a partial trace, then, through the larger circulation of cultural artifacts from which an evolving, adapting idea of region emerges. In their textual features and political histories, however, maps often assert for themselves a greater authority that should be regarded by critics with a certain skepticism. Benedict Anderson observes that if the museum is the objectification of cultural practice, the objectification of the space a culture occupies is the map. Certainly a trip to any of the many Dollywood gift shops to buy a Tennessee-shaped magnet illustrates how easily the map lends itself to logoization. Indeed, a growing body of scholarship is highlighting the ways geography and cartography have historically allied themselves with political positions, all the while denying the alliance through scientific or legalistic rhetoric. The acceptance of the cartographic definition of culture involves, like the colonialist museum, a refiguring of history, except that maps function not as a distancing but as a denial of the past. Maps rhetorically posit within their features an eternal, textual present, and even when the experience of the landscape by the traveler is at odds with the depiction, maps contain within themselves an argument for their own completeness and accuracy. The map user adopts a stance of deliberate naiveté about the authors' motives, which must surely be altruistic. (Rare—though not totally unheard of—is the map intentionally made to misdirect the user or obscure the terrain.) Yet to use a map is to some degree, at least, to acquiesce to its authority. It is tempting to do so unreflectively, as if maps were indeed windows on creation, authorless anomalies in the textual universe. And yet, behind this illusion of purely immediate representation lies immense authorial power—the power to write the very face of the earth.

In this light we should return to the maps on my office wall and note the many layers of authorship these artifacts involve. These are useful maps, wonderfully detailed maps, that have been of great practical value to me not only as an outdoorsman on my native ground but also as an evocation, far from home, of the places where I love to spend my time: Laurel Falls, Red Fork Falls, White Rocks, Zep Spot. But they are also—indeed, above all—government maps, and taken in that regard they are almost eerie in their detached, omnipotent gaze. These maps can seem spun out of the rhetoric of Michel de Certeau's "voyeur-god" who "must disentangle himself from the murky intertwining daily behaviors and make himself alien to them" (93), converting into data the contours of the land. The gaze is directed at the land, and the ways that it looks at the land necessarily depopulate it. The maps' pretense to timelessness is methodologically incapable of accounting for the movements, activities, and subjectivities of populations; a landscape superficially, at least, devoid of history is also a landscape devoid of sociality, of lived experience. As geographer J. B. Harley asserts, "the silent lines of the paper foster the notion of socially empty space" (284). All that remains are opaque representations of cultures, black dots that stand in for the habitations where we live in ways more complicated than correctly organized space can account for.

Looked at in a broader frame, however, these maps document social and political moments that connect to larger histories, conflicts, and questions that have profoundly shaped the experience of the places they depict. These particular quadrangles are, as the fine print notes, "Mapped by the Tennessee Valley Authority." It is oddly appropriate that the government agency that has arguably had the greatest role in rewriting not only the contours of the culture but the shape of the landscape itself is the agency to whom is given the authorial and authoritative (not to say authoritarian) task of describing the land, in comprehensive, objective, objectifying detail.

Just as the quiet remains of the Cade's Cove settlement belie the cultural and physical processes of removal that brought them to their current state, the dispassionate text of the TVA map seems inappropriately mute about the controversies and conflicts that have underwritten its very existence. Perhaps, however, we should move away from the features of the map proper, and consider those representational practices in larger contexts, or "move away," as Harley says, "from a history of maps as a

Rhetorics of Place and Region

record of the cartographer's intention and technical acts to one which locates the cartographic image in the social world" (303). The TVA maps' cool empiricism is undermined by the amorphous history of cartographic Appalachia, the progression of efforts at mapping the region itself, which mirrors the history of cartography in North America. Historian John Alexander Williams notes that "Appalachia is one of the oldest names on North American maps, dating from the early Spanish explorations of the United States. The name conveys the notion of a regional core somewhere in the highlands" (9). But Williams's term "notion" is to the point; he documents the multitude of geological, geographical, political, and cultural definitions that have converged, overlapped, and competed for status as the dominant definition of the region, extending its possible boundaries from Mississippi to New York, but excluding along the way selected sites that wished to disaffiliate themselves with the region's "hillbilly" connotations (Williams 9–13). Mapping Appalachia has been less about achieving a definitive set of boundaries than about a succession of acts of bounding, within which the TVA is an important but by no means dominant participant.

If the seemingly panoptical authority of the TVA's version of this place becomes somewhat less total considered in the context of its predecessors and successors, it becomes even less reliable when viewed as part of the TVA's larger project of cultural, economic, and geographical transformation of the region. First of all, maps are only one element of a complex of representations of the region that the TVA created to facilitate its work, from documentary photography and feature journalism to the 1940s motion picture *Valley of the Tennessee*. While these other representations are not themselves the kind of rationalist objectifications that maps are, they provide an affective context for encountering these maps, in the form of a triumphalist interpretation of the TVA and the presentation of the region's population as, in the words of cultural critic David Whisnant, "a ruined and spiritless people. . . . By contrast, TVA men are erect; their gazes are focused, analytical and direct. . . . They comprehend the system and command the technology, as their fingers knowingly trace charts, blueprints, and scale models" (*Modernizing* 273).

The TVA's use of maps, and the propaganda about its acts of mapping, depicted a monological, empiricist vision of the region's terrain that belies the conflicts within the history of this agency itself about what its disposition toward the region could or should be. The composition of TVA's founding triumvirate of directors during the New Deal suggests the multivalence of its cultural intervention: Arthur Morgan was a moralistic but progressive "social engineer" who spearheaded the TVA's cultural program; David Lilienthal, a pro-business rationalist who placed his faith in upgrading the region's infrastructure; and Harcourt Morgan (no relation to Arthur) was a social conservative and former University of Tennessee president whose commitments to local elites helped broker the authority's presence in local politics. Whisnant asserts, "TVA's actual social role would in effect arise out of the harmony (or conflict) among the [directors'] social and political views" (*Modernizing* 58). For historians Michael McDonald and John Muldowny, this interaction was marked mostly by conflict between Morgan's "community-oriented dream of an industrial capitalism reduced to rural proportions" and Lilienthal's goal of "bringing a 'backward' area into full modernity" (270). That the impact of TVA's intervention in the landscape has itself been ambivalent in its impact is thus not surprising. Socially progressive elements of the TVA's programs have gradually been stripped away, co-opted, or outmoded; while the agency did have success in bringing rural electrification to the region, arguably improving the standard of living for many rural and mountain dwellers in central and southern Appalachia, it has also created an appetite for electricity that outstrips its hydroelectric capabilities, meaning that the TVA has become a major player in the coal market that has caused economic turmoil and environmental catastrophe in Appalachia (Whisnant, *Modernizing* 48–56).

TVA has contributed to patterns of conflict, change, and motion in the region on the micro- as well as the macrolevel. Resettlement of people displaced by the creation of the TVA lakes, for example, has been a part of larger patterns of migration and motion that include the arrival of new residents, drawn by TVA-sponsored changes in regional culture. These migrations have, McDonald and Muldowny argue, had unexpected effects on the circulation of ideas about what the region is, and should be: "It is ironic that TVA's development has encouraged the process of modernity to the degree that new people have entered the Valley who want to preserve the region as it was, while those who lived in it as it was have either left it or have been unable, in many respects, to secure the advantages TVA was created to provide" (272). So, as with Cade's Cove and other historical sites that preserve a stable set of cultural practices as the definition of region, the abstracting, overdetermining power of mapping's rhetoric of definition catalyzes, rather than resolves, the ongoing debate over what exactly the region is.

Yet, again like the museum, the rhetoric of mapping operates as a denial of the dynamics of these historical, rhetorical engagements. Elizabeth Bishop, in her poem "The Map," says, that "mapped waters are more quiet than the land is" (3), a remark particularly apropos here as it captures the irony of those cool, uniformly blue expanses on, say, Boone Dam or Watauga Dam quadrangles. Indeed, even the quadrangle names (Watauga Dam or Johnson City or Elizabethton quadrangle, for example) promote technology and the urban settlements technology makes possible as the dominant feature of the landscape, its focus, its purpose. Beneath those waters are homesteads and graveyards and trails and valleys and hills to which the map does not admit as a past or present reality.

In Search of Regional Interconnections

Ultimately, maps and heritage museums work in roughly the same way in their quest to contain culture in an artificial and finite zone, which then makes culture available to unethical uses: commodification, exploitation, stereotyping. But they are also shot through by the same irony: their very existence is a part of patterns and processes of interconnection and change, of conflict and contestation, which undercut their surface claims to definition of and authority over place and region.

If the rational credibility of a finite, knowable region is questionable, however, there is some affective appeal to it. It is with some pride, I admit, that I look at the county-by-county map in the front cover of Paul Salstrom's *Appalachia's Path to Dependency* to discover that I am from "Older Appalachia," because Washington County, Tennessee, is shaded in a color signifying such status. But what would Salstrom say if he knew that there, in the heart of Older Appalachia, I grew up in a notably unrustic neighborhood of university professors known officially as Seminole Woods but informally as Scholar Holler—black dots and contour lines I can see on the map above my desk in Boston, undifferentiated from any other building on the map? What am I to make of the fact that my experience of Appalachia centers on a medium-sized city, and that the only times I have been around many of the items in Alice Faye Bragg's catalog of pieces of the true Appalachia—"the old hand-whittled shucking peg . . . [the] double shovel plow"—is in heritage museums? Is my experience of the region I claim geographically as the place of my birth rendered inauthentic by my place within the culture? My two models, curatorial and cartographic, are at loggerheads.

These misgivings are not, however, enough for me to believe that I never was an Appalachian; neither my experiences nor my culture has gone wrong, been conquered, disappeared here; rather, the available models of the culture I grew up in are too static to take into account the changes wrought in Appalachia over the years. Indeed, there never was a time of Edenic exemption from the processes of cultural change and evolution at any point in Appalachia or any other region, no moment of cultural purity. Recent historical scholarship points powerfully away from "the 'world we have lost' romanticism about a traditional mountain subculture" and toward "locating preindustrial Appalachia within the wider ambits of theoretical advances governing comparative historical scholarship of rural societies throughout the world" (Pudup et al. 18). Authenticity exists only as a construction of interested parties; as Raymond Williams argued in *The Country and the City*, every generation mourns the recent demise of the pastoral ideal, and the disappearance of the older, simpler ways—but for reasons that are entangled with the political conflicts of the day (12). It may be more useful, more accurate, and more ethically sound to regard the region as John Alexander Williams does, as a place that, like all places, "is a zone characterized by the interaction of global and local human and environmental forces and that regional boundaries inevitably shift with the perspectives of both subject and object" (12).

For all that is wonderfully or tragically unique about the region, there is at least as much that connects it with the experiences of other cultures and subcultures on a global scale. The influx of medical personnel into the Appalachian region from across the Indian subcontinent is one example that has already made its presence felt in the range of cultural texts that work to define the region. One of these immigrant doctors, Abraham Verghese (already himself a peculiar cultural hybrid: a Coptic Christian, ethnic Indian, raised in Ethiopia and practicing internal medicine in my hometown), has produced an account of his experiences in intercultural contact, tellingly entitled *My Own Country*—shifting regional, geopolitical, and discursive boundaries to reflect the perspective of the subject. This book is filled with scenes like this one, which neatly turns the tables on Stephen Greenblatt's experiences in Java:

> I had once tried to reach Dr. Patel, a cardiologist, to see a tough old lady in the ER. . . . I called his house and his wife told me he was at "Urology Patel's" house, and when I called there I learned he and "Pulmonary Patel" had gone to "Gastroenterology Patel's" house. Gastroenterology Patel's teenage daughter, a first-generation Indian-American, told me in a perfect Appalachian accent that she "reckoned they're over at the Mehta's playing rummy," which they were. (23)

Note here that not only have the "foreigners" expanded into an elaborate community, in which not only their work and their identities have merged, but also their own community has begun to merge, as it expands into a new generation, into the surrounding culture. With Greenblatt we might again ask, who is assimilating whom—especially as we recall the absolutely vital (as in "vital organs") role these newcomers play in their adopted home?

Given Verghese's atypical perspective, it is perhaps not so surprising that he produces a cultural study of remarkable nuance. In his book, we see a region distinguished not by uniformity but by the variety of its practices, a place that might be better characterized as Michel Foucault's "hetero-topia," which "is capable of juxtaposing in a single real place several spaces, several sites that are in themselves incompatible" (25)—the kind of "zone" Williams suggests facilitates a clearer understanding of the dynamic char-acter of Appalachia. This juxtaposition comes in part from the conflict between Verghese's both self-conscious and assigned "otherness" in the community—my community—that he attempts to make "his own," but it is intensified by the fact that Verghese's practice focuses on the commu-nity's first AIDS victims. The experience of reading Verghese's book is for me the juxtaposition of responses of familiarity, as he mentions people and sites well known to me, and unfamiliarity, as he becomes increasingly involved in the region's (heavily closeted) gay community, and this is the great value of this book: it simultaneously confirms and expands local perspectives.

A space in the cultural landscape of the region like "the Connection," the town's only gay bar and hence the only public "queer space," was for me, as a heterosexual male resident of the region, a taboo place, open for discussion with my peers only as a source of juvenile humor. Verghese experiences the same sense of socially cultivated aversion as he attempts to go there to give the region's first safe-sex presentation: "I thought the occupants of the car driving by were scrutinizing me. I stared straight ahead. My palms were sweating and I had to pee, though I had gone just before I left home. Did every man have to go through what I was going through in order to work up the courage to walk into the Connection?" (53)

However, where as a homophobic young person I was encouraged to see the Connection as an anomaly, an aberrant intrusion into my com-munity, for Verghese, the Connection is not only a queer space but is also specifically an Appalachian space. This crucial juxtaposition in this het-erotopia is made clear when Verghese encounters a person described as "neither a man in drag, nor . . . a woman" but "a spectacle, an east Tennessee queen" (57). Multiple tensions are intersecting in this place for Verghese, as indeed they did for me, a "native," although in a somewhat different fashion. The (aptly named) Connection becomes a contact point, a heterotopia, for multiple desires and spectacles, but also for dangers—specifically, the AIDS virus—that, as Verghese documents, threaten the regional population across lines of class, gender, ethnicity, and sexuality.

To the extent that Verghese's account of his life in east Tennessee during the rise of the AIDS epidemic exposes the fact that multiple publics make up the supposedly unitary region, he provides a valuable service. To a very great extent, region is in Verghese's account a porous and dynamic construct, with a heterogeneous population that opens cultural spaces for its particular, yet public, interests wherever and whenever possible. But Verghese's book illustrates how the cultural practices of groups excluded from a unitary version of the region find spaces in which to survive, and even prosper. The Connection is an example of this kind of social construction at work, but the Tri-City AIDS Project (TAP), the early days of which are documented in Verghese's book, shows something more like a critical regionalist version of a queer space. This advocacy and support group united (and continues to unite) gay and straight, infected and noninfected citizens into a regionalized site of discourse and social praxis that dislodged fixed social structures as it mobilized local interests against a larger problem—in other words, it transforms social construction into social action through social invention. Take the testimony of "Vickie," a working-class woman infected with HIV by her husband: "I have become a person I didn't know existed inside of me. I know I can make friends. I know I'm respected after people get to know me. And my heart is so full of love to them who need it. I'm so active in every organization I join. I'm now on the board of TAP! Can you believe it? An old country hick like me!" (334). Vickie's last interjection signals her awareness of her place in the existing order of traditional versions of the regional culture. But by participating in a space opened by locals on the margins—gays, working-class women and men, the "diseased"—she has gained perspective on the contingent nature of the models she previously worked within unquestioningly. Ironically, and sadly, this has come because of her terminal illness: the price at which she has gained her knowledge of the variety of cultures and subcultures, which compose the dynamic region she has lived in, is the end of her life. Her creation of a complex skein of political and social connections is not sustainable.

Nor is it for Verghese. While recording the struggles and successes of his AIDS patients, Verghese also documents the near collapse of his personal life, especially his marriage, which triggers a decision at the book's conclusion to move away. The collapse of Verghese's collective sensibility, the individualization of social problems with which his text concludes, resonates almost as an abandonment. This is not to criticize a choice that, for Verghese, must have been difficult indeed, or to belittle his personal conflicts; rather, this decision points to the ways in which a model that begins to take into account the variegated and dynamic nature of a place ends by invoking another limiting, stratifying trope of regional representation: apocalypse.

That Verghese's account ends with the individualization of social problems and a subsequent abandonment of the place where those problems transpire marks it as part of a tradition of regional representations, both fiction and nonfiction, that includes a good deal of this century's writing about Appalachia, picturing the region as "a place without hope" (Stanley 72n). This closing gesture on Verghese's part belies his depiction up to that point of a dynamic, multicultural landscape, engaged in crises afflicting both local and broader cultures, alive with desire, loss, and expectation, as well as tradition and continuity. The implications of Verghese's final decision are foreshadowed by his development (and publication, in the *Journal of Infectious Diseases*) of a "paradigm" for the migration of the region's gay men. What he discovers is that these men, having eventually reached gay communities in urban centers where they became infected, were coming home to die. However, rather than opening the presumptive stability of Appalachian culture to a new kind of scrutiny, the research culminates in a new *personal* appreciation of the divisions between the region and the rest of the world: "I will not be able to forget these young men, and the little towns they came from, and the cruel, cruel irony of what awaited them in the big city" (326). It is not surprising, given the stable inside-outside of this city-country model, that Verghese comes to this model by tracing migratory patterns on a map: "I could see a distinct pattern of dots emerging on this larger map of the U.S.A. All evening I had been on the threshold of seeing. Now I fully understood. The paradigm was revealed" (319–20).

The Trail, Made by Walking

Part of the problem with Verghese's conclusions, then, is its undercutting of hope through its substitution of personal for collective concerns. Part of it, though, comes from the attempt to think of the culture paradigmatically. This problem is intensified, indeed, perhaps even caused by the crisis surrounding Verghese's situation. Verghese's paradigm leads to a siege mentality that hinges on an "us versus them" pattern of thinking, the cruel world, the city and its dangers, encroaching on the organic community and its rich resources of traditional values. Clearly, elsewhere in Verghese's account, it is not traditional values but the reconfiguration of Appalachian culture in vital subcultures and new spheres of public life that sustains the culture against crisis. The search for a paradigm ends at a conclusion not too far afield from Alice Bragg's nostalgic claim that Appalachia is the heart's longing to go home again. Indeed, that is exactly what Appalachia has become for the author, in exile from "his own country," at the book's conclusion.

Verghese's tentatively dynamic and generative model is undercut, then, by conflicting impulses: toward individual emotional reaction, but also toward epic sweep. The collective culture in its various forms disappears into a background of doomed struggle, summarized in Verghese's paradigmatic map, and behind the tragic heroism of individuals brought too far into the foreground—transforming the text as a whole into a kind of museum, a pantheon of the honored dead. Verghese's story raises all the right questions about the need for our models of place to take into account multiple possibilities, migrations, experiences, and politics, but in the end, structurally and intellectually the book falls short of constructing ways of thinking about the region that facilitate this inquiry— the work longs too much for the paradigm to be revealed, and misses the point that his own material makes in abundance: that many paradigms compete for primacy in this space and that it is this multiplicity itself that constitutes the region. Verghese brings us to the point where, in the words of anthropologist Mary Anglin, "we are either left with images of rugged mountains and rich lore laced with superstition, or the recognition that we have limited understanding of a region cross-cut by complex histories, social relations, and cultural traditions" (177), and he defaults to the former. With Anglin, I am calling for "an alternate vision, a blurring of the lines between Appalachia and 'the outside' " which "would not displace Verghese's portrait so much as contextualize it. . . . In this rendering, Appalachia is a place where homosexuals, heterosexuals, and people of indeterminate sexual identities have lived amongst the contradictions of sexism, homophobia, and tolerance" (179–80).

But what would such a text look like, one that rejects the totalizing claims that the dominant genres and discourse of place seem to make tacitly and almost inevitably? What would a text about a place be like that searches not for the moment of enlightenment in which the place's paradigm is revealed but instead for what Michel de Certeau calls "its tireless but quiet activity" (31): the partial traces, artifacts, images, metaphors that provide clues and insights, incentives to further cultural production and debate? In the case of a region, as not simply a place but an aggregation of places, it is crucial that these moments of cultural production, ephemeral when considered in isolation, be seen not as relatively discrete and autonomous but as connected not only to each other but to broader patterns of the production of space, of history, of culture and politics.

The history of the Appalachian landscape includes one vital example of the kind of text I am arguing for here: the Appalachian Trail (AT). The trail resists attempts to understand the region as a stable, finite object. Rather, in both its current configurations and its history, the Appalachian Trail provides a way to understand region in terms of social construction, social invention, and social action. In other words, it facilitates a critical regionalist understanding of Appalachia. If the walker is, as de Certeau argues, a creative force whose very act of walking rewrites the cultural text of the urban landscape, the trail provides the kind of site in which the actions of walkers not only collectively produce a durable artifact that connects the meaning and purpose of their actions over time and across space, but it also provides a site that can be examined by the cultural critic as a locus of particular sorts of cultural production. The AT constructs a regional rhetoric for the production of representations that connect spaces together in specific configurations for particular purposes.

The Appalachian Trail is also an apt site for exploring critical regionalism as a cultural studies methodology inasmuch as its travelers produce not only the footpath itself as a durable artifact, but also a broad spectrum of texts employing a diverse range of representational practices. In this sense the AT (and its constituent texts) can be studied as an act of social construction. The AT and the varied experiences of walking it become a locus of collective, durable cultural production, even during the hiking of the trail itself, as many shelters are equipped with journals in which hikers create a collaborative text that mixes practical information about trail conditions with personal communication between individuals and groups and more philosophical ruminations. But after the hiking itself (or interspersed with it), hiker-authors continue to produce a remarkable range of texts. As David Emblidge notes in his *Appalachian Trail Reader*:

> Hikers' private journals stand next to scientists' close observations of the natural world, and these readings mingle with poets' evocations of the natural world and its spirit. Historians remind us of how Appalachian culture developed, and early explorers report the thrill of seeing uncharted territory for the first time. Some of the writings come from celebrated literary professionals; many come from enthused amateurs whose experience on the trail inspired them to capture what they could of it in words. (xiv)

Emblidge suggests that he has crafted his own work to resemble the experience of hiking the trail (xi), and other examples tend to mimic the trail's multiple significations and rambling shape. Robert A. Browne's *The Appalachian Trail: History, Humanity, and Ecology* is a representative example of a larger trail-centered genre: the thru-hiker's journal, a write-up of observations and adventures while hiking the entire length of the trail. A single page or two invokes the physical beauty of the landscape; an account of the impact of logging, as the trail coincides with the bed of an old narrow-gauge railroad; botanical and ornithological notes; contact with fellow hikers, both in person and in the form of another of the trail's literary genres, the trail shelter register; and a historical note on the life of a hermit whose cabin abutted the trail's current route (32–33).

Sponsoring the production of Browne's book and the work of other travelers is another trail text, the guidebooks produced by the Appalachian Trail Conference, a nongovernmental organization based in Harpers Ferry, West Virginia—roughly the trail's midpoint. Unintentionally parallel to postmodern works like Calvino's *Invisible Cities* in their atomized, intertextual, reversible format (each section presents the same information twice, north to south and south to north), the guides fragment the trail into individual moments distinguished by mileage notations. The significance of an individual unit varies widely, however. Some are directive ("0.2 Reach ridgetop and follow rocky crest"), others cautionary ("13.1 . . . *Caution*: If the [trail] is flooded, return to old railroad grade and walk downstream"), others scenic ("12.6 . . . This ridge, covered with pine, Catawba rhododendron, and mountain laurel, affords fine views of rocky gorge walls"). Unlike a map they are rooted in both the history and the current formation and reroutings of the ever-changing trail, constantly reissued to take into account the latest developments.

This multimodal form and procedural responsiveness to contingency signal an important difference between the approach to representing place in these guides and the strategies we see in both heritage museums and TVA maps: rather than attempting to discern and reify an objectified definition of a place, the guides take their shape from the place itself, but for purposes defined by its users. Instead of molding Appalachia (by forcing it into a preconceived mold?), both the texts and the walkers are molded by it. The guides' division of the AT into like sections defined by points of intersection with main roads is an arbitrary gesture on its face: why not segment the trail according to major peaks, trail shelters, water sources, or other objectives? But that arbitrariness is principled in that it is geared to the experience of the trail by a broad cross section of its users, tacitly undermining the fiction of "wilderness" that would serve to (seemingly) isolate the trail from other spaces, and instead emphasizing its connection to other networks of human travel and its relationship to car culture.

These texts are about access to Appalachia on the scale of human users in a working relationship to the region, of participants in the life of the place, not on the detached and dominating scale of the "voyeur-gods" of the TVA maps, and not in terms of a stable, binary insider-outsider relationship. The book as a useful book, as a basis for experiences, makes its text an experience in the tension between objectivity and subjectivity, an experience in reflexivity—just as the trail itself involves, at many points, the re-creation of what were once utilitarian experiences. The section of Browne's book that I summarized previously and the section of the trail guide I have just quoted both take place on a section of trail through Laurel Fork Gorge that not only follows the bed of an old logging railroad but also provided the route for the inhabitants of the gorge and the valley upstream to walk down to the community of Braemar, Tennessee, for supplies (*Appalachian Trail* 68–72). The text of the trail guide underscores this simultaneous utilitarian objectivity and individualist subjectivity as it continually addresses itself to the reader; unlike the trail journals, the guidebook is a persistent second person, acknowledging that the AT is not an entity itself but exists for the use of others. These texts embrace the partial role and implication in broader networks of social construction.

The AT would not in fact exist for anyone's use without acts of authorship and collaboration that link the trail to broader social histories. Benton MacKaye's 1921 essay "An Appalachian Trail: A Project in Regional Planning" emerged not only from the intellectual ferment of the larger collective of the Regional Planning Association of America (RPAA), but it was developed in particular consultation with the RPAA's philosopher-critic, Lewis Mumford (Simo 86), and Clarence Stein, its organizing force and the editor of the *Journal of the American Institute of Architects* in which MacKaye's essay appeared (Parsons 466). In this article and in his other writings, MacKaye makes clear that the AT is not, in his conception, simply a means of transportation or outdoor escapism, but a rhetorical enterprise in itself, an effort to convince as broad an audience as possible to reconsider and reconceptualize the way that the spaces of the North American landscape are organized in relation to each other. In other words, MacKaye and his collaborators conceived of and designed the trail as an act of what can be termed social invention.

Social invention is to social construction as walking in de Certeau's sense is to MacKaye's concept of exploration: a deliberate act of organiz-

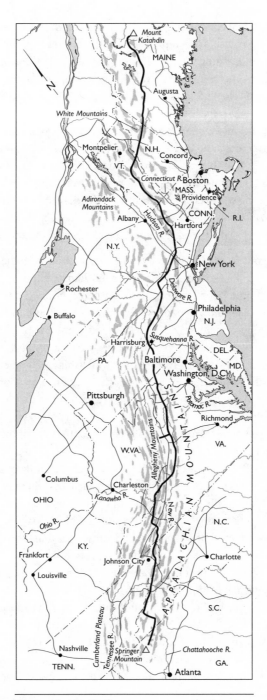

The Appalachian Trail

ing the contingent constructions that one can discern into formations that serve some purpose, into representations that create a deliberate and assertive meaning rather than one defined purely by cultural and political contingencies. The textuality of MacKaye's conception of the trail is underscored by Melanie Simo's suggestion that he saw the AT as a project comparable to his father Steele's experiments in the theater: "If, as Benton believed, Steele MacKaye had viewed the theater as a 'focusing lens' or telescope, to give people new perspectives on their lives, so Benton could try something comparable, to 'focus the people's vision' on the forces—economic, social, environmental—that were quietly, relentlessly shaping their lives" (83). Simo's assertion is borne out by MacKaye's remarkable thought experiment in "An Appalachian Trail," in which he asks readers to imagine a giant striding along the crest of the Appalachian mountain range:

> Starting out from Mt. Washington, the highest point in the northeast, his horizon takes in one of the original happy hunting grounds of America—the "Northwoods," a country of pointed firs extending from the lakes and rivers of northern Maine to those of the Adirondacks. Stepping across the Green Mountains and the Berkshires to the Catskills, he gets his first view of the crowded east—a chain of smoky bee-hive cities extending from Boston to Washington and containing a third of the population of the Appalachian drained area. Bridging the Delaware Water Gap and the Susquehanna on the picturesque Alleghany folds across Pennsylvania he notes more smoky columns—the big plants between Scranton and Pittsburgh that get out the basic stuff of modern industry—iron and coal. In relieving contrast he steps across the Potomac near Harpers Ferry and pushes through into the wooded wilderness of the southern Appalachians where he finds preserved much of the primal aspects of the days of Daniel Boone. Here he finds, over on the Monongahela side the black coal of bituminous and the white coal of water power. He proceeds along the great divide of the upper Ohio and sees flowing to waste, sometimes in terrifying floods, waters capable of generating untold hydro-electric energy and of bringing navigation to many a lower stream. He looks over the Natural Bridge and out across the battle fields around Appomattox. He finds himself finally in the midst of the great Carolina hardwood belt. Resting now on the top of Mt. Mitchell, highest point east of the Rockies, he counts up on his big long fingers the opportunities which yet await development along the skyline he has passed. (326)

Here on a grand scale is an experience similar to that of the individual hiker in the Laurel Fork Gorge of upper east Tennessee, in which natural attributes and processes, economic and cultural histories, and legacies of political conflict enmesh to create a complex and dynamic intersection of forces in a distinctive and geographically specific network of places. The region emerges not as some boundaried whole, but as a complex relationship among places—a relationship that emerges through the creative perception of the observer, for the purposes of creating an argument about how relationships among places should be perceived.

One might see in this gigantic perspective something similar to the TVA's (at least superficially) monolithic view of the region as power resource. But MacKaye's giant sees more than "natural resources" available in the mountain range, and instead the possibility for full employment, for abundant food, for relief to social problems of crowding and crime and environmental problems of pollution and waste that emanate from the fractured metropolitan landscapes of the eastern seaboard. For MacKaye the solution to these problems would come in part from a series of camps that would create a new kind of social order for which the AT would be the backbone. "Shelter Camps" spaced logically along the trail would begin the changing settlement patterns by encouraging walkers to see the camp as a space of inhabitation, not merely retreat. "Community Groups" would grow up around the shelter camps to provide the goods and services the itinerant campers (some of whom would cease their wandering) would require, and "Food and Farm Camps" would, in a final stage, be established to provide the provisions these groups would require, making them self-sufficient: "The camp community is a sanctuary and a refuge from the scramble of every-day worldly commercial life. It is in essence a retreat from profit. Cooperation replaces antagonism, trust replaces suspicion, emulation replaces competition. An Appalachian trail, with its camps, communities, and spheres of influence along the skyline, should, with reasonably good management, accomplish these achievements. And they possess within them the elements of a deep dramatic appeal" (328–29).

As that last sentence makes clear, for MacKaye the AT is a medium for presenting to the American public the idea that a self-sufficient and environmentally sensible life is in fact possible. Thus the primary function of the trail was as a rhetorical practice, as a means of representation and of persuasion. As historian Paul Sutter writes, "[W]hat MacKaye really hoped the AT would encourage was perspective, the essential link between mere recreation and a more thorough re-creation of modern living" (566). This purpose is clear in the way MacKaye ends his essay not with a ringing vision of his Utopia realized, but with a discussion of the "Dramatic Appeal" of the AT and the "scouting life" it facilitates. In a point that resonates in the present time, MacKaye argues that the attempt to live amid more generative and useful relationships among people and landscapes is a less sensational struggle than war. But he optimistically concludes that "There is but one reason—publicity. Militarism has been made colorful in a world of drab. But the care of the country side, which the scouting life instills, is vital in any real protection of 'home and country.' Already basic it can be made spectacular. Here is something to be dramatized" (330).

MacKaye's sense of the "dramatic" potential of the Appalachian Trail suggests what region could be, when freed from the dominant sense of place as a discrete geographical thing or finite set of cultural practices. He engages region, and indeed the idea of place itself, as a practice of representation, a way of rhetorically linking spaces into complex configurations that serve particular purposes. In this form, region, as a term that describes the relationship of multiple places, has the potential to be a social invention envisioning better ways of ordering places, peoples, and cultures, a "focusing lens" that can help identify, scrutinize and respond to complex intersections of labor, environment, politics, and economics in particular sites on the landscape—intersections that point toward interconnections with other places, peoples and cultures.

Keeping this discussion in the conditional tense is important, however. Despite its rich socially constructed network of representations (including the AT itself), and the deliberate social invention underlying its inception, the AT has not, by any means, fulfilled MacKaye's vision for reordering the American landscape, and indeed has not approximated the form he described in his foundational essay. The Appalachian Trail may certainly be seen as one of the most remarkable and enduring monuments to MacKaye's vision of regionalism and to the entire work of the RPAA; to this day it represents a complicated, evolving collaboration among government and private citizens as its maintenance and protection depends on the combined work of the National Parks Service, U.S. Forest Service, the nongovernmental Appalachian Trail Conference, local AT clubs, and the landowners across and beside whose lands the trail passes, not to mention the hikers who use it daily. And on a more conceptual level, as Sutter argues, the AT embodies a more complicated vision of the relationship between culture and nature, between society and wilderness, than much of the thinking about these issues before or since (555).

From the early stages of the construction of the AT, however, it became apparent that MacKaye's grand vision of a socialist Appalachian region that would provide not only a refuge from urban environments but indeed "a retreat from Profit" would not come to pass. On the contrary,

Rhetorics of Place and Region

the promotion and coordination of the construction of the AT fell to urbane professionals like Milton Avery, a Harvard-educated lawyer who served as chairman of the Appalachian Trail Conference from 1932 until his death in 1952. Just as the TVA's social mission fell away as its leadership became increasingly controlled by directors who saw its purpose in strictly utilitarian terms, the AT became increasingly seen by the professional and managerial classes who became its stalwarts as a venue for recreation—in the attenuated meaning of the term MacKaye worked so vigorously against. As geographer Ronald Foresta writes,

> Although MacKaye envisioned the trail as a cooperative endeavor of working people, guided perhaps by social reformers, the project became avocational for professionals who were assisted by managers of public lands. That appropriation of leadership was crucial in determining the character of the trail. . . . Neither group had any interest in a broad societal mission for the trail in the manner of MacKaye and the other founders. (80)

Indeed, one thing the early organizers of the AT worked expressly against was the idea that squatters would take up residence along its route.

If the Appalachian Trail failed in its instrumental function, it may also have failed more profoundly in its rhetorical function. Rather than energizing radical politics, the political potential of the AT has been largely ignored by radicals; meanwhile, corporations and what Foresta terms "a contented segment of society" have endorsed and promoted the AT as an opportunity for individualist, escapist leisure (84). In this sense the Appalachian Trail repeats the pattern common to many of the works of the RPAA of failure to achieve in execution what was envisioned in theory. The other major monument to MacKaye's vision, for example, is the Route 128 bypass of Boston, a project that MacKaye conceived as a greenbelt to thwart the kinds of development he termed "wayside fungus" and that has become today a worst-case scenario of suburban sprawl (Spann 193).

But the comparison of the AT to Route 128 can also show that it is possible to overstate the case. The Appalachian Trail has certainly not assumed the physical form MacKaye originally proposed for it. But if we consider its success in terms of the rhetorical properties that MacKaye considered its most immediate and important function, we might see it as a qualified success. If indeed the radical potential of the AT has been co-opted by the class affiliations of many of its enthusiasts, one cannot doubt that it has caused an ever-growing number of people to walk the Appalachian ridge crests like MacKaye's giant, and it is perhaps impossible to measure the extent to which the AT's adherents have adopted the "tendencies" toward viewing in a new light the relationship of populations, landscapes, and lifestyles MacKaye saw as the immediate outcome of the AT experience—physical transformation of North American settlement patterns being a secondary result at best. In drawing the professional classes into a new and working relationship with the mountain region, MacKaye's AT may have ultimately done some good, even if it falls short of his ultimate, transformational goals.

Indeed, it may be important in and of itself that the AT has not assumed a form dominated by one man's idiosyncratic theories and plans. Instead, as the constellation of representations that mediate the larger, collective experience of the AT indicates, the AT-as-text is a palimpsest overwritten with the practices of its many users over time. And it has afforded certain kinds of advocacy as well: in sites from Saddleback Ridge in Maine to the high balds of the Tennessee–North Carolina border, the AT and its protected corridor have become rallying points for not just narrowly defined "wilderness protection" but broader struggles over environmental politics, industrialization, and development. The answer to the question MacKaye posed in 1921, "Would the development of the outdoor community life—as an offset and relief from the various shackles of commercial civilization—be practicable and worthwhile?" (327), can be a confident yes.

In fact, I assert that the answer is even more strongly affirmative because the AT has proved malleable in its means and purposes over time. In other words, the AT could be and in various if limited ways has been a site of social action. If the AT has failed as of yet to become a vital political rallying point for the average resident along its route, its demonstrated ability to transform over time suggests that it could yet do so. For example, Hot Springs, North Carolina, and Damascus, Virginia, are both towns whose economic base had dramatically contracted, the former with the disappearance of the "medicinal springs" tourist trade that once was the main form of the leisure economy in the region, and the latter a former outpost of the timber industry. More recently they have evolved into "Trail towns," providing hospitality to hikers and other outdoorsmen, echoes of MacKaye's ideal of the "community camp," "something more than a mere 'playground'; it should stimulate every possible line of outdoor non-industrial endeavor" (328). Rather than becoming centrally planned worker's utopias, however, the trail towns have evolved out of a mix of hiker needs and locally perceived opportunities. That these changes were not dictates of the AT and its founding visionaries, but rather emerged from patterns of its adaptive use and reinterpretation over generations of users, suggests that in a more socially active way than its planners originally conceived, the AT has fulfilled MacKaye's assertion that "If . . . people were on the skyline, and kept their eyes open, they would see the things that the giant could see. Indeed this force . . . would be a giant in itself. It could walk the skyline and develop its varied opportunities" (327). Perhaps these trail towns might become as well seedbeds for new kinds of grass-roots social organization taking place across the lines of class and culture that undoubtedly intersect in the interactions between the "hiking classes" and their local hosts? Or will they become outposts of a regional subspecies of gentrification, spurring second-home development and a boutique economy that serves the wishes of the contented classes and squeezes locals ever further into the margins? How might the AT provide a perspective that affords views of just and equitable solutions to such dilemmas?

Whether or not the Appalachian Trail is completely successful in the conversion of its purpose as a social invention into a vehicle for social action, it represents a powerful model of an alternative perspective on place and on region—one that embraces the rhetorical function of a region not as a thing itself or set of things but as a way of talking to people about the relationships among places and convincing them what those relationships should be. The AT also makes clear by contrast the fallacy in the approaches to understanding place that I outlined earlier in the chapter—the mistake of trying to think about a region as a thing, rather than a way of thinking about and representing the spatial relationship of things and people, of texts and authority. If it is necessary to think of place as a complex and dynamic relationship among different images and experiences of the space it occupies, in the particular case of a region the imperative is even more absolute. By definition, when we speak of region we are talking not about any one location but a group of locales, brought into a relationship by a factor or set of factors: politics, economics, culture, history. A region is not either a geographically bounded slice of terrain or a finite set of representative cultural practices, but is a way of describing the relationship among a broad set of places for a particular purpose; the larger identity of a region is not defined by any single definition but emerges from the dynamic, historical relationship of these acts of definition. Neither Lares nor Penates, to recall the example from Calvino with which I began, are indeed the true essence of Leandra; rather, their interaction creates and sustains the city. Perhaps, at the time that the picture of me writing that early draft of this chapter was taken, I was not in Appalachia in any meaningful way, but that picture itself is (now) Appalachian, inasmuch as it has been drawn into the representational history of the region, the sometimes convivial, sometimes agonistic circulation of texts postulating and questioning what exactly the region is.

Understanding this circulation of meanings and engaging with it is what critical regionalism can do. In its participatory, purposeful, and political acts of regional definition, the Appalachian Trail suggests what critical regionalism can be: a way of using region deliberately to make visible the forces that intersect and intercede to create a network of places, not to isolate them from the larger movements of culture, politics, and history but to enmesh them in these movements intricately and inextricably. More important, the Appalachian Trail shows both the potential and the perils of articulating a vision of how else the region could work amid these forces, to mediate them in such a way as to catalyze the creation of a better kind of place.

Places are not things to be found out there in the world; they are ideas about spaces that are constructed by people, in acts of observation and interpretation, and more durably in writing, in visual arts, in the built environment. Places come to seem like things because over time multiple interpretations and representations begin to coalesce around specific spaces, building on each other in ways both convivial and agonistic. Regions are a particular sort of place, a kind of meta-place that emerges from analyses and descriptions of how specific sites within a group relate to each other. Like the more localized places of which they are composed, the appearance of a permanent and stable form derives from the aggregation of different, sometimes competing, sometimes collaborating, versions of what that region is. These descriptions and analyses are created by different people and groups of people for particular reasons, and they shape not only how the region itself is understood but also how the places that make up the larger region are understood. If place itself, then, is a complex and contingent social construction, region is a social invention for describing the political, cultural, historical, and economic relationships among places.

In this chapter, I look at a couple of spaces that draw on specific elements of the traditional representational vocabulary of the Appalachian region, for example, log cabins in public parks and trash dumps in remote mountain hollows. Looking at these particular sites will point toward the ways that critical regionalism can be useful in examining how the movement of people and things, of images and ideas, can be seen to constitute these places as part of broader spatial configurations. Chapter 1 was devoted to understanding the idea of region as a (apparent) whole, how the concept of region itself forges metonymies on a broad geographical scale. Chapter 2 examines how regional relationships shape and are shaped by specific places, for the purpose of creating new understandings of these places that challenge spurious and often oppressive common-sense notions about the social, cultural, and political hierarchies of these places.

The spaces under consideration in this chapter share a superficial appearance of being apart from more important forms of life and work: spaces of escape or of disposal, spaces where meaning is eluded or cast off. From a layman's perspective, public parks, with their recreational facilities and historic exhibits, may seem to be relatively innocuous spaces for play and leisure, and dumps may appear to be purely utilitarian, but here I examine each as complex texts that produce a variety of meanings about the relationship of the places they are part of to larger political, historical, and cultural geographies.

The community under consideration in this chapter is the town where I grew up, Johnson City, Tennessee. As the setting for Abraham Verghese's *My Own Country*, it was described in chapter 1, but some more detail is in order. Johnson City is a city of about 50,000 located in the extreme northeast corner of the state, part of the Tri-Cities Metropolitan Statistical Area that includes neighboring Kingsport, Tennessee, and Bristol, Tennessee-Virginia. In the heart of the Great Appalachian Valley running from southeast Tennessee into southern Pennsylvania, the city nonetheless has historically served as a kind of interface between the southern Appalachian region and larger cultural and economic systems, the economic power of its local elites exerting a major shaping force over the history of its surroundings and the people who live there. In the words of historian Tom Lee, "If there has been a common theme in the story of the Tri-Cities area, it has been the power of a set of businessmen, professionals, and civic leaders to define a vision for an entire area" (267).

Like many relatively young cities, Johnson City is a community with few intentionally public spaces. Founded along the rail right-of-way in the latter half of the eighteenth century, Johnson City has become a town without a center. It has not always been thus: its downtown was once a thriving center of the economic, social, and political life of the city. The railroad depot at the center of downtown's Fountain Square was not only a site of public history, the literal point of origin for a community that began as a water tank on the rail line, but also a site for public discourse about matters local, regional, and national, for political speeches by candidates on whistle-stop tours, for parades, and for other rituals of community.

Johnson City's downtown, however, like many in cities of its size and age, is in a general state of decline; instead, the city's business and cultural landscape is dominated by the generic suburban sprawl of North Johnson City, where wide arterial streets connect chain restaurants, shopping centers, and car dealerships across expanses of parking lots. And it is worth noting that this area of greatest development—around the junction of U.S. 11-E and Tennessee 36 near their junction with Interstate 26—is also marked by the fewest public parks.

I do not mean to wax nostalgic about Johnson City's past. First of all, it is a past I never really knew; by the time I was an adolescent in the late 1970s, the shift in cultural and economic power from downtown to strip mall was pretty much complete. And I am circumspect about the fact that the robust civic life that used to play out on Fountain Square was part of a civic order dominated by a system of privilege and race and gender discrimination—its public life was in most respects the practice of white supremacist capitalist patriarchy. But the strip mall district, with its homogenizing power literally steamrollering the local landscape as it carves it into private, restricted spaces, is a pretty sorry version of the public space where, as landscape studies scholar John Brinckerhoff Jackson writes, "the role of the individual in the community is made visible, where we reveal our identity as part of an ethnic or religious or political or consumer-oriented society" (18). In this district, the role of the individual as anything other than a consumer of goods is largely obscured, just as the relationship of this landscape to its natural and cultural contexts is concealed. Even though the older versions of public life were flawed, this new order does not offer a better alternative, reflecting so little of the problems and priorities of locals and localities, denying the interconnectedness of different aspects of the landscape.

But it cannot be wished away. Critical regionalism must confront the land as it lays even as it seeks "the best life possible," to use Lewis Mumford's words. Moreover, Jackson, in the same discussion quoted earlier, goes on to assert that the strip mall and the other relatively recent developments of the vernacular landscape might have public functions that as yet we are not capable of recognizing: "What is left of the old political landscape vanishes," he writes, "but as yet we have no name for the one which is taking form around us" (21). Naming this new set of representations and relationships is what critical regionalism is for, in sum, even though naming is not an end in itself but part of a larger project of social invention for social action that can move the city and the region toward a better future. If the American cultural landscape is increasingly dominated by consumer and recreational forms, as the example of Johnson City's recent development suggests, then trying to understand these landscapes of recreation and consumption in their historical and political dimensions becomes an important project—especially since, in their deliberate devotion to a uniformly pleasant and entertaining sensory experience, in playing to the least, most common denominators of their human constituents, these spaces seem to try so vigorously to deny the continued significance of history and politics.

The problem, in other words, is not one of place versus placelessness; this situation is not a crisis of the erasure of the local, even in the form of historical and political conflict. Rather, the challenge here is how to discern the local—its history, its politics—in these new configurations, to understand how its constructed space links these particular landscapes to larger issues, larger struggles, larger histories—in other words, how the specific site is implicated in broader regional relationships. The first half of this chapter thus devotes detailed attention to new spaces for sport and play that have appeared in Johnson City in the last decade, with special attention to the ways the relationship (or lack of it) of local history to broader patterns of political, cultural, and social change is encoded and interpreted in these at least superficially apolitical and ahistorical landscapes. In the late 1980s the city of Johnson City developed two new recreation areas, Winged Deer Park, which opened in 1991, and Buffalo Mountain Park, which opened a few months later in 1992 ("Parks and Recreation"). Both parks, I argue, create landscape narratives of abiding conflicts in local identity that foreground the community's sense of its place in the region and the nation.

Playgrounds of the Pioneers

At least as early as Frederick Law Olmsted Sr.'s 1880 essay "The Justifying Value of a Public Park," landscape scholars, designers, and enthusiasts in the United States have recognized the importance of parks as formal leisure spaces to people, to communities, and to culture (Simo 118). In his central work *The New Exploration* (1928), Benton MacKaye asserts that one key distinction in human activities is the difference between "recreation" and "decreation," the former being a kind of play that is productive in some way, what he terms "constructive relaxation," the latter a mere escapist "undoing and unraveling" (126–27). MacKaye hoped that spaces like the Appalachian Trail might transform mere idle leisure into more useful, socially inventive forms of cultural production, harnessing play into the "re-creation" of lost connections between inhabitants of a place and their history and environment ("An Appalachian Trail" 325–26). As we shall see, one might surmise that MacKaye would be somewhat less than pleased with the design of the parks under consideration here: Winged Deer Park focuses its design on team sports of the sort that, in the uniformity of their practice from place to place, have little to do with their specific context, while Buffalo Mountain Park offers only the most basic infrastructure for what MacKaye termed "the scouting life" with a network of trails built on a mountainside.

But MacKaye's categories are perhaps a tautology, for something is created in these parks, even if not a critical or even deliberate sense of regional interconnections. Though a space for sport and play, seemingly apolitical activities, these are public spaces that represent a formative aspect of the collective identity of the communities they serve. As civic spaces, creations of and for the community, these spaces can and should be the focus of a critical regionalist critique as sites that should encourage the practice of democracy. As sites of collective landscape construction and shared experience, they should be part of a process of social invention facilitating the connectedness of the local landscape to larger histories and the imagination of better futures. Public spaces present landscapes that can be made the object of public debate, a place to begin the task of inventing region anew. But without critical reflection on the design and construction of these sites, not only as public spaces for the practice of community life but also as places to imagine and achieve the complex interconnections between the specific community and the rest of the region and the nation, parks become social constructions whose de facto social inventions suggest no vision at all. They substitute instead a narrow, parochial, and atomized version of region that cannot facilitate social action.

Spreading across former pastures, Winged Deer Park is an expansive and impressive multipurpose facility on the city's northern edge, beside the Tennessee Valley Authority's Boone Lake—a location that automatically links this place to the modernist landscape ethic of "official" Appalachian regionalism. Organizationally, the park centers on well-appointed softball and soccer fields, which host annual tournaments that draw in visitors from across the region, even the nation. A four-lane U.S. highway provides principal access to the park and becomes North Roan Street, the arterial serving North Johnson City, the mall, car dealerships, discount stores, and chain restaurants. The development of the park has been part of, and surely a catalyst for, a remarkable building drive in this area. Property already enhanced in value by its proximity to the lake has increased even further; huge houses fill the many new subdivisions that are springing up all across this former farmland. These new suburbs are classic examples of the "exclusive" developments of which cultural critic Alexander Wilson writes, "The exclusions are many, for this landscape overwhelms both the land and its history" (201).

Buffalo Mountain Park is a drastic counterpoint even in its geographical location, as it lies on the city's southern border, and consists of the northern face of the mountain for which it is named. (Winged Deer, by contrast, received its name via a contest among local schoolchildren.) The park itself provides space more for individual play than competition, with a network of hiking trails and a modest picnic area. It seems more akin in many ways to the traditional, informal recreational space of the "fields beyond the city walls" than it does to Winged Deer's more deliberate civic parkland. Indeed, on some of the other faces of this same mountain, the winding roads through the hollows are lined with turnouts where for decades working people from both the city and the surrounding countryside have pulled off to drink, smoke pot, shoot guns, have sex, and so forth. From Buffalo Mountain's slopes one can look out across all of Johnson City, on a clear day seeing even Winged Deer, but in the foreground are mixed-income neighborhoods, light industrial areas, the regional university, the faded downtown district.

The contours of the conflict between these two parks is superficially clear: Winged Deer represents an extension of the same thinking that produced North Johnson City, an enterprising link to the broader currents of American culture, an invitation for the development patterns typical of car culture and the service economy to erase local distinctiveness, a space of "decreation." Meanwhile, on the south side of town, Buffalo Mountain Park helps "recreate" connections between the community and its past, its traditions, with its subdued use of local landforms and practices, its continuity with the preexisting social and geographical dimensions of the landscape. Winged Deer's facilities for nationally popular, competitive team sports; its contextualization by the TVA lake, emblematic not only of the top-down project of modernization in Appalachia but also the rise of the "recreational landscape" in North America; and its conversion of working landscape into leisure space all imply an erosion of the distinctly "local" characteristics of Johnson City, just as North Johnson City, like strip-mall districts everywhere, silenced the once-thriving public spaces of downtown.

At Winged Deer, play becomes an "activity," zoned and segmented into "facilities": softball on the softball fields, soccer on the soccer fields, nature on the nature trails, and history a single site on one corner of the park. On the drawing board for future expansion are more discrete leisure "nodes": an amphitheater, an aquatics center, a lakeside restaurant (J. Watson 1). Local history is constructed here more in terms of "tradition," defined by Alexander Wilson as "whatever can be expediently retrieved from the past understood only as a justification for the present" (214). In Winged Deer Park a monument to early settlers and a log cabin serve to certify this version of progress-as-assimilation as the manifest destiny of the community. One remarkable feature of the monument, a bronze compass indicating the direction and distance of eight historical sites, quite literally places Winged Deer at the center of local history. And yet the historical trappings themselves are, in the larger design of the park, quite peripheral. No direct walking route leads from the softball bleachers to the "historical zone," for example; chain link fences without gates block all the most logical approaches.

Regional Connections

Massengill statue at Winged
Deer Park; Robert Young house
is visible in background.
Photograph 1998 by the author.

The "centering" of history upon Winged Deer is particularly ironic in light of the fact that its two most prominent historical icons were moved to their present location. The cabin, known as the Robert Young home, is one of Johnson City's oldest surviving man-made structures, an artifact of one of the area's original homesteads. Built in 1776, it was the home of Robert Young Sr., whose original land purchase of 2,000 acres included much of what is now Johnson City. Young's home has made a remarkable trek this century from its original location, stopping once at Optimist Park, a half-mile or so north of its original site (Stahl 18). Its recent move to Winged Deer, right beside U.S. 11-E, with a beautiful view of Boone Lake, is quite an upgrade: the house is, for the first time in a century or so, back on prime real estate, and it finally has electricity.

The Massengill statue had considerably less ground to cover, but its movement is no less significant. It once stood at the confluence of Tennessee 36 and U.S. 11-E that is now the very heart of North Johnson City's commercial development district (and desert of public space). While its public accessibility was highly limited as it stood in the center of a major intersection, its significance in that site was perhaps more instructive.

Regional Connections

Bronze compass at base of Massengill statue, Winged Deer Park. Photograph 1998 by the author.

Henry Massengill, the founder of the family commemorated on the statue, was, like Robert Young, a major land speculator, plantation operator, politician, and patriarch in the earliest days of white settlement of the Johnson City area. The thriving commerce that sprawls across his former land holdings represents, in many ways, the culmination of a process he set in motion. Thus a monumental depiction of him in that site, his gaze fixed upon Lowe's and Arby's and Dan's Fan City, upon the acre of unused parking lot that for years surrounded the abandoned, former Wal-Mart that has become a Super Wal-Mart only a mile away, comments, in however an oblique fashion, on the historical connection between his original ambitions and their present-day results. In the words of Tom Lee, "There can be little doubt that the development of the Tri-Cities brought opportunities and benefits to the people of the area, but the distribution of those benefits was often inequitable" (267).

At Winged Deer, this legacy seems simply to confer pioneer vigor on a good game of softball. A pamphlet describing the relocation of the monument is careful to note that "As at the original location, the statue faces west, portraying the westward movement of the pioneers." And, indeed, reading the description of Massengill's family inscribed on the statue's base indicates that his sons and their sons (except for Ailsey, of whom all we learn is that, despite two marriages, he "died without issue") headed west to establish three counties, found the medical department of the University of Nashville, and cast the Great Seal of Tennessee.

But that westward gaze now stares across the regimented leisure landscape of the park; the view from Robert Young Sr.'s front porch is now of the softball complex. Though the relationship of the historical landmarks and the playgrounds might be appropriate (in ways that will become clear momentarily), it is thoroughly mystified. This presentation is monumental, schoolbook history, literally carved in stone, with only a positional relationship to the other forms of play here. History as events, as experiences, as struggles, is curiously detached; instead, heritage serves a decorative, commemorative role in the broader experience of managed pleasure. In this sense, the historical decor represents an even more profound variety of "decreation" than the playgrounds and playing fields. With no commentary on how that history created the park, history is only an element in the leisure to which this landscape is so thoroughly dedicated. How surprising is it, then, to find elsewhere a log cabin as part of the accoutrements, amid the sleek modern plastic toys, of these playgrounds of the pioneers?

The Redneck Public Sphere

By contrast, Buffalo Mountain Park appears to resist this trend, constructing a more accurate version of local history in its public space. The very fact that the park provides the visitor the opportunity to understand visually the patterns of settlement and the organization of the city as a whole suggests this park's more organic relationship to the community. The summit of the mountain, a precipice called White Rocks, is carved with initials and dates back to nineteenth century—a set of barely legible writings and overwritings that exist in stark contrast to the monological, literally monolithic stone inscriptions of the Massengill statue. This precipice, an historiographic palimpsest, affords views not only of westward expansion but also, to the south and east, back in the direction local culture came from, toward Iron Mountain and Limestone Cove, one of the very earliest settlements in the region, part of a network of small, interconnected farming and mining communities eclipsed by the growth of Johnson City in this century (Hsiung 61).

Like the stone, the landscape one perceives from this vista reveals itself as a complex set of overwritings and revisions; like the views from White Rocks, the forms of play on Buffalo Mountain seem to locate the participant in the historical progression of the uses of this space. Many of the trails are simply upgrades of paths worn on Buffalo Mountain by generations of hikers, hunters, even moonshiners—all pursuing timeworn recreational pursuits with historical ties to the work of settlement. Buffalo Mountain Park's recreation thus seems to be the preservation—perhaps the evolution—of a local tradition that generally thrives only on the margin, a place for the people Jack Temple Kirby terms "retro frontiersmen" and whom most people call rednecks, to ply their time-honored trade of hanging out in the woods. This class-coded practice, Kirby notes, has in recent times been curtailed by the rise of posted land. Whatever else may be conservative or even reactionary about rural white southern culture, there is at least one small element of resistance here, a kind of critique of private property and reclamation of public space. The privatization of the wilderness that is contested in these spaces is a syndrome of which Robert Young Sr. and Henry Massengill were founding fathers. A sign at one of the woodland turnouts I mentioned earlier, by the Nolichuckey River on Buffalo Mountain's southwest side, is an artifact of that conflict: private landowners have posted a warning sign to discourage use of a riverside turnout, but someone has taped a handwritten rejoinder to it: "GREED GREED GREED" the note taped to the sign proclaims, and goes on to imply that the "danger" at this site is just a ruse to get "dumb stupid college students" to pay to hang out at the campground on the other side of the river—a campground, one might note, operating on the grounds of the house, now a Mexican restaurant, that was formerly the home of the mine operators whose work created the conditions that facilitated the landfill development discussed later in this chapter.

These turnouts are outlaw parks, unofficial landscapes of play that share a mountain and a constituency with Buffalo Mountain Park. They are dangerous spaces, rogue places, in the white-middle-class imagination of the community's dominant interests. Moreover, as the frequent illegal dumping there implies, they are "white trash" spaces, violating and challenging dominant standards of propriety and civility. They are places I was warned about growing up middle-class in Johnson City, places where the sheriff's deputies will shake down your car if they find you there, and if you look, as I do, like one of "them dumb stupid college students," they might lecture you on how you can get yourself murdered up there. They are places that periodically have a county-owned backhoe unleashed on them to make them unusable, but a combination of four-wheel drive and weather inevitably opens them back up again. They are not places anyone will ever set up a granite monument to prosperity and expansion, and they are not places whose forms of play can be regimented into facilities—although, significantly, these spaces are with few exceptions carved out of the public land of the Cherokee National Forest.

Warning sign at turnout near Embreeville, Tennessee. Handwritten note taped to sign reads, "GREED GREED GREED / Greed human owner of Chuckey Trading Co. [restaurant on opposite side of river] said has made a fortune by overcharging the dumb stupid college students: patsys." Photograph 1998 by the author.

These are public spaces created by and for people excluded from other public spheres, spaces where the cultural codes of civility that govern behavior in official civic spaces is everywhere defied and defaced.

Recognizing this history that is both metaphorically and geographically behind the forms of recreation at Buffalo Mountain Park leads in one respect to an analysis that notes, in dismay, that the park is a way of displacing further these transgressive spaces, co-opting them into the discourse of civic propriety that has governed the design of public parks in general back to the days of Frederick Law Olmsted. And, indeed, a quick scan of park rules reveals that many of the key elements of redneck countercultural practice—fires, guns, alcoholic beverages—are now prohibited in the park's confines. Prohibitions can only do so much, however: recently Buffalo Mountain Park has been embroiled in a controversy over drinking and drug use in its confines and, more specifically, over its adoption by the region's queer community as a cruising site, suggesting that the park is fulfilling in practice what its design suggests, that the very shape of the terrain facilitates the interaction and indulgence of populations that normally fall under censure by community standards. Indeed, local property owners now voice strenuous objections

Regional Connections

to the existence of the park itself—the *Johnson City Press* reports one resident stating "It was much more safe before it was a park"—and of people "using the park for drug use, as a hangout and a place for couples to have sex. And they say homeless people have made the park their home" (Saylor, "Residents Concerned" 1). Increased police surveillance resulting in conflict with park patrons and multiple arrests confirms that the park is not simply a space for apolitical leisure but the center of local confrontations over class-coded behavior and general criminality, and sexuality (Saylor, "Five Arrested" 1). That the confrontation is framed in terms of landowners versus transients locates this confrontation in that broader history of retro-frontiersmen versus posted land, even if the articulation of it is in somewhat more contemporary terms.

Wearing its cultural conflicts on its sleeve in a way unimaginable in Winged Deer's landscape of propriety, Buffalo Mountain Park represents, even in its regulated, conflicted, and covert and transgressive way, a recognition of a rough-hewn, ungoverned form of play that is native to this place and its particular physical, social, and cultural landscape. This continuity, because it emerges from evolving cultural practice, does not require a display of objects—monuments and log cabins—to certify its role in local history.

It is possible to examine these parks as entities unto themselves, and to contrast them to each other in terms of their disparate approaches to integrating history and leisure. But recognizing their interrelationship as public spaces emerging from the same community is just as important or more so. It is not that Winged Deer is "false" while Buffalo Mountain is "true"—each is a version of the relationship of local and regional history best understood in relationship to each other, against the backdrop of broader regional narratives. While Johnson City is physically located in the historical and geographical heart of southern Appalachia, the city itself was born of the Industrial Revolution, of the very kind of economic expansionism of which North Johnson City is only the latest manifestation. Its origins were as a water tank on the rail lines connecting western North Carolina and southwest Virginia with the commercial corridors of the Tennessee Valley and the Valley of Virginia, facilitating mining and the timber industry in the region in the late nineteenth century—including the mines operated by the supervisors who lived in the house by the Nolichuckey, mines that would, when they had outlived their usefulness, achieve a new significance in regional history as dumping grounds.

The evolution in recent times toward a service economy represents a logical if problematic extension of that same pattern, not a disruption. Ironically, the fiscal success of North Johnson City makes the develop-

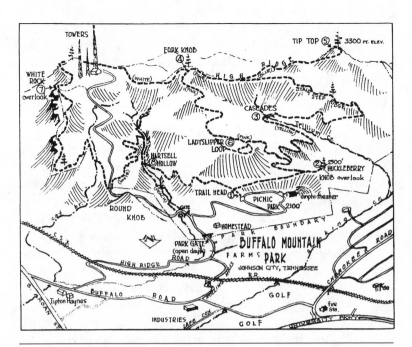

Drawing of Buffalo Mountain Park by local architect Frank Knisley, later distributed by Johnson City Parks and Recreation as a trail map. Courtesy of Frank Knisley.

ment of new public spaces, like Buffalo Mountain Park, possible. In this light the conflicting public memories of Johnson City's parks, rather than canceling each other out, represent an important reflection of the community's liminal status, its history as an interface between a deeply interconnected local ethos and the broader cultural developments that have always interpenetrated it. To look at the sprawl of North Johnson City, you would believe it to be a classic example of what urbanist Joel Garreau has famously termed an "Edge City," but rather than the edge of a larger metropolitan area, Johnson City is the "edge" of the metropole, the contact zone between it and the rural spaces that, mythologically, at least, have challenged and resisted the city's modernizing power.

In other words, in a backhanded way, the disingenuous use of history to certify progress in Winged Deer's heritage decor reflects an accurate, if somewhat cynical, view of Johnson City's history, because the history of Johnson City has always involved the reconfiguration of Appalachian identities. It would be even more cynical for the city to try to claim direct descent from some nostalgic version of an Appalachian folk culture. As David Hsiung notes, Johnson City and Johnson Citians have often, from their earliest history, defined themselves against the mountaineer culture surrounding them, even though they themselves were in many cases descended from it (186). These complex lines of division cloud easy judgments one might make, then, about the "authenticity" of Buffalo Mountain Park as set against the "intrusion" of commerce and competition represented by Winged Deer, the false versus the true. The juxtaposition of these recreational spaces instead shows the ambivalence of a community that, like all communities, generates multiple versions of place within a single space. The public spaces, appropriately, then, depict this conflict about history and identity as they offer, in the seemingly ephemeral form of recreation, an opportunity for citizens of the community to explore and consume, to re-create—not, as MacKaye might have it, to de-create—multiple versions of their community's identity. What critical regionalism can do is make clear what is at stake in the design and construction of these landscapes, so that they can be understood as social inventions that expand the possibilities for a generative cultural engagement with the dynamics of politics and history in the supposedly inert spaces of the geographical margin by demonstrating how the built environment encourages "tendencies," to use MacKaye's term, toward understanding the relationships between the local site and broader spaces. To do so, however, requires a more nuanced appreciation of the workings of local public discourse, the production, consumption, and circulation of representations—including (perhaps especially) the built environment of public space—in specific places.

As important as these public spaces are, however, critical regionalism must also be attentive to less visible sites, spaces where, even though they are not designed or constructed to embody civic values or accommodate collective, public activities, nonetheless play a significant role in social construction of regional relationships. Benton MacKaye would doubtless label the turnouts lining the roads on Buffalo Mountain where good ol' boys drink and smoke, or the queer cruising in the park itself, as spaces and practices of "decreation," asserting as he does that "publicly abhorrent" conduct of "the drunkard and the wastrel" is the prime example of "destructive relaxation" (*New Exploration* 127). But, as we have seen, those practices connect in significant ways to local and regional history, and relate in a dynamic if not convivial way with the configuration of public leisure spaces in the community. Something is re-created there, an important if transgressive and covert rendition of the community's evolving meaning.

The image of decreation plays to white, middle-class, and socially conservative ideals of region. In the (necessarily) furtive way these community standards are transgressed, the acts of transgression, while changing the meaning of the place through tacit processes of social construction, are easily labeled deviant by law enforcement authorities, landowners, and newspapers. Conservative community standards are undermined in these situations but not necessarily challenged in a durable, meaningful way. The question the contrast between Buffalo Mountain Park and Winged Deer poses is how an alternative rendition of the community's implication in broader social struggles might be powerfully challenged, what alternative cultural practices might articulate a new and different image of the meaning of the cultural conflicts. How could Buffalo Mountain Park and its adherents create a set of representations that calls into question who has access to public space and public discourse, and who should? How could the nature of the conflicts that converge on Johnson City's public parks be described in a regional rhetoric of social invention, leading to forms of social action that make the tacit challenges posed in this space explicit and purposeful? In the remainder of this chapter I look at an even more preterit, decreative site on the landscape to explore possible answers, looking at the discourse of trash and dumping, and some recent historical moments in which area landfills inspired new forms of social construction, social invention, and social action that transformed images of regional places as "wasted space." In the first half of this chapter, we have seen how the landscape is itself a representation that models certain forms of region; in what remains we shall see how the regional creation and circulation of representations creates particular kinds of landscapes, and how the actions of people on those landscapes can change the meaning of the representations of it.

"There Ain't No Lower Class"

In 1976 the state of Tennessee began an advertising campaign to discourage littering and raise environmental awareness statewide. The ad agency contracted for the task, Bill Hudson and Associates, decided to make a humorous spot and created a character called "Tennessee Trash." Tennessee Trash (as played by the late Nashville actor-musician Irving Kane) is a scruffy, dirty white guy, balding, sideburns, sunglasses, cigarette; he rides along through the sixty-second spot in his 1964 Corvair (vanity plate reading "TRASH" attached to a bumper rigged with magnets to fall off on cue) "messing up the highways . . . junking up the byways," according to the lyrics of his country-rock theme song, which culminates in the refrain, "Lord, there ain't no lower class than Tennessee Trash" ("History of Tennessee Trash," "Tennessee Trash Lyrics"). He is a hillbilly revision of Iron Eyes Cody's famous "Crying Indian" (from Keep

America Beautiful's 1971 ad "People Start Pollution, People Can Stop It"), a counterpart to the vanishing Noble Savage, the retro-frontiersman wallowing in his own filth.

In 1976 I was an eight-year-old growing up in a middle-class subdivision in Johnson City, Tennessee, and I thought Tennessee Trash was hilarious. My brother and I sang the song together; we would point at junky cars on the road and sing the refrain. We were hardly alone in our enjoyment. The ad was highly successful statewide, and its title character passed into the local vernacular, most people, I think, using it not unlike my brother and I did, as an appellation for people and places not up to our town-folk, middle-class standards, shorthand for all those rednecky little communities we would see from out the windows of our family station wagon when we drove through the country.

In 1976 the late Hobart Story lived in little house in a bend in the road in Bumpass Cove, a holler opening on to the Nolichuckey River valley ten miles from Johnson City, the kind of mountain community my brother and I might have pointed at and snickered, "lord, there ain't no lower class. . . ." Story saw those ads too, and I wonder what he must have thought of them, with their heavily class-coded and individualized version of the causes of the environmental crisis in America. Every day Story witnessed a parade of gigantic dump trucks that headed up the holler full and came back empty, dumping thousands of pounds of garbage each into a landfill operated by Waste Resources. What Hobart and his neighbors were starting to figure out, and what they would soon bring to the attention of the region, was that those trucks were hauling not only garbage that Waste Resources had legally contracted to dump in a landfill in Bumpass Cove, but also barrels of illegal toxic waste that were tossed in the landfill and stashed in abandoned mines.

Story was discovering a cause of environmental and human crisis not accounted for in the "Tennessee Trash" campaign. That ad suggests that bad, junky, poor people were messing everything up with their low-class behavior. If we could all just be good, the ad pleads—and by good, clearly, we mean "high class"—our homeland would be clean. Just individual effort and upwards identification were needed. What Story and his neighbors were witnessing, though, was that "Tennessee Trash" had it exactly backwards, from their perspective. The problem was not that trashy people were running loose in polite society, messing up the highways and the byways for the rest of us, but that powerful interests could identify places as trashy, as waste and hence wasted space, and use that cultural identification as a rationale to go way beyond littering, to creating potentially fatal toxic environments. Story was learning the hard way that "Tennessee Trash" is not only a cautionary tale but a self-fulfilling prophecy, a moment in an ongoing cultural and political process of hierarchical stratification of places that has specific, material consequences.

Critical regionalism can engage in a specific way with the history of dumps and dumping in my hometown and in places like Bumpass Cove by examining the ways the cultural devaluing of exurban spaces can result in a serious political disempowerment and disenfranchisement. What a regional approach to analysis of this situation confronts is that the problem is not simply "environmental" in a narrow sense but is a broader problem of cultural politics that has a particular geographical and spatial structure. As Robert Bullard has documented in his multiple editions of *Dumping in Dixie*, trash begets trash, and identifying these "waste spaces" in the geographical margins of the American terrain and exploiting them economically, politically, environmentally, and culturally—through the creation, maintenance, and circulation of representations that limit the possibilities for anyone seeing these sites in a generative relationship with larger social structures—is a crucial component in the maintenance of an unjust and unsustainable social and economic order. Envisioned and depicted as politically inert, regional communities are acted upon as such, and become thus.

Clearly, more than cultural criticism, however vigorous, is required to redress these grievances. As examples such as the "Tennessee Trash" campaign and others I offered in the rest of this chapter indicate, however, the cultural imagination of regional spaces—generally rural, frequently poor, and often racialized as well—plays a powerful role in the political and material fate of regional communities. What critical regionalism could offer in such situations is a new way of describing the relationships between these occluded regional sites and the larger networks of cause-and-effect of which they are a part, by creating a systematic challenge to the images that obscure these relationships. Just as critical regionalist methodologies can be used to discern the intersection of larger historical connections in the seemingly discrete and politically inert civic spaces of sport and play in the parks of the first part of this chapter, reinterpreting and reimagining these spaces as sites of vital engagement with regional development—that is, critical regionalism—can also develop a representational vocabulary of region to transform the processes of social construction present in the cultural imagination of dumps and dumping, such that they become not "waste(d) space" but social inventions that can catalyze new forms of social action.

A Reciprocal Relationship

Perhaps no single site evokes the social construction of places as fully as the landfill—formerly known as the dump. The dump is the place where results of cultural production, compiled and accrued from all across the community and the region, quite literally reshape the terrain. Residents of southwest Ohio (I was recently one) know that the highest peak in the tri-state area is the summit of Mount Rumpke, a massive landfill, the state's largest, operated by Rumpke, Incorporated. Standing 1,075 feet high as of this writing, Mount Rumpke accepts 6,200 tons of trash every day. But its operators claim they need to expand the facility to accept almost 10,000 tons a day, adding another 95 acres to its 440-acre tract, if Hamilton County is to avoid becoming a solid waste exporter, paying to dump elsewhere (McNair). Mount Rumpke, not purely a utilitarian facility by any means, is a representational space as well: it not only has permanently altered the viewshed of the region but is also a kind of tableau, its peak the improbable site of the patriotic spectacle of a giant, illuminated American flag year round and, seasonally, of holiday decorations as well.

Though few communities have such a visible, landmark landscape of waste, dumps can almost always be read as an image of community, places where the shared business of casting off the old seemingly knows no class distinctions, where everyone's belongings mingle on an equal if humble basis. For archaeologists dumps are especially significant: a portrait of a place and the social practices and patterns unique to it, local cultures depicted and defined by their leavings. As self-styled "garbageologist" William Rathje (an archaeologist by training) notes, "what people have owned—and thrown away—can speak more eloquently, informatively, and truthfully about the lives they lead than they themselves ever may" (Rathje and Murphy 54). But as with so many other aspects of community life, the dump is no longer a matter of purely local interest. Like an increasing number of local spaces, the dump is a point of global commerce, this putative waste space a productive site of commerce for progressively fewer and fewer companies as mergers reshape the handling of waste in America. Writing about Mount Rumpke in the *Dayton Daily News*, Jeff Nesmith reports that "the country will [likely] enter the next millennium with two companies in control of picking up, hauling off, dumping and recycling more than half its municipal and industrial solid waste," splitting $18 billion in annual revenue for doing so (13A).

With this much money involved, it stands to reason that dumps and dumping have become important political concerns. One of the most interesting debates of recent times, from the standpoint of place and culture, involves a conflict between the state of Virginia and the city of New York, in which place identities and dumping became a matter of highly visible public debate. When grass-roots groups in rural Virginia stirred political debate about the operation of huge commercial landfills that received bargeload upon bargeload of trash from the metropolis, Mayor Giuliani of New York responded with characteristic tact that "this is a reciprocal relationship" because "people in Virginia like to utilize New York because we're a cultural center, because we're a business center" (Melton A1).

Here is the politics of cosmopolitanism in its plainest and harshest terms: the Metropolis is the unquestioned proprietor of all forms of culture and commerce, and communities beyond the city walls should receive with gladness the garbage of the City, out of respect and gratitude for its cultural power, and the desire to give something back. The condescending metrocentrism of Giuliani's remarks certainly was not lost on Virginia's leading citizens. Led by Republican governor James Gilmore, who sternly declared "there is no relationship or obligation as a result of the excellence of New York City" (Melton A14), Virginia's politicians rose in defense of their native land. Republican state senator William Bolling was perhaps most oratorical, declaring, "Mr. Mayor, listen closely. You worry about what's going on in New York. We'll worry about what's going on in Virginia. But make no mistake about it. We will not stand idly by and allow the Commonwealth of Virginia to become a dumping ground for New York City and New York State" (Melton A14).

Place and politics are indistinguishable in this confrontation, but the situation is not as simple as it seems. Gilmore's and Bolling's rhetoric is exactly the kind of oversimplified, parochial posturing that an unreflective politics and poetics of place falls prey to. Bolling and Gilmore are disingenuous, to put it mildly, on several levels, most importantly that, as members of Virginia's ruling class, they are, of course, in no danger of having landfills put in their neighborhoods, near their homes. Landfills in Virginia, as elsewhere, are generally located in low-income rural areas, where the struggle for basic economic survival makes the Faustian bargain of trading a few jobs for tons of trash seem desirable. As Robert Bullard writes, "Historically, toxic dumping and the location of locally unwanted land uses . . . have followed the 'path of least resistance,' meaning poor and black communities have been disproportionately burdened with these types of externalities. . . . This pattern has proven to be the rule, even though the benefits derived from industrial waste production are directly related to affluence" (4–5). The politicians' indignant responses erase the politics of race and class that have made dumping a political controversy within Virginia long before Mayor Giuliani entered the fray.

Their place rhetoric further works to obscure the fact that, as Republicans, their tacit support of their party's long-standing policies of privatization, deregulation, and opposition to environmental controls have sponsored the rise of the waste industry. The waste industry certainly knows this history: the *Washington Post* reported that Governor Gilmore received $100,000 in campaign contributions from waste industry lobbyists during the 1997 gubernatorial election, and Senator Bolling certainly benefited from the $26,000 the industry gave to the GOP Senate Caucus between 1995 and 1998. Browning-Ferris Industries and Waste Management, the two companies scheduled to merge into America's waste-handling superpower, were both among the ten biggest givers to Virginia political campaigns (Melton A14).

The populist politics of place deployed by Republican politicians on both sides, either naive or cynical, obscures the intricate and often contradictory political, cultural, historical, and material connections between city and country, between center and margin on the American landscape (to say nothing of the hypocrisy of the politicians themselves). One of the important facts lost in this spat is that the landfill is itself a business center, a place where something important is happening, where large-scale political conflicts between states and among multinational corporations, conflicts that only occasionally make for good political theater nationwide, are being played out in relative obscurity. A critical regionalist reading of this power play not only brings these connections to light, but considers as well how cultural formations with specific histories and applications—like the image of exurban spaces as dumps—are being mobilized and utilized in deliberate ways, not just socially constructed but socially invented.

It is a curious contradiction that the act of throwing away has become so productive, that the pariah spaces of public life have such massive private, financial value. It is a contradiction that indicates, backhandedly, how the margins of the American landscape are perhaps more complex and more productive than one generally presumes. Certainly it demands a reconsideration of how we think about waste spaces, about how we think about who is dumped on, and what that action means. For though dumping has increased in its value to the service economy, its cultural capital, the dump in the American imaginary, has not really changed much at all, as the Virginia squabble indicates. "Dump" is still an unambiguous put-down to apply to a place, and though the mega-mergers of the waste industry suggest that owning a dump might be profitable, being a dump is not.

The dump, then, as a geographically circumscribed site for the storage of the useless and unwanted, is particularly potent as an image of regional life, and an especially persistent image of the southern Appalachian region, a presumptively trashy landscape presumably populated by white-trash people. Indeed, for me, growing up in east Tennessee, our nearby neighbor Virginia represented not a no-place best used as New York's dumping ground but a cultural step up, a place of dignity and sophistication. The "Great Man" brand of history we learned in school taught us that Virginia gave the country George Washington and Thomas Jefferson, Founding Fathers, visionaries; we produced Andrews Jackson and Johnson, a rowdy redneck and an impeached, sullen tailor. And if we needed further reminding of the possibility for atavism in our state, we had "Tennessee Trash" reminding us "he's a little bit of you, he's a little bit of me," and we would turn into him if we weren't vigilant, tidy, and, well, more like Virginia.

I am not alone in having seen my own accustomed places as a dump; the image's persistence and power in southern Appalachia extends even to the region's own authors. One of the most recent Appalachian authors to deploy the dump emblematically is Pinckney Benedict, whose interest in the preterit and ruined aspects of the southern mountains is summarized in "The Wrecking Yard," the title story of the collection in which it is found. "The Wrecking Yard" is a series of vignettes set in and around an auto junkyard, whose employees struggle to be creative amid the detritus of American car culture, building up muscle cars out of the wrecks and relics they handle by trade. Benedict's would-be artists are scavengers, variously described as "undertakers" (24), "vultures," and "parasites" (28), who live in a historically asynchronous, precapitalist world of barter, swindling, and theft amid stacks of crushed cars that form a bleak, go-nowhere landscape of "cool dark alleys and blind corridors" (32).

Benedict's "wrecking yard" imagery is not confined to the physical space of the junkyard, however—soon it maps out across the rest of the local landscape. In the story's two principal vignettes, protagonist Perry and his aptly named partner Weasel journey up onto Big Lime Mountain to salvage brutal wrecks—the first a cattle truck that has rolled off the road and down the hillside, scattering living and dying cows all through the woods, and the second the wreck of a fellow hot-rodder who has, perhaps accidentally, perhaps intentionally, missed a turn and plummeted off a cliff. In both cases the two main characters (and supporting characters as well) exhibit a remarkable indifference to life, both human and animal, just as they ignore the often grim fates of the former drivers of the cars they scavenge in the junkyard.

Indeed, the mountain landscape itself becomes a junkyard of both mechanical, animal, and human wreckage. In the second trip up to Big Lime, Weasel and Perry are engaged as much in the search for a missing woman passenger in the wrecked car as they are to retrieve the wreck itself. And the searchers for the woman's body, conversely, gather up auto parts as they work. Human and mechanical salvage begin to blur: Perry asks Weasel, "Did they find anything yet?" and is told, "Nothing but pieces of car. They found a rearview mirror with a pair of shoes tied to it and a headrest off one of the seats and the radiator fan. But no girl. . . . I got all that stuff in a box in the back of the car. I figure I'll take it to the yard with me when I go" (36). Appropriately, then, the story ends with Perry engaging in a pointless gesture, littering the landscape by tossing a hubcap over the cliff:

> The hubcap flies beautifully when it leaves his hand, light as a tin pie plate. The wind catches it, and for a moment Perry imagines that it will spin out and out, across the valley and the fire road and the tame little stream, to land in the trees on the other side. Instead, abandoned by the breeze, it arcs suddenly downward and to his left, and disappears with a dull clang into the bushes somewhere below him, coming to rest in a tangled wooded place that he cannot see. (39)

The zoom-out in Benedict's conclusion expands and confirms an evocation of the mountain landscape itself as a wrecking yard, a dump. A moment of potential (if modest) beauty, perhaps a memorial gesture to the loss of life Perry has just witnessed, becomes mere littering. Not only does this scene conclusively deflate any potential for Perry, much less the other scavengers and vultures of the wrecking yard, to be creators of hopeful cultural forms, but it situates him in a bleak landscape that in itself, in the wind that abandons the flung hubcap, cannot even support a feeble symbolic gesture, much less sustain a movement for positive change. In this story Benedict presents a mountain region that is not cast upon but just is the ash heap of history, the emblematic junk heap extrapolated across the larger landscape.

The conflict between Giuliani and the state of Virginia suggests that there is a certain degree to which this observation is denotatively true. Economic desperation has led to a proliferation of landfills, scrap yards, and other junk heaps throughout the mountain south. But Benedict takes the image a step further, transforming it into an emblem that identifies the people of the region as passively acquiescent, even parasitically enthusiastic about these changes, when they should be more justly seen as only one interested party in a pattern of cultural and landscape conflict and change that links them to rabble-rousing state politicians, recalcitrant big-city mayors, corporate mega-mergers, and the creative writing graduate program of the University of Iowa (attended by both Pinckney Benedict and Abraham Verghese). Potteiger and Purinton claim the wasteland disconnects the space from history altogether: "The growth of a landfill forms layers and epochs, and its future can seem limitless. When the deposition on landfills stops, and they are capped for indeterminate afterlives, the wasteland becomes a sublimated and buried history. Fenced and removed from the center of daily life, many waste sites, in a sense, exist out of time" (216). The question is how to put that place back into historical time, how to redefine the junkyard so that the larger picture it evokes is one of a politically engaged, historically nuanced, and culturally vital network of regional interconnections. As it stands the dump is an image of the hopelessness, uselessness, and ineffectiveness of cultural life on the geographical margins. How might this part be seen as pointing to a different whole? How might this site signify a different point in time and space, one located within a narrative of historical change and future possibility, instead of a no-place out of the flow of time?

"The Dump Is Full of Images"

In Wallace Stevens's "The Man on the Dump," it is garbage that supplies the raw material for an artistic vision: "The dump is full of images," the speaker declares. But artistic vision is not a goal in itself; it must confront the materiality of the world, where "Everything is shed; and the moon comes up as the moon / (All its images are in the dump) and you see / As a man (not like an image of a man), / You see the moon rise in the empty sky." Stevens teases the reader here with the possibility of an encounter with an unmediated reality, but not quite: when you see as a human, but not like the image of a human, a simile still remains where once there was a simile and a metaphor.

Even in the dump, for the people of the dump, where the hard facts of existence are laid bare, representational practices persist, and can still serve some purpose. Stevens writes, "One sits and beats on an old tin can, lard pail. / One beats and beats for what one believes." More than just shoring fragments around ruins, Stevens suggests, the dump can possibly be a cultural resource, can be the site in which culture and society can be reconfigured in new and vital ways. Even a reductive and degrading label like "white trash" can be appropriated to a critical project; Roxanne Dunbar, for example, redefines it as a critique of the bloody project of the U.S. conquest of North America romanticized in the frontier myth, identifying the "white trash" label as a function of the loathing of a society founded on conquest for its tools: "We dregs of colonialism, those who did not and do not 'make it,' being the majority in some places (like most of the United States) are potentially dangerous to the ruling class: WE ARE PROOF OF THE LIE OF THE AMERICAN DREAM" (76–77).

The history of dumps and dumping in and around Johnson City supplies examples that suggest that, like Stevens's poetic dump, the trashing of Appalachia could be a starting place for social action, if recognized as a social construction and reconfigured as a social invention. Twice in my lifetime landfills have become generative sites of regional politics and public life in which the potential for new forms of social organization and collective political action emerged, if only fleetingly. Recovering these histories of dumps and those dumped upon might transform the image of the region by appropriating and redeploying one of its dominant tropes. Recovering the history of local trash in this way means understanding the moments in which the dumped-upon used that very status to search for new modes of collective organization and new possibilities for the future of their communities.

The dump moved to the center of local public discourse most recently when, in the early 1990s (while I still lived in the area), the city of Johnson City contracted with Waste Management to construct and operate a landfill in the city limits of Johnson City itself. This civic project, which brought the global politics and economics of the waste industry to the local landscape, wore its class politics on its sleeve, as the proposed site on Johnson City's southeast borders overlooked the Broadway area, a district of working-class neighborhoods, and the Keystone public housing projects. As Jim Wozniak reported in the *Johnson City Press* in 1995, the appearance of environmental racism and classism was accompanied by a more scientific distress about the site's location on the headwaters of a stream and the potentially unsuitable geology of the landfill's shale foundation. Opposition to this project hinged not just on issues of site selection, however, but also on the fact that the dump was to be a privately operated, for-profit facility, taking in trash from across the region. This aspect presented not only an image problem (though those terms figured prominently in public debate), but also the problem of Waste Management's dubious record in the region: the nearby town of Erwin had recently filed suit against the company over disposal rates. Even the name of the new dump, the disingenuous "Iris Glen Environmental Center," came in for criticism: of course there are neither irises nor a glen on the site, just a big and growing heap of garbage. As with the design and naming of Winged Deer Park, the representational practices surrounding the creation of this site seemed devoted to disconnecting it from cultural politics, thwarting critiques of the issues of space and of class that are so vital in this situation.

Despite local dissent, Iris Glen opened in 1994 and has operated relatively uneventfully thereafter—though it's no Mount Rumpke, the earth-and-garbage mound of the supposed "glen" has joined Tannery Knob and Masters Knob as visible landmarks on the city's eastern skyline. The controversy surrounding the project now is its relative unprofitability: ironically, the site has failed to live up to its trashy reputation. A year after opening Iris Glen was receiving about 840 tons of garbage per day, considerably off its projected 900–1,200 ton daily rate. The culprit was Waste Management's principal rival, now potential merger partner, Browning-Ferris. Taking advantage of the delays in Iris Glen's construction caused by local controversies, Browning-Ferris opened a landfill in neighboring Hawkins County—as one of Tennessee's poorest counties, a rival "white trash" space—luring away some of Waste Management's potential customers, including Greene County, Tennessee's 150 daily tons of trash (Wozniak, "Iris Glen" 5). This pressing need to increase the amount of waste flowing into these landfills, which will be intensified in the near future when the same company owns both Iris Glen and the Hawkins County sites, has dire implications for the future: will the waste-handling megacorporation continue to provide curbside recycling, for example, when it needs tonnage for its landfills to turn a profit? Will it expand its search for garbage, perhaps accepting toxic waste to meet its quotas?

This controversy illustrated the complex and socially constructed nature of the local landscape, as the conflict simultaneously invoked matters political, economic, cultural, and environmental, revealing the convoluted and complex nature of waste and wastelands. But, more notably, it also led to new forms of social and political organization: grass-roots opposition from the affected neighborhoods evolved into a more formal movement, Citizens for Responsible Government. This grass-roots group became better known as the Carter Coalition when its organizing resulted in the election in 1993 of a new (and, notably, female) mayor, coalition leader Mickii Carter; headlines in the *Johnson City Press* read "Keystone votes give a boost in Carter's win" (Wozniak, "Keystone" 1). The people of Keystone and Broadway, so marginal to civic life that the city government believed it could readily dump trash on them, both discovered new ways to represent their opinions and perspectives in public discourse (despite the failure of that effort to achieve its desired end of blocking the landfill) and changed the patterns of representation in civic government.

As a catalyst for new forms of political organization, the Iris Glen incident was not unique, but part of a history of connections between trash and dumping and grass-roots organization. This history also lends credence to concerns such as those raised about what waste-handling companies will resort to to turn a profit. In 1979 Hobart Story led residents of Bumpass Cove, a hollow about ten miles from Johnson City, in organized protest against the misuse of a landfill on the site of former manganese and iron mines. The history of absentee ownership and resource extraction in Bumpass Cove dates back to the nineteenth century and has left visible marks on the terrain: abandoned mine entrances and traces of old equipment and structures mark the hillsides, and the house (now a restaurant and campground) built in the 1880s for the English mine owners still stands near the mouth of the cove, across the river from the turnout discussed earlier in the chapter, where retro-frontiersmen defaced the "Danger" sign. Further up the holler, the company town built by the Embreeville Freehold Land, Iron, and Railway Company, Ltd., has faded into the hillside, now a rural crossroads called Embreville (Lee 36). It is a landscape that preserves a visible record of exploitation throughout its modern history: a place of resource overdevelopment and human underdevelopment. Mine and iron forge closures left Bumpass Cove a poor but enduring mountain community, with little in the way of business or industry in the Cove itself until Waste Resources of Tennessee obtained a permit for a landfill on a former mining site in 1972 (Couto 114–15). Waste Resources discovered one other function Bumpass Cove, stripped of all other available resources by outside interests, could perform for industry.

By the mid-1970s, however, the residents of Bumpass Cove began to fear for their health and safety, and suspected misconduct by the landfill operators. On 25 July 1979 torrential rain caused flash flooding across the region, and Hobart Story, who had begun a largely unsuccessful campaign of letter writing to newspapers and government offices to raise regional awareness about Cove residents' anxieties, went to the landfill, concerned about its ability to weather the storm. He arrived in time to witness parts of the landfill washing into a nearby creek, including barrels that gave off strong odors and released suspicious substances.

Disturbed and frightened, Story began to organize. By Monday morning, residents of Bumpass Cove and Embreeville just downstream were sitting in the road in front of Story's house, blocking trucks carrying up to 80,000 pounds of garbage apiece to the landfill. This direct action to physically obstruct the only public route into the Cove—sometimes with picket lines, but sometimes by covertly scattering nails on the road—manipulated the same marginality and inaccessibility that made the site suitable for landfill development to block the illegal dumping.

Later the residents would use the act of interpreting the local landscape to their advantage again, as a basis for public, legal action. Their demands that the county enforce an eighteen-ton weight limit (flouted by the forty-ton haulers) on a bridge in the Cove successfully shut off the flow of waste for a while. When Waste Resources attempted to circumvent the problem bridge by using a back road that led to a cemetery, residents obtained a restraining order by claiming that it was an act of desecration. The evolving, adapting local opposition resulted in the closure of the landfill by year's end.

The damage, however, had been done—though only the activism of the local residents brought that damage before the public. Groundwater testing by East Tennessee State University chemists revealed extensive heavy metal contamination. Polychlorinated biphenyls (PCBs) were detected in groundwater at the landfill. Barrels of toxic waste were discovered in abandoned mines near the landfill itself. Medical assessments (at a health fair organized in part by the landfill opposition movement) indicated that twenty-five of eighty-six residents had liver problems. And on 22 August 1980 an eight-month-old infant, Dana Townsend, died suddenly of indeterminate causes, which naturally fed speculation about the toxicity of the Bumpass Cove environment (R. Wilson, Sanders 3).

However, something else had also happened: a community had learned quite a bit about not only how to operate as a collective, but also how to present its localized concerns to broader publics. The Bumpass Cove Citizens Group incorporated on 26 November 1979, providing a locus for strategy development and a forum for community concerns. It raised money at public events and (appropriately enough) at roadblocks and hosted cookouts and covered-dish suppers that brought a new degree of coherence to the community. The events in Bumpass Cove even encouraged cultural productions like a songs, videos, letters to the editor, and the scrapbook of newspaper clippings kept by Cove resident Roxy Wilson. The Bumpass Cove residents used representational practices designed and constructed in response to local exigencies to create new forms of knowledge about their home that depicted it not as an isolated "white trash" space, a chronotope situated outside of history, but as a local manifestation of a broader set of political and cultural conflicts. People who, prior to this incident, were generally perceived as marginal

Police escort Waste Management Incorporated heavy equipment out of Bumpass Cove, 16 February 1980. From Appalachian Photographic Archive, courtesy of Archives and Special Collections, East Tennessee State University, Johnson City, by permission of the *Johnson City Press.*

members of their own community had become public writers and spokespeople in ways they might never have imagined: Hobart Story, who had a reputation as a drinker, had for years been dismissed as paranoid but found himself and his home at the center of a popular movement. Women of the community like Mary Rogers, Gail Story, and Linda Walls who had little formal schooling and had up to that point limited their concerns to domestic work became powerful voices and planners of community change (Couto 115–17).

The transformation of the community was not limited, however, to the transformation of individuals. New networks of collaboration with regional sites of intellectual resources and cultural production emerged from the crisis, a particularly significant development given the stereotypes of illiteracy that cling to places such as Bumpass Cove. As noted, East Tennessee State University chemists supplied technical assistance and empirical knowledge that reinforced resident's claims; ETSU's Archives of Appalachia preserves a collection of documents and artifacts, including Roxy Wilson's scrapbook. Various programs from Vanderbilt University's Center for Health Services provided financial and human assistance. The Highlander Center, a "citizenship school" founded in the 1930s dedicated to supporting grass-roots organizers, provided impor-

Regional Connections

94

tant training not only in the logistics of operating a community group but also critical, cultural skills of research and writing that enabled residents to locate, interpret, and re-present relevant information from often baffling and unhelpful state records and archives, honing their skills in public argument. Cove organizers expanded from their local group to help create Tennesseeans against Chemical Hazards, or TEACH (Couto 116–17). The naming of this group is significant, I think, in that it signals the way that those who were once acted upon now saw themselves, and the place they inhabited, as actants in political and cultural narratives, teachers whose local knowledge could have broader applications and implications.

That a site of a type so widely imagined to be a cultural void could become a kind of pedagogical space points toward the fact that Bumpass Cove itself became, at least fleetingly, a different kind of landscape, a regional landscape: a particular site that opened onto a broad spatial and discursive network of vital relationships. The residents of Bumpass Cove were able to transform this preterit "waste space" because, in the words of Richard Couto, "They had a vision of a new and better community. They also had new insight into the politics of their problem and the limits of their power" (117–18). Finding the means to represent their new understanding of their place and its role in larger regional configurations, the people of Bumpass Cove engaged with the implications of the received, socially constructed understanding of their community and, through acts of social invention, created a foundation for social action.

Partial Victories

Both of these episodes in the history of my community and in the history of waste and dumping have the unhappy corollary that the popular movements that came out of them were not sustained. In the case of the Bumpass Cove Citizen's Group, Red-baiting that centered on the role of the Highlander Center in the organization of the community led the group's first president, Skip Foss, to resign from the group and try to unincorporate it secretly, claiming concern about Communist infiltration. The group disintegrated in the turmoil that followed. Its basic goal to clean up Bumpass Cove also went unachieved. In an ironic twist, the attempts to remove the toxic materials proved to be more dangerous to Cove residents, folks living along the route by which materials would be removed, and anyone living wherever the waste would be removed to, than simply leaving the barrels in their current, moderately dangerous location (Couto 119). Gail Story simultaneously relays her own disappointment and her broader geographical consciousness when she states, "To leave it in was safest. It wasn't safest for us, it was safest for the rest of the world" (quoted in Couto 119).

The Carter Coalition likewise collapsed under its own success. Though Mickii Carter was elected by her fellow commissioners to a shared mayorship, she served only one term on the city commission before the group lost its momentum along with the fight against Iris Glen. The Carter Coalition encountered an even more profound defeat when it attempted to rewrite the charter for the city of Johnson City, in order to have an elected mayor and alderman in place of its current commission–city manager system. While the coalition succeeded in forcing the election of a charter commission, its slate of candidates was soundly defeated; only two candidates, including Mickii Carter's husband, campaigned successfully on a reform platform (Wozniak, "Pro-Status Quo" 1). A charter commission made up of candidates publicly dedicated to the status quo predictably allowed the matter to die quietly. The electorate had rallied around criticism of the landfill, a battle that had already effectively been lost, but remained unconvinced of a need for broader, structural change. Unable to move from a single, relatively finite issue to an energetic broader debate, the Carter Coalition soon ceased to be a significant force in city politics.

Each case presents the dense profusion of interconnections among different kinds of struggles, political, cultural, economic, and legal, as well as among different interests on different geographical scales—Iris Glen, for example, is not only a civic matter and a matter of social class but also a local instance of the ongoing competition and consolidation of the waste handling industry. Yet in each case, the struggle was diluted when it expanded beyond a single site, beyond the landfills in question, to engage in broader political conflicts with city government as a whole, as with the Carter Coalition, or to develop the community rather than oppose its destruction, as the Bumpass Cove Citizen's Group was trying to do—it had just purchased an abandoned building for a community hall when Foss engineered the group's dissolution.

This problem, I suggest, represents the flip side of the grandstanding, homogenizing statism presented by Mayor Giuliani and his Virginia counterparts earlier. On the one hand, place broadly and generally conceived, like the Great State of Virginia, lacks the nuance and complexity, the diversity of interests and backgrounds, the tense, dynamic and evolving character that emerges from the multiple and competing versions of place always in play at any moment in its existence. On the other hand, the kind of community brought into existence only in response to a specific and (relatively) finite crisis like opposition to waste disposal practices lacks the durability, the expansiveness, the breadth of consequence and connection to endure beyond the particular manifestation of conflict that brought it into existence.

Critical regionalism must attempt to negotiate between these two poles, linking individual moments of cultural struggle to larger patterns of history, politics, and culture, by understanding how they are linked not only in time and in the nebulous networks of discourse but also in space, through relationships of power that can be material (in the form of garbage, for example) and cultural (the idea that exurban spaces should willingly accept garbage). This reconsideration is particularly important in the case of the geographical margins of American culture, where conflict is not supposed to happen, whether that inert nature is because the people of marginal places like the southern Appalachians are a nostalgic reservoir of conservative values—the persistent myth of "Small Town U.S.A"—or because the illiteracy and depravity of exurban populations, as seen archetypally in John Boorman's *Deliverance* and its inheritors, preclude their meaningful participation in public life. These assumptions are common to both right and left: Marx remarked that one positive contribution of the bourgeoisie is that it "rescued a considerable part of the population from the idiocy of rural life" ("Manifesto" 477), and that rural workers form a class "much as potatoes in a sack form a sackful of potatoes" ("Eighteenth" 608).

Critical regionalism is thus not intended to supplant other aspects of identity-driven cultural critique, but rather to augment and extend it, providing what Patricia Nelson Limerick calls "an unexpected approach to the seemingly intractable divisions of history, a way to find, quite literally, common ground in seemingly detached and separate narratives" (95). Doing this means developing critical strategies capable of recognizing conflict and struggle in forms unique to specific landscapes, and creating tactics for intervention and action specific to those landscapes. As I have tried to show by picking through the cultural politics of trash and dumping, crucial struggles, matters literally of life and death, are playing out in spaces and places occluded by enduring images of city and country, center and margin, metropole and region. Yet despite these disjunctions in the American cultural imagination, multiple linkages bind the experiences of disparate geographical sites. Region, then, is a way to describe the socially constructed intricacy of these interactions; critical regionalism is a way of harnessing these new tactics of description, these acts of social invention, in projects of social action.

In 2001 the state of Tennessee revived the "Tennessee Trash" advertising campaign, once again bringing to the foreground an explanation of environmental destruction that mystifies the structural inequalities and political economies of dumping and waste even as the waste industry continues to grow and consolidate, even as the siting of undesirable and hazardous facilities continues to endanger those with the least economic and political clout. As the stories in this chapter suggest, the cultural resources exist for the vernacular landscape to become a powerful rallying point for resistance to these and other structural injustices. Both the Iris Glen and the Bumpass Cove episodes, however, demonstrate the limitations that local organization without regional identity and awareness face in creating a sustained movement toward social transformation. In both those cases, I would like to suggest, we see the occurrence of social action engaged in a social construction of place with only an attenuated role for a socially invented vision of region in the future.

This juncture is where critical regionalism can most usefully intervene. While cultural critique is no substitute for the kind of grass-roots activism illustrated in this chapter, academic work could usefully augment the citizen actions that rally in response to specific, local exigencies. For just as academic work in itself is seldom enough to create popular movements for social change, popular movements might benefit from the integrative power of academic analysis. The Bumpass Cove incident in particular exhibits the potential for a fruitful university-community collaboration, in the ways that health screenings and groundwater testing, for example, among other intellectual, human, and material resources provided by Vanderbilt University and ETSU, facilitated the efforts of the Bumpass Cove Citizen's Group to support their claims and to make their case effectively to broader publics. This sponsorship of Bumpass Cove's rhetorical project augmented the more traditional humanitarian role academic workers played in alleviating, even in limited ways, the physical suffering of the Bumpass Cove residents.

As a cultural critic I wonder, what would the cultural equivalent of the public, scientific intellectual work done in the Bumpass Cove case look like? How might academics with training in cultural criticism have been able to offer their intellectual and human resources to assist in this case, in the same way that chemists and public health researchers did? Without making too grandiose a case for cultural critique, I want to conclude this chapter by suggesting critical regionalism, practiced by academic intellectuals willing and able to reclaim the supposedly tranquil or inert places of the geographical and cultural margins as vital sites of intervention, might be able to help people see the relationships between isolated nodes of resistance to injustice and larger patterns of politics, history, and culture.

Negation, in other words, is not enough; the practice of critique should always be accompanied by the development of principles for cultural production. Critical regionalism can provide a research and writing methodology to enact this place-centered investigation of the forms and issues that create connections between the supposedly parochial interests of regional communities with broad patterns of conflict and struggle. For this methodology to be truly transformative for the geographical margin, however, this project must be taken up on a broader scale by the people of these communities, and must be transformative not only of communities but of the academy as well, drawing academic practice into new areas of public life by making it part of the local cultures in vital but also vernacular ways. We have here a tantalizing vision of the kind of "civic professionalism" that Herb Reid and Betsy Taylor assert is a central aspect of critical regionalism: "professional identity and training that includes the experiences, ethics, and skills to be accountable to a regional public and capable of collaboration, communication, and identification with local communities" (24). To paraphrase Lewis Mumford, regionalism may only be an instrument, but its aim could be the best life possible.

However, a rhetoric of landscape, a language of images, that originates largely outside the community itself, plays a powerful deterministic and often obfuscating role in the practice of local public discourse. The disingenuous use of the log cabin, for example, to link Johnson City's contemporary development patterns to a heroic narrative of westward expansion appears to rely more on a discourse and a definition of Appalachia originating in metropolitan popular culture forms than on any careful consideration of the history of the southern mountains. The next necessary movement in the development of critical regionalism, therefore, must be to consider the factors that shape the production and reception of representations in communities on the geographical margin. This move is especially important in light of the fact that, for people living and working outside the twin metropolitan centers of American culture on the east and west coasts, the dominant and pervasive representational practices of mass media not only focus attention away from their homes but do so in literate forms to which these people are deliberately and systematically denied access. From the mediated places of representation then, we will turn to media representations of place.

When folks from Johnson City like me—upper-middle-class white kids who do things like go to college, move to larger cities, and use their attenuated sense of cosmopolitan to define themselves against the locals —talk to each other about our experiences of their hometown, they often do so with reference to movies and television. Director David Lynch's Lumberton (the setting for 1986's *Blue Velvet*) and Twin Peaks (depicted in the 1990–92 television series of the same name) are two particularly popular points of comparison; although they were not made as portraits of Johnson City or Appalachia, they rang true for us high school cult-film types, whose parents were not likely to be from there, and who viewed the surrounding area from the sheltered standpoint of cul-de-sac subdivisions. Their resonance was not necessarily in the details of the landscape (though Lynch's talent for rendering strange such familiar details as trees, stoplights, and neon signs somehow hit home for me, at least) but in the vision of how the place worked. Both *Blue Velvet* and *Twin Peaks* show small-town worlds in which the good and the depraved, the normal, the transgressive, and the deviant, operate side by side, often oblivious to each other, sometimes starkly juxtaposed, but always having multiple points of connection and zones of overlap. We used the narrative and social structures of work like Lynch's as the basis for creating our own understandings of our homes that were drenched in weirdness. Each new oddity learned about Johnson City and its environs was integrated into our overall picture of Johnson City as a place that was absurdly and dissonantly menacing, as the bland homogeneity of its Edge City landscape butted up against the mass of contradictions that is the surrounding Appalachian landscape. A story like the Hanging of Murderous Mary, for example, would make us shake our heads and say, "David Lynch would love this place."

Johnson City seemed never to disappoint in providing new examples that confirmed our Lynch-ian version of it—though I suspect we could have found enough strange stories to sustain this theory in almost any place we lived. The things we chose to examine collectively in conversation, to emphasize in our description of the place to others we would encounter as we moved away from Johnson City, were the ones that fit with the tendencies of movies and television programs that we admired precisely because they asked us to challenge the dominant meanings of our community, to see things in the local landscape that we might not have noticed seeing it solely through the filter of the typical, bland strip mall development and 1960s ranch houses that were our native habitat. Just as important, through these media representations we were taught to see the increasingly uniform and sterile spaces of our city's contemporary landscape development as potentially weird themselves: their tedious, authoritarian qualities fissured but also intensified by their proximity to rural spaces with a reputation for peculiarity.

Perhaps the most important new possibility media texts like Lynch's opened up to us was that there were multiple ways not just to think about our place and region but to represent it. A different kind of vocabulary, a heretofore unrealized rhetoric was available to us as we went about the daily work of interpreting and enfabling our experience of home. Those who wished to use work like Lynch's to intensify their withering (and, to my thinking, elitist) critique of the town could do so, but if you brought some of the visual richness, enigmatic mood, and sense of the base complexity of human interaction that characterizes Lynch's vision to your own perceptions, it seemed suddenly there was something there to be described.

Both *Blue Velvet* and *Twin Peaks*, for example, are structured around investigations, in each case showing sophisticated young people (Jeffrey Beaumont [Kyle Maclachlan] and Sandy Williams [Laura Dern] in *Blue Velvet*, or Audrey Horne [Sherilynn Fenn] and Donna Hayward [Laura Flynn Boyle] in *Twin Peaks*) working toward the revelation of intricate social webs whose meanings shape and are shaped by the landscapes they overlay. At least part of the appeal of media texts like *Blue Velvet* and *Twin Peaks* for people like me growing up in a place like Johnson City must have been in the way they communicated the idea that people like us— bored kids feeling cut off from Culture—could make vital knowledge from local materials, could find something in the spaces at hand, seemingly so far from the cosmopolis, that was worth learning. Moreover, the films powerfully underscored that we (like Jeffrey and Sandy and Audrey and Donna) could have access to the cultural resources to grapple with the weirdness that was around us, just beyond the dull patina of daily life, and that we had the skills to discern and describe it.

I had David Lynch back in my mind recently, reading about a horrific murder case in Johnson City with more than a few Lynchian overtones. According to *Johnson City Press* reporters Gregg Powers and John Thompson, the story opens on 11 October 2002, with the discovery by two fishermen of a severed head and a pair of hands in Boone Lake, near a boat ramp at Winged Deer Park—a reprise of the opening of both *Blue Velvet*

Bodies by the lake: Sheriff Truman (Michael Ontkean) and Doctor Hayward (Warren Frost) discover the body of Laura Palmer (Sheryl Lee) in ABC's *Twin Peaks* (1990–92). Image © CORBIS SYGMA.

and *Twin Peaks*, as the former begins with Jeffrey Beaumont finding the severed ear of a kidnapping victim on the ground, and the latter with fisherman Pete Martell (Jack Nance) discovering of the body of Laura Palmer (Sheryl Lee), wrapped in plastic, washed up on a lakeshore. Unlike the faddish obsession with "who killed Laura Palmer?" that swept the United States during *Twin Peaks*'s first season, however, this Johnson City story is somewhat lacking as a whodunit: only five days later city police identified the head as that of a missing seventeen-year-old Georgia boy named Adam Chrismer, who, along with his wife of two months, Samantha Lemming, sixteen, was last seen in the company of a fifty-one-year-old man named Howard Hawk Willis who was in federal custody in New York State at the time the body parts were found, charged with dealing cocaine.

Willis and Chrismer had been spotted in a Wal-Mart in Fort Oglethorpe, Georgia, on 5 and 7 September, by store security cameras. The duo was caught in the act of using the credit cards of Willis's stepfather, Samuel Johnson Thomas, who was reported missing on 5 October (Thompson and Wozniak). Thomas's dismembered body would later be found on the Georgia side of Lookout Mountain, near Chattanooga, Tennessee. By the 17th, authorities announced they would indict Willis for the murder, having discovered the rest of Chrismer's and Lemming's

Howard Hawk Willis.
Photo courtesy of the
Johnson City Press.

bodies in a storage unit in downtown Johnson City rented by Willis's mother, Emma Hawk, who would be named an accessory to the crime (Wozniak, "Body parts").

Reconstructing this story through the local newspaper accounts, it was hard not to think that all you need is a Log Lady and a one-armed man (trademark eccentrics from *Twin Peaks*'s cast of characters) and you've got quite a television show. Not just the brutality of the murders transfers them from the realm of the seamy into the spectacular, though. There is also something about the way expectations about the local landscape are violated by the course of events, the way Winged Deer Park, that the self-proclaimed center of triumphalist local history, and haven for safe, sanctioned forms of recreation, was transformed into the epicenter of what one local reporter memorably described as a "panorama of gore" (Thompson). By contrast, a stabbing at Buffalo Mountain Park the previous April seemed a more routine tragedy: when Mack Lawson stabbed John Garland on 21 April 2002, it was "only" a lover's quarrel (Spradlin, "Area"). The fact that both lovers were men served only to intensify criticism of deviant behavior at Johnson City's "outlaw park." This latest episode fit neatly with the long-standing terms of Buffalo Mountain Park's landscape narratives and, in so doing, reinforced, rather than challenged, the structure and meaning of that landscape.

But how to make sense of the jarring juxtaposition of the calculated but surreal brutality of the dismembered corpses alongside the narratives of unmitigated progress represented by the TVA lake and the park's proud display of civic propriety? The day after the discovery of the body parts, the sheriff of Washington County, Fred Phillips, observed that the murders appeared "ritualistic" (Spradlin, "Sheriff"). Raising the specter of Satanism in the Bible Belt is a volatile rhetorical move that reflects what a significant disruption to the dominant image of the community had occurred. Moreover, it suggests that the murders themselves were being perceived as a kind of composition, not unreflective human action but a performance designed to create an image of its own. Not only were people killed, they were killed in a way that created an intrusive cultural phenomenon—a "panorama of gore" rewriting the landscape of Winged Deer and Johnson City, connecting it in the most sordid ways to a network of swindles, abuses, and atrocities from the Fort Oglethorpe Wal-Mart to the New York State penal system.

The police emphasized the trail of evidence, articulating an empirical, positivist view of the regional connections the case revealed. For them the story was an immediate, material matter, but for everyone else (myself included) the news of the Willis case was just that: news. It came to us through media outlets that performed the initial work of narrativizing an extraordinarily unruly chain of events into a cogent whole. But as audience we had to plug in the story details needed to make the reportage into a fully coherent, recognizable narrative—the affective elements of the incident, the questions of how and why this group of people came to do the things they did. For that, I turned to David Lynch, and I am sure that many other folks in Johnson City and beyond called to mind images from whatever media texts they had seen that seemed relevant, to try to find the means to construct for themselves a narrative structure that could somehow make comprehensible events that defy not only the most basic standards of human behavior but a community's dominant understanding of itself. I, and likely many of my fellow Johnson Citians, tried to make sense of this social construction of our place and its broader regional relationships by working to integrate it within a broader field of representations.

Critical regionalism must search for the kinds of texts that can facilitate the most expansive possible thinking in situations like this, in which circumstances challenge people's ability to make sense of their places' interconnections, even (especially) when those connections run counter to the assumptions underlying "commonsense" versions of local and regional landscapes. A film may ostensibly be "set" somewhere else, but local problems and priorities are always a part of what Edward Said has termed the "field of attitude and reference" (64) for how those representations are received, and the range of uses to which those texts might be put.

Much of the content of popular film represents a powerful rhetorical project against an understanding of exurban places as vital spaces of public life. The depiction of communities outside of the metropolitan center imagines them as altogether too unified, whether for good—nostalgia—or for ill—horror. Perhaps because The City has become the site of intense intercultural struggle, a polyglot and polysemous place, the regions beyond (including, paradoxically, many cities) are seen as simultaneously unitary and, as such, entirely different from the cultural life of the city. And yet, because the urban experience is the organizing principle of American culture (again, for good and for ill), regional life can appear either as the lost unitary language of American culture or as entirely illiterate and bizarre. Either way, whether through sepia-toned sentimentalism or chiaroscuro terror, regional communities, Other Places, are held by both left and right to be entirely separate from the central political and ethical struggles of American culture, and hence neutralized.

Returning to the story of the killings in Winged Deer Park, the latter section of this chapter will examine how films such as *Fargo* (1996, dir. Ethan Coen) and *Pulp Fiction* (1994, dir. Quentin Tarantino) might be read from a regional perspective that challenges this exclusion of the local concerns of exurban communities from the vital concerns of public life. But first, by examining the relationship between literacy and region in *Deliverance* (1972, dir. John Boorman), *Apocalypse Now* (1979, dir. Francis Ford Coppola), and *Cape Fear* (1992, dir. Martin Scorsese), we will take a closer look at how one particular synecdoche of American popular film's "landscape narrative" of regional life, illiteracy, works to disconnect exurban spaces. However, the very terms of that exclusion can also function as a metonymy, pointing toward broader regional interconnections.

Never Get Out of the Boat

Deliverance has supplied American culture with its most enduring imagery of the geographical margins in the visual age. For most Americans, *Deliverance* is one of those movies for which there is no first viewing: American popular culture is replete with direct and indirect references to this film: allusions abound in other cultural texts to albino banjo pickers or quotations of the film's most famous line: "Squeal like a pig!" Even a movie as drenched in urban cool as *Pulp Fiction* goes so far as to appropriate the rape scene, replete with redneck thugs, to its urban underworld —to point to the next level below the world of Tarantino's bored, cynical murderers. The screen place the film envisions has become a permanent location in the national imaginary; "Deliverance Country" is colloquial shorthand for the whole of the southern Appalachians, indeed, for any place deviating from the expected urbane patterns of modern and post-modern cultural development. These invocations abound even as we move beyond the thirtieth anniversary of the film's 1972 release.

Nothing testifies to *Deliverance*'s staying power more than the resurfacing of the sexually deviant, randomly brutal hillbilly character twenty years later in director Martin Scorsese's 1992 remake of the noir classic *Cape Fear*. In both of these films, literacy (and the lack of it) is at once a synecdoche that totalizes and essentializes the Appalachian region's identity as a space apart, but ironically it also links stereotypes of the mountain South—a region representative (indeed, the apotheosis) of the ways areas outside the privileged urban sites of American cultural production acquire the tag of illiteracy—to representations of other marginal populations. To dramatize how this regional connection works, how the places evoked by film interconnect, forming broader spatial networks, we will move to a discussion of *Deliverance* and *Cape Fear* by way of another film, about another trip to the backwoods: director Francis Ford Coppola's *Apocalypse Now*.

All three are river movies, landscape narratives about finding far upstream from "civilization" a degraded, tribal population that embodies a dark, barbaric side of "human nature." The river, like the highway, is a prime component of a landscape narrative, linking space and time into a chronotope. But in the case of these films the upstream movement defies the normal associations between the flow of water and the passage of time; here the travelers move against time and, indeed, out of time. Place comes to serve in the ahistorical, even antihistorical way that literary critic Roberto Dainotto describes (2). As the travelers move upstream, the trappings of progress individually of cultural "development" fall away and the travelers enter a timeless space, where the landscape and its inhabitants are seen through the eyes of the travelers and understood in terms of their vocabulary of cultural meanings and interpretations, juxtaposing a cosmopolitan, mobile sensibility with its apparent, isolate opposite.

The films not only share a landscape narrative structure, they also use a parallel visual vocabulary to create the idea of their cultural others, a fact that suggests commonalties between the southern Appalachians and other marginal places and sheds light on the way the people of the mountains are imagined from a cosmopolitan standpoint. The prime element of this visual vocabulary involves the depiction of the landscape and its relationship to the film's main characters. In a revision of Joseph Conrad's *Heart of Darkness* set in the Vietnam War, Captain Willard (Martin

Sheen) is sent via a navy patrol boat with a small crew far upriver into Cambodia in search of a rogue Green Beret operative, Colonel Kurtz (Marlon Brando), with orders to "terminate with extreme prejudice." The landscape of *Apocalypse Now*, for example, presents an ever-present menace; an important early scene culminates in the humane, unassuming Chef (Frederic Forrest) learning the lesson "never get off the boat"—an apt epigraph for *Deliverance* as well. He and Willard, venture into the jungle to gather mangoes—to live off the land, as it were—in a scene constructed of long shots that alternately dwarf the men in a vast, decadently lush setting, and tracking shots that seem to stalk the two men, implying that "the hills have eyes." An important stylistic device here—one that is used to great effect in *Deliverance* (Cunningham 125)—involves obscuring the camera's view with vegetation. The presence of the leaves and branches in the line of sight enhances the stalking effect and emphasizes the landscape as a confusing and impenetrable place. The sudden leap of a tiger from the verdant backdrop, and the resulting mayhem, shocks but does not surprise, given the elaborate visual setup.

That the tiger is initially believed by the characters (and the viewers) to be a "Charlie" suggests the thin line drawn between the debased humans and the natural world. The strategy here is reductive, depersonalizing: the land and the people are one. Later—much farther upstream—the boat is attacked by aboriginal enemies who rain arrows down on them, but the camera offers only fleeting glimpses of the actual assailants, presenting instead images of the arrows hurtling out of the line of trees—the boat is attacked by the land itself. Perhaps this comes in response to the film's opening shot in which a line of jungle suddenly bursts into flame, under attack by American helicopters. In both cases the landscape is interchangeable with the Enemy. However, when later Willard arrives at the compound where Colonel Kurtz rules the aborigines, this tactic is reversed: in several different shots Kurtz's followers carpet the terrain, providing a backdrop like the trees and plants in the tiger scene (for example).

Kurtz himself is a curious mediating figure between the raw savagery of his followers and the "civilization" Willard represents. The precise quality of Kurtz's menace will have important resonance for Scorsese's *Cape Fear* twelve years later, for Kurtz represents the threat of someone who embraces both literacy and savagery—a culturally unacceptable hybrid. Kurtz is constantly associated visually with books and representational technologies of other kinds—photos, tape recordings, and so forth. For most of the movie he exists for Willard only as a dossier, and even after the two men meet, Willard studies Kurtz's books and photographs to try to understand him. But Kurtz has linked his fate to the hostile landscape, which, in its chaos and excess, is antithetical to the ordering principles all these texts imply. Kurtz has gone mad trying to balance the two, and the movie generally suggests that attempting to do so violates deep, abiding taboos, recalling white cultures' prohibitions against miscegeny. "Civilization," "progress" mean choosing the text over the terrain, and never going "back" to nature.

As literacy studies scholar Peter Mortensen has shown, this use of illiteracy in representing the lives and experiences of mountain people has its roots set in a social Darwinism, which, while never factually accurate, has shaped public perception of the region, as well as public policy affecting the region, throughout American history. Perceptions of illiteracy have shaped the relationship not only between the mountain South and the metropolitan cultural centers of the United States as a whole but also, as Mortensen shows, within the U.S. South itself. Literacy is one of the ways the traditional political and economic divisions of Tidewater and Frontier, of plantation South and mountain South, are mapped onto cultural practices ("Representations" 106–8). There is an anxious undercurrent to this process, though, that what is feared here is not so much illiteracy itself as the idea of alternative literacies, outside of the standards and control of the dominant culture. It is Power's fear of sedition that is allegorized here, expressing itself by trying to demonize and belittle what it cannot understand. As a social invention, this tactic represents a morally suasive rhetorical position by which to control the terms and techniques by which public discourse is carried out, an attempt to centralize the valid languages for public life based on the fear that linguistic and literate plurality destroys, rather than invigorates, the workings of community.

This fear is precisely what *Deliverance* encodes, working visually, like *Apocalypse Now*, to suggest that its hillbillies are an extension of the prediscursive landscape that is their home. When four Atlanta professionals take a weekend trip to canoe a whitewater river that is about to be dammed for a hydroelectric-generating lake, they find themselves fighting for their lives against a pair of hillbillies who sexually assault two members of their group, and against a more unforgiving river than they expected. The use of vegetation to obscure line of sight recurs throughout this movie, heightening the sense of entrapment, hostility, and constant surveillance. Low camera angles peer at the canoe party from underneath and behind natural obstructions. In both of the encounters with the sadistic hillbillies on the river, the assailants appear first at a distance, well back in the depth of field (hence nested in the surroundings), viewed through tree branches as they move toward their victims. As cultural historian Rodger Cunningham writes, "the first rapist is initially seen moving *within* a wall of green, as if belonging to it, a 'living extension' of its threat; and the rape scene itself is played with the campers in long shots, surrounded by the entangling, viny, loamy gloom" (125). Like the Asians and the tiger in *Apocalypse Now*, the mountaineers appear as a force of nature, ungoverned by system or reason.

But they are not just a force of nature, as comes out in the first encounters of the city boys with the hillbillies. The interaction is marked by confusion created by the inability of the city boys, and apparent unwillingness of the hillbillies, to adapt to the different forms of literacy they all encounter. In the now-iconic "dueling banjoes" scene, *Deliverance* starts to suggest that music can provide a "universal language," but quickly and completely scuttles that optimistic note. The communication proves confrontational; the banjo duels instead of duets; what seems to be a moment in which difference can be overcome proves otherwise. At the conclusion of the showdown, the guitarist from Atlanta, Drew (Ronny Cox), extends a hand to the deformed and albino banjo player (Hoyt Pollard), but his hand goes unacknowledged as if the gesture was part of a foreign vocabulary. The failure of this contact has been foreshadowed before the end of the duet, as Drew admits "I'm lost" and the boy plays on without him.

When the hillbillies do speak, they are oblique and often unintelligible —dialogue is halting and marked by repetition and misunderstanding when it occurs at all. Meanwhile, the vacationing men from Atlanta exhibit a kind of logorrhea, talking and laughing heedlessly, indiscriminately. We hear their voices even before the Warner Brothers logo has given way to the film proper, which opens with an assault on the landscape that anticipates the opening shot of *Apocalypse Now*. As Appalachian Studies scholar J. W. Williamson points out about *Deliverance*, this image represents a kind of admission that whatever assault is perpetrated against the cosmopolitan travelers, the exurban landscape itself is undergoing an assault of even greater magnitude and devastation, an environmental catastrophe (157).

Though the early sections of the film are marked by the puerile chatter of the vacationing suburbanites, *Deliverance* (like *Apocalypse Now* and *Cape Fear*) moves on a vector toward a silence broken only by natural sounds. The silent, final encounter with the enigmatic albino boy—accompanied now only by the sound of the river—presents the locals' mute nature as a major factor in the larger pattern of misinterpretation and misrecognition: as the boy stands on a log bridge over the river, he sways his banjo slowly back and forth. Drew, mistaking this for a kind of wave, smiles and waves back, receiving no response. What did this gesture mean? A warning? nothing? The film leaves the enigma unresolved—vaguely but indisputably frightening, untranslatable. But the boy serves as a marker for their transition into a saturnine landscape that seems to preexist language.

Appropriately, it is Bobby (Ned Beatty), the rape victim, who is least successful at crossing the cultural and linguistic gulf, and who is most voluble in the early scenes, full of self-important but hollow swagger. His attempts to communicate are stupidly condescending, and his reactions always attempt to mask his own confusion and insecurity in ridicule (Williamson 158). He tells the man pumping gas, "I sure do like the way you wear your hat," and is told, after a long pause, "You don't know nothing." Instead of considering the implications of this oblique but cautionary remark, Bobby turns, chuckling, to Ed (Jon Voight) and murmurs, "Ask him about his hat." Bobby's nonstop chatter and general disrespect are answered point for point in the grueling rape scene: he is stripped of both self-respect and human language when he is forced to "squeal like a pig."

There's Nothing More Dangerous Than an Educated Redneck

Bobby is a scapegoat, but he also serves as a kind of everyman here, or at least an every-suburbanite, and the assault is portrayed in such feral, brutal terms that he must command some measure of sympathy, even if that sympathy is coerced by playing upon the homophobia and class prejudices of the audience. In *Cape Fear*, attorney Sam Bowden (Nick Nolte), his wife Leigh (Jessica Lange), and daughter Danni (Juliette Lewis) are stalked and terrorized by ex-con Max Cady (Robert De Niro), who believes (correctly, as it turns out) that Bowden mishandled his defense against sexual assault charges some years before. In this film an ambivalence similar to that generated by Bobby's assault in *Deliverance* is resolved in favor of the bourgeoisie: Bowden brings Cady's revenge campaign upon himself, but the audience's allegiance must ultimately lie with the Bowdens as Cady's retributive methods become increasingly barbaric, as he abandons working within the world of discourse—here, embodied by law—to achieve his revenge.

The way the character of Cady is shaped by the same devices used to create the menace of the foes in *Deliverance* and *Apocalypse Now* suggests that Scorsese recognized that the same quality that made Kurtz and his minions so terrifying—the mixture of literacy and savagery—could easily

be transferred to an Appalachian character. Cady is the perfect complement to Kurtz: rather than the literate man gone savage, he is the savage
man gone literate. He has come downstream, to the tidewater, instead of
the audience, vicariously joining a group of travelers gone upstream to
the backwoods.

His savagery is repeatedly underscored in images of landscape. Not
only is he repeatedly identified as being "from the hills" of north Georgia
—literally, "*Deliverance* country"—he is visually associated with dark,
forbidding locations, and often framed against trees. Shots of wind in the
branches outside the Bowden's windows signal his menacing, unseen
presence. And during the film's most tense centerpiece scene, the encounter with the Bowdens' daughter Danielle (Juliette Lewis), Cady is in a
stage set with a gingerbread house and trees: a mythic, folkloric woodland villain. When asked where he is from, he replies, "the Black Forest."

True to form, these natural images are played off against textual images. Indeed, the first we see of Cady is not him per se, but his jailhouse
collage of jarringly incompatible images, and the tattoos that turn his
body itself into a text. Later, police Lieutenant Elgart (played by Robert
Mitchum, who ironically is both a son of eastern Kentucky and the actor
who played Max Cady in the original version of the film), seeing Cady
strip-searched, remarks, "I don't know whether to look at him or read
him." Cady's first line in the movie is his reply to a guard who asks him, as
he leaves prison, if he wants his books; he replies, "I already read 'em."
His literacy is the product of a prison self-education (a la Malcolm X),
and before his transformation, his defense attorney Bowden played upon
Cady's illiteracy, concealing potentially helpful depositions from him to
guarantee his conviction—an act of literal prejudice, prejudgment, motivated by horror at Cady's savagery.

Like *Deliverance*'s Bobby, Bowden is forced to reap precisely what he
has sown, as Cady manages to turn the entire system of law—the regulation of nature by the written word—into his vengeful tool. For lawyer
Bowden this is a vision of apocalypse. The narrative is fueled by Cady's
ability not only to remain within the law but to turn it against its own
agents. Cady's literacy becomes a vehicle for his sexual menace as well: his
seduction of the Bowdens' daughter involves masquerading as a teacher,
and in that guise (and even after the act is exposed), granting her access to
forbidden texts, such as Henry Miller's *Sexus* trilogy. What this bourgeois
family is menaced by here is that those down by law, down by all kinds of
contingent, discursive structures, will come to understand the structures
without being assimilated by them—gaining knowledge but leaving rage
intact. Cady himself spells out the threat in no uncertain terms in a

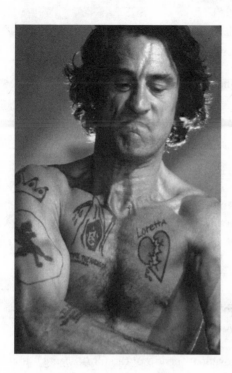

Body as text: Max Cady (Robert
De Niro) in *Cape Fear* (1992).
Image © CORBIS SYGMA.

stirring soliloquy, delivered after he has just brutally dispatched three
goons the increasingly desperate Bowden hires to dispatch him. "You
ain't better than me!" he bellows. "I'll outlearn you, I'll outread you, I'll
outphilosophize you! It takes more than a few blows to the guts to take
this good old boy down!"

Like *Deliverance*, though, the problem is not just that he will acquire
literacy, but that its acquisition will somehow be deformed in the act of
translation (of which his tattooed body is symbolic). Cady was not unlet-
tered before his prison stay, but differently lettered; more than once it is
noted that Cady comes from Pentecostal roots—a speaker of strange, and
to cosmopolitan ears, imaginary tongues. These "archaic" practices signal an overall lack of "development" that on the film's terms ultimately
precludes a successful acculturation—clearly a tendentious way of portraying a religious practice that is historically class coded. As cultural
critic Matt Wray writes, "In general, charismatic Christianity brings a
sense of spiritual power and righteousness to those who, because of their
positions within capitalist economic structures, suffer from a fundamen-
tal lack of social and economic power" (Wray and Newitz 207). Instead,
charismatic religious practice is attributed to the body, much as genetic

deformity characterized the native population of *Deliverance*. Cady tells the Bowdens of how his daddy handled serpents and his mama drank strychnine to explain his apparent indestructability, noting he has "a genetic advantage." Thus a historical body of religious practices—a socially constructed, class-specific, literate strategy for representing and interpreting the material world—becomes a racialized, bodily trait.

Given the film's hysterically essentialized portrayal of his difference, Cady's attempt to emulate and participate in this foreign society is necessarily imperfect; his outcast status is signified externally in bad suits and a ludicrous haircut as well as being portrayed in his personality, his tattoos, and his accent. This film says Cady is separated from the society of the Bowdens by a gulf no amount of literacy can overcome, because their differences are not cultural and constructed, but natural. The crime Cady is immediately guilty of upon leaving prison is his attempt to participate in the society that has clearly rejected him. Indeed, though all three of these movies do a certain amount to build viewer sympathy with the savages, albeit as tragically deformed, all eventually stack the deck against them so high one has to revert to supporting the side of (white, patriarchal, urbane) "civilization." In all three cases the savage practices become so bizarre and brutal that no moral, ethical viewer can possibly justify them except through a willful counterreading of the kind I am staging here. This extremism, too, is part of these films' argument against the cultural margin. Of course, in each case it is less argument than emotional and ideological manipulation, which both reaffirms the normative status of the center and suggests that the margin is pathologically unfit to participate in public life—and therefore must be ruled, incarcerated, inundated, exterminated. Both *Deliverance* and *Cape Fear* have their hillbilly menaces swallowed up by rising waters: reintegrated, as it were, with the landscape from which they were never really separate (a precise inversion of the memorable scene before the climax of *Apocalypse Now*, of Colonel Willard rising from the water, having made his resolve to kill Kurtz and reject his mad hybridity). But *Cape Fear* and *Deliverance* also end with the haunting suggestion that they might someday return, implying that a more permanent, intentional solution to the "hillbilly problem" would perhaps have been desirable. The controversy over the ending of *Apocalypse Now* further underscores this ambivalence, as two different endings were filmed and released at various times: one in which we see an air strike destroy Kurtz's compound, and another in which Willard flees the ruins of the encampment into the night.

These films react to transgressive and deviant local literacies not just with censure but with fear and hostility. Audiences are actively discouraged from entertaining the possibility of multiple literacies, for example, but instead urged to see deviation from the cultural norm as just that, a deviation that presents the threat of destroying "order," which becomes an end in itself, beyond reproach. Even traditional, assimilationist, American "melting pot" ideology is rejected here; even the idea that, Pygmalion-like, these populations could be adapted to a centralized, dominant literacy is discredited. Only the very hysteria of this representational strategy suggests that literate plurality might open society to more democratic participation in public life by a broader cross section of the citizenry.

Apocalypse Now centers this argument on race, a tactic all the more unsettling for the film's remarkable aesthetic achievements. But the same can't quite be said of the other two; rather, one can observe a very interesting use of the hillbilly figure in racial configurations: as a substitute, a white site for the expression of fears typically reserved for blackness. Note in *Cape Fear* especially that in a movie that supposedly takes place in the tidewater South, virtually no African Americans appear, but traditionally racist motifs do: cannibalism, that signature atrocity of the cultural Other, attributed to Cady at least twice; and, predictably, miscegeny—he is, after all, coming for the Bowden's daughter. By linking linguistic and other cultural differences with what *Deliverance's* Bobby calls "genetic deficiencies," embodied in albinism, retardation, and, in Max Cady, sociopathic mental deformity, these movies suggest that these literate and material differences are permanent and bodily. Thus the highly contingent and socially constructed qualities of class and region become naturalized, biological.

Deliverance's use of albinism, and the way it has been totemically appropriated to so many other locations, sums this point up. It implies that whiteness in the South is not all one thing, that some are in fact too white—their whiteness a part of an entirely other culture, another race. It also supplies a provisional answer to the problem literary critic Henry Shapiro explores, "that conventional modes of resolving the dilemma posed by the perception of 'deviance' from the American norm by a region of people . . . could not be utilized to explain the 'deviance' of white, Anglo-Saxon, Protestant, native-born Americans living in the present and within miles of the older centers of American civilization" (x). This strategy reinforces whiteness's cultural authority, by postulating that any deviation from white-supremacist capitalist patriarchy is tantamount to biological mutation. The whites of the Appalachian region (the poor ones, anyway) are not "bad" whites, it says—in fact, they are not "regular" white people at all. The possibility of alternative forms of whiteness that have a different, potentially resistant political valence is foreclosed, its threat neutralized, by disconnecting the spaces in which such alternatives might thrive from broader patterns of history and culture, stigmatizing the places in which such unsettling transgressions might occur as deviant (Cresswell 24–25). Such a construction of regional identity thus authorizes an occupation and exploitation of the landscape's natural resources, and paternalistic control over and utilization of the people's human resources, such as has characterized the history of Appalachia within the project of modern and postmodern development, as was the case with Bumpass Cove (in chapter 2). Note that both *Cape Fear* and *Deliverance* focus on "new" Southerners—prosperous, cosmopolitan—but both films are anxious about the basis of that prosperity. Bowden's career includes a history of exploiting the poor; *Deliverance* opens with images of dam construction, extracting power from the mountain landscape to support the urban expansion of Atlanta.

The racialization of regional people and the class alliances indicated by *Cape Fear* are part of a broader complex of other associations, mapping a kind of discursive region within and among these films. Clearly, homophobic anxiety is central to the plot of *Deliverance*; as cultural critics Michael Ryan and Douglas Kellner write, "The homosexual attack can be interpreted as a projection of the fear that inhabits . . . male-on-male group relations. It is fitting that the film should end with a man in bed with his wife, having a nightmare of the return of the repressed" (150). We are similarly made to know early in *Cape Fear* of the fact that Max was sodomized in jail, a fact that adds queer sexuality to his menace (rather than building sympathy for him as a rape victim: he does not use the word rape to describe his assault).

As film scholar Pam Cook points out, this queer threat is also incorporated in *Cape Fear*'s dark and paradoxical view of femininity. In the same conversation, Max, who eventually even appears in drag (in racial "drag" as well—disguised as the Bowden's Latino maid), notes he has been "getting in touch with his feminine side." As Cook argues, part of Max's horrific nature is the way in which he figures as the avenging angel for all of Sam Bowden's chauvinistic uses of women, including his tenuous but domineering assertion of authority over his wife and daughter. Like Colonel Kurtz, Max is an unacceptable hybrid, not only of literate practices but of gender identifications and sexual practices as well. Despite a superficial critique of Sam, and of the patriarchal order of which, as father, lawyer, and eventually as stone-wielding barbarian, he is representative, "Scorsese still adheres to a negative notion of the feminine. The real horror in *Cape Fear* is feminization: the contamination of positive 'masculine' values (heroism, integrity, honour and so forth) by 'feminine' values of weakness, prevarication and moral laxity" (Cook 15). In *Deliverance* (and *Apocalypse Now*) women are excluded from the narrative almost entirely, making clear that the most important cultural crises are those pertaining to bourgeois white men in which the maintenance, protection, and unquestioned dominance of white masculinity are to be achieved.

Counternarrative and Social Reinvention

Indeed, perhaps the most subtle ideological pattern in these films, all of which played in broad national and international release and are available on DVD in practically every video store in the nation, is that they are not really concerned with the problems of Appalachian people, of women, blacks, Latinos, queers, or working people at all. Instead they are addressed almost entirely to the anxieties, neuroses, and hysteria of a relatively small section of their audience: prosperous, straight, cosmopolitan white men. Marginal populations are used here only to reflect these men's own images, however troubling that image may be. For members of marginal populations, for regional audiences that do not share the attenuated cosmopolitan values that define the ways of reading the good and bad, the heroism and horror in these films, an uncritical viewing of these films could only produce a kind of communal self-loathing: our community has atrophied because the people here are awful. In this scheme the only way to let yourself off the hook is by identifying "up" and internalizing the centralized, metropolitan values that have created the unsustainable patterns of development that undermine exurban communities to begin with. The social construction of regional exceptionalism, embodied in the trope of illiteracy (or, at best, deviant, hybrid literacy), becomes through the rhetorical force of the films' dominant meanings a social invention that thwarts, rather than facilitates, social action for expanding the possibilities for democratic culture.

That these films are all cautionary tales of who or what might be awaiting an opportunity for revenge, amassing its strength for a counterattack, does, however, have the ironic side effect of making these works available for appropriation and interrogation within local contexts, a project of social reinvention, reading the counternarratives in these films to envision new regional networks of solidarity among the varied populations these films work to disempower. Critical regionalism should not argue for more "positive" portrayals of regional life, which serve ideological ends by sanitizing conflict and valorizing assimilation of local cultures into a coercive cultural unity. To see what kind of film that strategy produces, watch director Michael Apted's *Nell* (1994), in which stereotypes of Appalachian illiteracy persist, but in a nostalgic rather than horrific guise, as feral child Nell (Jodie Foster), despite her mental incapacity, proves to have magical powers of "healing" broken patriarchal family structures. This film merely trades the horrific historical Appalachian stereotype of "a strange land and peculiar people" for the nostalgic historical Appalachian stereotype of "our contemporary ancestors"; these are, of course, the region-specific adaptations of the images of native-as-savage and native-as-innocent familiar from other histories of American modernist expansion. In keeping with the racial resonances of the other films discussed previously, *Nell* offers an Appalachian rendition of the "Magic Negro" phenomenon exemplified in such recent films as *The Green Mile* (1999, dir. Frank Darabont) and *The Legend of Bagger Vance* (2000, dir. Robert Redford), in which histories of oppression and cruelty serve (through a benevolent supporting character) to heal the psychic wounds of members of dominant culture, without challenging in any way the structural inequities that produced the oppression in the first place.

This Appalachian version—the Magic Hillbilly?—offers regional life as the container of traditional values that are above the fray—a tactic that serves reactionary purposes, proposing that cultural conflict is a problem that must be suppressed (and troublemakers like minority races, labor organizers, feminists, and queers therefore must be silenced, deported, or worse) rather than acknowledging conflict's role in an ongoing process of defining human rights and responsibilities through the critical practice of democratic, public life. Instead of demanding condescendingly laudatory versions of regional life, critical regionalist scholarship about Appalachia can work to identify films about the Appalachian region and its diverse populations that take plurality, cultural conflict, and structural inequality seriously, engaging these historical phenomena by mapping the connections among varied places and challenging the cultural practices that work to obscure, and by obscuring sustain, these political problems. For example, Haskell Wexler's *Medium Cool* (1969), Barbara Koppel's *Harlan County U.S.A* (1976), or John Sayles's *Matewan* (1986) all enlist practices of social construction into projects of social invention, creating challenging representational tactics that address broad conflicts as they play out in specific places, exploring the pressures upon and resources for public life and its participants while they acknowledge their own constructedness, and hailing viewers not merely as objects of the film's preconceived notions but as (potential) agents of social action.

While each of these films is no doubt problematic in its own particular ways, they all strive to conceive of agency in terms of social organization larger than the individual, to represent the struggles of populations not normally taken seriously in mass media forms, to take local knowledge seriously by giving careful attention to processes of place construction, and to deploy self-reference and self-consciousness about representational practices in a purposeful way.

Wexler breaks down the fictionality of his film, as the film's central characters, including an urban Appalachian working mother and her child, roam Chicago during the 1968 riots, the actual event caught on film during location shooting. Evenhanded about gender, attentive to detail about the lives of the working poor, Wexler's film, though urban in setting, juxtaposes political, economic, and cultural crises in America to one another and indicates the relationship, rather than the disconnection, between urban and rural cultures. Koppel breaks down the (purely artificial) truth effect of documentary form by invoking some traditional narrative strategies in her depiction of a Kentucky coal strike lending the story a pedagogical coherence it might otherwise lack, clarifying the film's status as a public argument rather than an anthropological study. At the same time she is careful to chart the structural nature of a crisis connecting diverse places and populations; a narrative about the challenges of local cooperation, agency, and collective action takes place against a backdrop of economic, political, and geographically integrated relationships. Sayles breaks down the expansionist trappings of the western genre by relocating its conventions to the coalfield wars of the 1920s and 1930s, attempting to revise public memory by reconfiguring the western within a narrative of the regional costs and cruelties that support an urban industrial culture. While clearly allegorical and genre-driven in many respects, Sayles also pays careful attention to regional history, especially in dismantling the myths of ethnic and racial homogeneity. The film uses these neglected historical facts to argue for a social vision of a community that conceives of diversity as a resource for collective action but also powerfully depicts structural, cultural impediments to that vision.

In all three of the films, what we can term their socially inventive qualities are a matter of both content and form, with no guarantees on either. The deciding factor in every case needs to be the local and regional crises in which one seeks to intervene. In that act of intervention, the media texts are used within tactical formations, rather than grand strategies, and subjected to ethical readings that ask what kinds of representational decisions were made, what kind of rhetoric the films employ in the vision of social order they offer intentionally or by default. The first half of this chapter has examined how representations of a particular place might shape its role in the popular imaginary, and how the terms of representations that isolate and detach a region from broader currents of public life might be read against the grain to reveal how not only the places but the texts that depict them are part of, and indeed create, larger spatial networks of meaning and connections to other places and representational practices. But critical regionalism must not confine its concerns only to the representations of the particular region in question. Indeed, it may be an even more valuable project to approach cultural criticism from the opposite direction, and ask how depictions of other places, seemingly beyond the realm of the place in question, might be examined in specifically regional terms.

I have implied the importance of this project by suggesting, for example, that *Apocalypse Now* can be read in terms of its relationship to stereotypes of literacy and the potential for cultural production in Appalachia. In the rest of this chapter I make explicit what has thus far been implicit: that critical regionalism can be a way not only of understanding texts about a region but of understanding texts that depict other places from a regional perspective.

Crime, Violence, and Community: A Critical Regionalist Project

Popular culture not only offers interpretations of literacy but is a literate practice itself, one that, not unlike academic writing, persuades its readers toward particular interpretations of their own circumstances. It is not coincidence that movie theaters and lecture halls share the same basic design principles, for, as cultural critic bell hooks writes, "even though most folks will say they go to the movies to be entertained, if the truth be told lots of us, myself included, go to the movies to learn stuff" (*Reel* 2). While popular debate persists in discussing mass media as an empty cultural form, or even a mind-draining one, the media industry has persistently extended the reach of its powers of social invention, using its disproportional influence over processes of social construction to encourage particular versions and visions of how the world works or should work. Versions of place and region in film can function in much the same way as Benton MacKaye's ideal for the Appalachian Trail, to create particular perspectives on regional relationships, to encourage "tendencies" in popular understandings of the landscape—as opposed to dictating the knowledge itself to a passive populace.

An understanding of film as a form of social invention helps us to account for the fact that, as bell hooks writes, "whether we call it 'willing suspension of disbelief' or just plain submission, in the darkness of the theater most audiences choose to give themselves over, if only for a time, to the images depicted and the imaginations that have created those images" (*Reel* 3). And yet, at the conclusion of the film, those same people reemerge into the world they seem to have left behind. Recognizing film and other media forms as social invention means seeing them as a kind of pedagogy, and it suggests as well that formal schooling is not the only site of "instruction" for the populace and that media pedagogy is no more monolithic in its influence than classroom instruction. Rather, media texts are elements of a broad continuum of representational practices (including academic writing of the sort I am doing now) that instruct, persuade, affect, and effect people on how their worlds work—and how to work in their worlds. George Lipsitz notes that "cultural forms create conditions of possibility but they also engender accommodation with the prevailing power realities" (16). In terms of place, this accommodation involves subsuming isolating local histories from broader national or global narratives, as I have argued in the first half of this chapter, hierarchically positioning the local below or outside the realm of vital cultural conflict and public debate, and thus mystifying the relationship between the actions and decisions of small groups of citizens and broad patterns of economic, social, and political change.

Creating conditions of possibility, on the other hand, involves offering viewers perspectives and tendencies to see local places as part of broader networks of cause-and-effect, historical change, economic interdependence, and political dynamics. Encouraging and discouraging certain representational practices, valuing certain literacies of place and discrediting others, mass media affects its viewers at the level of what Frederic Jameson, following the lead of geographer Kevin Lynch (in *The Image of the City*), calls "cognitive mapping," "a way of linking the most intimately local—our particular path through the world—and the most global—the crucial features of our political planet" (xiv). Controlling place is a highly significant part of maintaining social order, of keeping everyone in their place, and this management is carried out through regimes of representation that attempt to control place imagination (Harvey 22). As geographer Jeff Hopkins writes,

> The pleasure of film lies partially in its ability to create its own cinematic geography, but so too does its power. The cinematic landscape is not, consequently, a neutral place of entertainment or an objective documentation of the real, but an ideologically charged cultural creation whereby meanings of place and society are made, legitimized,

contested, and obscured. Intervening in the production and consumption of the cinematic landscape will enable us to question the power and ideology of representation, and the politics and problems of representation. (47)

Even if a media text does not map the viewer's own place, it can teach practices of cognitive mapping that can encourage or discourage critical regionalist tendencies toward understanding the relationship of one's particular place to more expansive geographies. Understanding how this aspect of media as social invention operates requires examining not just how a particular media text constructs a particular place, but how it constructs ideas about place, region, and world, and the methods it teaches viewers for doing so, whether tacitly or explicitly.

To understand how media's pedagogy of place operates as a social invention demands that we examine its operations within the parameters of a specific project, to look at how it exerts its influence in the ongoing struggle over the meaning of a particular place in the context of a specific issue or set of issues. We might therefore ask what elements of a place's history a specific film or television program might operate on, and how, in return, the history of that place operates upon that film. The example to be explored here, which juxtaposes film representations of the relationship between place and violent crime with a "true crime" story from Johnson City, the murder story centered on Winged Deer Park with which this chapter began, reinforces the point that even largely dissimilar memories and experiences can impact the interpretation of media's models of place, and vice versa. Indeed, given the geographical centralization of both media production and media representation, if viewers drew connections with only those screen places that made specific reference to their own, most would never recognize anything they see.

What happens, though, when people see other places, and other ways to construct and represent a place, next to events in their own place (and representations of those events)? The Howard Hawk Willis murder case (which I refer to simply as "the Willis case"), for example, is a story that was part of the region's recent history, part of my experience of that place, and also part of a broader, mediated discourse about it—as I noted earlier, most residents of Johnson City or east Tennessee, myself included, had no direct experience with the Willis case, but experienced it through a constellation of images on television and in newspapers. Rather than being a distinct, isolated local experience, area residents and other observers encountered media representations of the Willis case not only from several different sources but amidst a broader field of representations of media culture, which saturate communities like Johnson City just as they do all others in these times. There are elements of these other representations that will register with the viewer or reader of the Willis case, other sources for reflection on the meaning of crime and violence in specific communities, other perspectives on how to discern the root causes of violent conflict within the structures of the place.

What critical regionalism can do is reconfigure this geographical relationship: reading media texts from a local perspective instead of reading local places through media texts. Instead of asking how media changes the behavior of people in specific places, we can ask what resources media texts make available to people to understand their own places in ways that recognize the dense networks of spatial relationships that intersect at any site on the landscape. To read *Pulp Fiction* and *Fargo* through the lens of the Willis case, as I do in the remainder of this chapter, is not to contrast an "actual" event to "fictional" ones and simply judge whether the fictional narratives are "accurate" or "true-to-life." Instead, it is a question of how one kind of mediated narrative can be read in the context of other kinds, and what resources for the production of new versions of local spaces can be discerned in the relationship between the local narratives and those in broader spatial circulation.

To geographers Jan Penrose and Peter Jackson, "The process of [place] construction is most clearly revealed in moments of crisis. . . . [C]risis (or the perception of crisis) serves as the catalyst in dislodging entrenched constructions, opening the way for alternative readings" (203). The Willis case powerfully dislodges entrenched constructions, starting with the human body itself. Indeed, the dismembered body parts become a kind of map themselves: in addition to the head and hands of Adam Chrismer, parts of Sam Thomas (Howard Hawk Willis's father-in-law and apparent first victim) were found not only on the side of Lookout Mountain on the Tennessee-Georgia border, more than 200 miles to the southwest, but also in Winged Deer Park, buried a few hundred feet from the boat ramp where Chrismer's body parts were found. The landscape narrative of the Willis case hinges on people disappearing and bodies appearing in disconnected pieces across a broad swath of the southern mountains. This dispersal of the human body across broad regional landscapes reflects the way the narrative of the Willis case chronicles the collapse of other seemingly "natural" entities. Families turn on each other in ways both brutal and conniving: not only does Willis turn on his father-in-law, he has more recently blamed his mother, Emma Hawk, for the killings. "It sounds like there's a lot of love there," prosecutor Joe Crumley has remarked (Wozniak, "Ex-wife").

Meanwhile, his ex-wife Wilda Willis, to whom Howard Hawk Willis continues to make jailhouse confessions (and professions of love) despite the fact that she promptly turns information over to the police, has reported being threatened and harassed by Willis's mother and aunt, Marie Holmes. Willis's mother has been charged for her alleged role in dismembering the corpses, but she and her sister have also been arraigned for attempting to intimidate Wilda Willis into destroying audiotapes she made of Howard Hawk Willis confessing to the crimes (Wozniak, "Emma Hawk"). This pattern of social destabilization resonates across progressively broader degrees of spatial scope: disrupting the landscape narrative of Winged Deer's civic space; creating a network of communities based on destruction, even desecration rather than exchange and interdependence. Even different sites of the justice system have been drawn into less-than-convivial relationships with each other in the course of this narrative: authorities in Johnson City are still, at this writing, awaiting the disposition of the federal drug charges for which Howard Hawk Willis was imprisoned in New York after the Chrismer and Lemming murders and are growing increasingly impatient in their desire to see Willis held accountable for his actions in their jurisdiction (Wozniak, "Willis' case").

The Willis case certainly seems ripe for treatment as a screenplay. Howard Hawk Willis, the murderous trucker, seems right down to his name like a crazy hillbilly character on a par with Max Cady, *Deliverance*'s unnamed rapists, or *Blue Velvet*'s resident psychopath, Frank Willard (Dennis Hopper), for sheer malevolence. His creepy mother, who, along with her sister, takes cleaning up after her boy to the point of threatening witnesses and mutilating corpses, combines the scarier features of Jimmy Cagney's smothering Ma (Margaret Wycherly) in *White Heat* (1949, dir. Raoul Walsh) and Norman Bates's mother in *Psycho* (1960, dir. Alfred Hitchcock). The teenage newlyweds caught up on a road trip with a madman that accelerates toward their destruction only slightly revises the formula of *Natural Born Killers* (1994, dir. Oliver Stone), another film that set off nationwide debate about violence and representation. The defiant ex-wife who stubbornly spurns Willis's jailhouse overtures, constantly turns his confessions over to police, and even defies the will of the mother is a part made for Holly Hunter in sassy, redneck *Raising Arizona* mode (1987, dir. Joel and Ethan Coen).

With their remarkably twisted and sensationally violent plots, the deeply ironic and hyperviolent crime films of the nineties, of which *Pulp Fiction* and *Fargo* are arguably among the most widely recognized examples, provide for me, and for their viewers in the southern Appalachian region, a part of the broader cultural backdrop, a "field of attitude and reference" (Said 64) for the events that unfolded from the discovery of Adam Chrismer's body parts on the shores of TVA Boone Lake at Winged Deer Park. Like the Willis case, these films contentiously engage the "cognitive maps" of crime and violence their viewers bring to them as they foreground violence—visually and thematically—in ways that ask viewers to reconfigure their normal approaches and reactions to depictions of violent acts. Just as Haskell Wexler, Barbara Kopple, and John Sayles integrate their challenges to the conventions of the film medium and the relevant genre conventions into the narrative of their work, so the works of the Coen brothers (*Fargo*) and of Quentin Tarantino (*Pulp Fiction*) pose challenges to conventional methods of Hollywood representation and "classical" Hollywood in their technique, even though they still emerge from the power structures of Hollywood's major studios and their cosmopolitan celebrity culture, whether they like it (as Tarantino appears to) or not (and the Coens seem not to). As such, they are part of the national cinematic culture, or "First Cinema," but stylistically, they have preserved some allegiances to the more aesthetically self-aware, independently produced, "Second Cinema" (MacDonald 28–29).

This dual status—Cinema One-and-a-Half?—signals the respects in which the work of these films attains to the status of social invention. The resistance to convention on the part of both films suggests that they might be teaching the viewer something different about violence, its social causes, and the larger frameworks of social relations of which those causes are a part. By complicating the viewing experience through experiments with form and style, these films seem to engage the viewer in the act of producing meaning from the text, making the film less a pure exertion of influence over the viewer, as Steven Heath envisions in "Narrative Space" (410), and more of a cooperative enterprise, a dialogue between film and viewer. But their citation and invocation of some of classical Hollywood's conventionality poses their technique as an inquiry and a challenge to, not a rejection of, dominant narrative forms.

The passive, rapt viewing experience Heath's landmark essay describes, and which the more passive, accommodationist, social construction of classical Hollywood technique encourages, is an example of what critical education theorist Paulo Freire describes as "banking-model pedagogy." Freire's description of this ideological mode of instruction recalls in many respects Heath's lonely spectator:

> Implicit in the banking concept is the assumption of a dichotomy between human beings and the world: a person is merely *in* the world,

not *with* the world or with others; the individual is spectator, not re-creator. In this view, the person is not a conscious being . . .; he or she is rather the possessor of *a* consciousness: an empty "mind" passively open to the reception of deposits of reality from the world outside. (*Pedagogy* 56)

By making films that foreground their own constructedness and high-light, by way of contrast, the repressive conventionality of First Cinema, Tarantino and the Coens may (but merely may, as we shall see) be work-ing toward a social invention aligned with Freire's liberatory "problem-posing" approach, where the educator's, or here auteur's, "efforts must coincide with those of the students to engage in critical thinking . . . [and] must be imbued with a profound trust in people and their creative power" (*Pedagogy* 56).

These two mass-distributed films have challenged their audiences more so, perhaps, than any Hollywood films released since the experi-mental period of the late sixties and early seventies, which ended with the rise of Spielberg and Lucas. Typically, Hollywood movie plots use vio-lence formulaically, as a means to an end, placing it in frameworks that make the viewers' reactions polarized, predictable, along lines of good versus evil. The message of these depictions seems to be that violence is, in the right hands, a manageable tool; its power is fully containable within appropriate structures; its emergence into public life and public space is generally temporary and reversible (unless there is potential for a sequel); in sum, it is not meaningless, as some would argue, but stable and conventional in its meanings. *Pulp Fiction* and *Fargo* each generated considerable discussion for the ways the films violated these conventions, presenting us with messy, wayward, grotesque, and irresolute violent spectacles. But given an actual episode of hyper-real violence—surely the Willis case qualifies as such—we can contemplate each text's pedagogy by examining the perspectives the texts encourage, and the understandings they offer, of the relationship between communities, regions, nations, and other social structures and these violent landscape narratives.

Pulp Fiction: Welcome to Nowhere

Quentin Tarantino's *Pulp Fiction* shares with the Willis case not only a high body count but also an emphasis on chance, coincidence, and con-juncture in its story. In the search for narratives that can help a commu-nity meaningfully respond to its true-life explosions of violence, *Pulp Fiction* is a complex case. One point about the Willis case that *Pulp Fiction* helps illuminate is the wayward, contingent nature of violence. Perhaps the most famous (or infamous) scene in the film involves the accidental shooting by professional killer Vinnie Vega (John Travolta) of a fellow passenger in a car. Vega is in midsentence when his gun goes off and literally blows the head off of his companion at point-blank range. The sudden incursion of violence into an otherwise ordinary situation (as ordinary as situations get for Tarantino's hired guns, anyway) mirrors, in a way, the sudden appearance of a human head and a pair of hands floating in a recreational area beside an apparently tranquil lake. The lesson seems to be, one minute you can be fishing, relaxing, sunbathing, when the culture of violence can intrude upon "normal" life.

Pulp Fiction is filled with such moments of sudden reversal of fortune, change of direction, twist of fate. Butch the Boxer (Bruce Willis) happens to spot the gangster boss he has double-crossed, Marcellus Wallace (Ving Rhames), strolling across the street in front of Butch's car, giving Butch a perfect opportunity to run Marcellus over, resulting in a gun battle that takes down several unsuspecting bystanders, and ending when the combatants tumble into a storefront concealing an sadomasochistic dungeon where they are taken captive. Society in this film seems governed by no clear sense of destiny, no standard plot form, no master narrative. *Pulp Fiction* does not appear to be bound for any tidy resolution; indeed, its very plot structure—which fractures an overarching linear plot into subsets of anecdotes, out of temporal sequence, only tangentially related to one another—seems designed to frustrate the ability of the audience to anticipate plot developments according to standard narrative or genre conventions.

However, the film's insight into the random and capricious nature of crime in our society is really only the patina of the film's statement. Its seeming "problem posing" proves to be only a shaggy-dog story; the film maker exerts not less but more control over the apparent indeterminacies of the film by inducing confusion about the connections between what are actually very tightly interwoven events. The seemingly alinear chronological form, for example, actually covers for a rather tightly wound narrative; linear progression is only temporarily set aside in a kind of reverse dramatic irony—the film is moving toward a resolution that is strongly predetermined but known only to the film maker. Traits like this suggest *Pulp Fiction* is a cynical, manipulative film, an example of Michael Ryan and Douglas Kellner's argument that experimental form does not guarantee progressive meaning (267–68). Contingency is only a veneer, beneath which the suggestion quickly vanishes that violence is a phenomenon with broad societal implications because it might erupt at any moment, in any place.

Amid these cynical strategies, place becomes the coordinating concept of the film's pedagogy. *Pulp Fiction* locates violence in an imaginary urban subculture outside of history, a self-contained world with its own internally consistent rules and regulations; despite the surface impression of the rule of misrule, Tarantino portrays a social world that operates with a high degree of stability and self-governance. Indeed, the lengthy discussion between Vinnie Vega and his partner Jules Winfield (Samuel L. Jackson) on whether being thrown out a window is appropriate punishment for giving another man's wife a foot massage demonstrates that not only is there something of a code at work, but there is even deliberative debate, which signals virtue of community, about the justice and propriety of that code. The distinctiveness of this underworld, its autonomy, is strongly underscored by the film's distinctive visual vocabulary. The film's career criminals are always artificially lit, denoting that their natural setting is the nighttime world, but underscoring as well their artificiality, their "unnaturalness." This lighting strategy is particularly clear in the film's last segment, "The Bonnie Situation," in which Jules and Vinnie seek the aid of a suburban househusband (Tarantino) to dispose of the body of Marvin, the victim of the accidental shooting. Reverse shots show Jules and Vinnie in artificial light while their suburban friend is bathed in daylight. This entire segment, in which the gangsters must dispose of the body before the wife returns home, underscores that Vinnie and Jules are virtually aliens, their lives totally foreign to the priorities and crises of everyday life, and hence their debates about codes of behavior a parody rendered harmless by their total irrelevance. Thus it is appropriate that Winston Wolf (Harvey Keitel), the "fixer" called in by Marcellus Wallace to clean up after the accidental killing, is wearing evening wear first thing in the morning: he is the interface between these creatures of the night and the daytime world.

One common thread to all of Tarantino's narratives is the appearance at various points in the vignettes of a briefcase, whose secret contents motivate much of the film's killing; it is the property of underworld boss Marcellus, stolen by rivals against whom he dispatches Jules and Vinnie. But it becomes not just a plot device but an emblem of the way violence is isolated from sites of social interaction and mystified beyond understanding. This talisman, and the fact that its contents are never revealed, save that they are mesmerically beautiful, suggests that the violence of this film is motivated by metaphysical causes, that despite the kitsch and

The monochrome underworld: hitmen Vinnie (John Travolta) and Jules (Samuel L. Jackson) in *Pulp Fiction* (1994). Image © Bureau L.A. Collection/CORBIS.

camp among which these characters move, and the contrived banality with which they converse, there is a higher, abstract purpose to their actions, a metaphysics. This suggestion is hinted at again by the fact that the motorcycle by which Butch the Boxer eventually flees Tarantino's violent microcosm—the vehicle, literally, of his salvation—is named "Grace"; and the suggestion is confirmed by Jules's "conversion" in the film's final scenes. These supernatural trappings mystify for the viewer the relationship of the film's violence to social conflicts in the places they inhabit, by making violence a cosmological occurrence rather than the local manifestation of broader cultural crises—and hence they make violence something that is not subject to human agency or intervention.

In Tarantino's underworld, however, even the potential of divine intervention is trivialized: when Jules, planning his postconversion life, remarks that he will wander the world like Cain, he is referring to Keith Carradine's character in *Kung-Fu*. This satirical moment reflects a complex double-movement in the content of *Pulp Fiction*—to suggest an otherworldly mysticism underlies these violent actions renders individual agency a moot point, but then to undercut even the metaphysical grounding of these characters' actions leaves them bereft of any grounding at all. Or, perhaps more accurately, there is a master narrative, but it is just a joke. Banality conquers all.

In this context it makes sense that the temporal grounding of this movie is unstable, not only in the disjointed narrative form but in the historical location of the action as well. The assassins' Blues-Brothers uniforms are part of the broader pattern in the film of a kind of historical aphasia, induced by stylized citations of popular culture with little regard to its time of origin—further detaching Tarantino's underworld from the lived experience of place, which, as I note earlier, is so intimately linked to the experience of history. Most critics note Tarantino's kitschy admiration of the seventies, but in point of fact references are made to various decades with no consistent pattern, starting with the soundtrack to the opening credits in which sixties' surf-rock suddenly transforms into seventies funk. In this case, it is interesting to note that Tarantino's soundtrack music is often rationalized, in this case as songs being played on the radio; this fact underscores that there is no historical grounding for the cultural practices of the film's characters. In this respect the world of *Pulp Fiction* is not unlike "Jackrabbit Slim's," the fifties-nostalgia restaurant Vinnie Vega and Mia Wallace (Uma Thurman) visit on their ill-fated evening out, which Vinnie describes as "a wax museum with a pulse." Community is in *Pulp Fiction* a bloodless pastiche of useless cultural forms—nowhere, and, we might say, no-when.

This hermetically sealed, impossibly detached community is at the root, I believe, of the film's other failures of vision: its treatment of women, gays, and blacks, for example, which bell hooks (*Reel* 47–51) and Henry Giroux (308–10) both note drapes reactionary statements in the trappings of the avant-garde. In this vision of community, a kind of mythopoetic rendering of Los Angeles with scant connections to any material place (and yet a vision that is nonetheless received in specific, material places), slurs and smears aimed at races, genders, and sexual identities seem (but plainly are not) detached from the historical, cultural, physical violence these populations have endured. More generally, the film pedagogically asserts that violence is a phenomenon unto itself, that crime and criminals inhabit an insular counterreality, a closed community in which actions have no consequences or relative value. This last point is confirmed by the fact that what is arguably the film's most visceral act of violence is, ironically, an act of compassion, as Vinnie Vega must plunge a giant needle into the heart of Mia Wallace to save her from an accidental heroin overdose. The heroin dealer's girlfriend Jody (Patricia Arquette) supplies us with the moral of this story and, indeed, the only lesson *Pulp Fiction*'s impoverished model of community is capable of teaching: "That was fuckin' trippy."

Body Parts

Which, indeed, is how one might initially respond to the Willis case. However, closer examination of this story reveals a high degree of interconnectedness of the people and places that make the entire narrative possible. In short, the Willis case, as a frame of reference for a person in a specific community and region, renders *Pulp Fiction*'s theory of community untenable, as the film configures violence and crime in self-contained social organizations, precluding useful scrutiny of the narrative's nonfictional counterparts.

The shape of the plot of the Willis case thus far is in nature quite similar to *Pulp Fiction*, as it provides a glimpse into a brutal criminal subculture whose inhabitants prey on each other as voraciously as they victimize elderly retirees for their credit cards. The social world of the extended Willis family seems as wholly alien to the sunny recreational world of Winged Deer Park as Vinnie and Jules are to the suburban setting of *Pulp Fiction*'s "The Bonnie Situation." But critical regionalism requires that we do more than just enfable the Willis story in some hermetic Otherworld; rather we must work to understand the larger, regional relationships the Willis case both creates and draws upon, and to create a "cognitive map" of greater discursive and material awareness and complexity. For example, in "The Gold Watch," the segment featuring Butch the Boxer's flight from *Pulp Fiction*'s underworld, east Tennessee is the destination to which Butch flees. Tennessee is offered up as a "good place," in contrast to the film's violent nowhere, a place exempt from the reach of the criminal syndicates Butch double-crosses—and, not coincidentally, the place where Quentin Tarantino was born (in Knoxville, about 100 miles west of Johnson City). And yet, far from exempt from violence, east Tennessee is the route of Howard Hawk Willis's murderous migratory path, its hyperviolence an exurban counterpart to Tarantino's trendy underworld, cosmopolitan and parochial by turns.

As the regional cultural network of the Willis case binds a diverse group of individuals to each other, it also reveals broader patterns in the landscape it maps: the murky, predatory depths of capitalism are revealed in the greed that motivates the relatively petty thefts that apparently caused the chain reaction of murders. Gender roles structure the web of conflicts enmeshing the various women—mothers, aunts, ex-wives, daughters. All are located in the narrative relative to the nature of their association with Willis, who as son, ex-husband, father tries to take advantage of each in her own way. In a narrative in which missing bodies are an important trope, Willis's first wife, Debra Willis, plays an important role: she disappeared in 1987, leading authorities to speculate, in light of more recent events, that Willis likely killed her and concealed her body as well (Thompson). The women in his own family appear to be the first place Willis has directed his violent behavior. But this tale is not purely a story of female submission to male dominance. Wilda Willis has thus far spurned her husband's jailhouse professions of true love and cooperates with authorities (Wozniak, "Ex-wife"); while the big break in the Sam Thomas murder came when Willis's daughter, Kelly Willis Chancey, told authorities that she called Thomas's cell phone after his disappearance and it was answered by Willis (Thompson).

But the narrative of the Willis case also relies on a landscape that is physically as well as discursively interconnected with larger historical trends. One detail of the Willis case that is perhaps not especially relevant to the ongoing investigation but is important to understanding this story as a kind of landscape narrative is that Willis was a trucker. The landscape narrative of his crimes relies on a dark reinterpretation of the transportation infrastructure, the highway once again a metonymy that connotes material interconnections among places and denotes lines of cultural, historical, social, and political connection as well. Willis's role in the movement of goods and the provision of services in a capitalist economy helped create the distinctive spatial form of his misdeeds, his deliveries of body parts a perverse reflection of his more legitimate employment. That Willis was a convicted cocaine dealer is also important to recall.

His illicit employment—another shadow of his ostensible profession as a truck driver, facilitated by his involvement in moving other kinds of freight around the country—ties him into even broader patterns of politics and culture, the global drug trade. On the surface, there appears to be little connection with the violence of American foreign policy in Colombia, but the killing of Chrismer and Lemming is connected, if tangentially, to the war between Colombia's right-wing government and left-wing guerillas, fueled by the black market economy's predatory capitalism, of which Willis was an agent. A critical understanding of the regional landscapes shaped by and shaping Howard Hawk Willis's criminal existence requires piecing together the individual parts of the Willis case to reveal not a weird, isolated anomaly but a highly organized set of connections and interconnections across a socially dense landscape, among a network of places—a map that is at once cognitive, material, and political.

Attention to *Pulp Fiction*'s social invention of region, its pedagogy of place, on the other hand, reveals the lack of an integrative term, a critical vocabulary for talking about the complex web of relations, vividly revealed through violent crises, that constructs places and communities not as discrete, insular bodies, self-contained and stable, but as connected through common struggle even though local material and discursive conditions of cultural strife vary significantly.

Fargo: "This Is a True Story"

Perhaps the first clue that *Fargo* supplies what *Pulp Fiction* lacks—namely, the idea of region as a way to think critically about the interconnections of places and problems—is the fact that its title, while, significantly enough, a place-name, is not the name of the place where most of the film's narrative is set. Only the first scene of the film is set in Fargo, North Dakota. But this act of naming indicates what the body of the film goes on to reveal more plainly: that this is a tale in which various communities are linked to one another by a series of events. Though the film is often casually described as being about small-town life—critic Paul Arthur, for example, lumps *Fargo* in with a passel of recent films "aimed at re-populating a realm . . . nearly erased from the cinematic map: Small-Town America" (30)—it is more about the dynamics of relationships, revealed by violent crises, between and among the different communities that constitute a specific region.

Like Tarantino, the Coens make the place of their upbringing a part of their cinematic place—but the difference in treatment is instructive. From the film's opening shot of bleak, snowy countryside, the terrain of central Minnesota figures prominently in the visual vocabulary of the film. This opening shot, however, makes an interesting and unconventional statement as a reconfiguration of the predictable establishing landscape shot that is de rigeur among opening scenes of films about region, whether gently reactionary (*Nell*), violently reactionary (*Deliverance*), or even progressive (*Matewan*). *Fargo*, instead, begins with a white-out, an un-landscape. The blank expanse nonetheless turns out to be terrain, as emergence of the headlights of Jerry Lundergaard's (William H. Macy's) Cadillac reveal that we are not looking at a blank screen but a snowbound prairie. The implication is that the terrain only becomes a place when human action (here, the initiation of a criminal conspiracy) inscribes it with meaning and purpose. However, the fact that we enter the narrative *in medias res*, with Jerry already en route to his rendezvous with the kidnappers, suggests that the landscape is not a blank slate (though perhaps the idea is being played with), but a site continually reshaped by narratives always in motion. It is a landscape that is harsh and forbidding, but out of which people always emerge, as when the kidnappers, trying to dispose of the body of a state trooper they have killed along a seemingly remote highway, are caught in the headlights of a passing car—whose occupants are then hunted down and killed.

This same idea is revised visually later in the film, as kidnapper Carl Showalter (Steve Buscemi) attempts to hide a briefcase full of ransom money along a fence line. In this case we see the idea of the landscape as a tabula rasa critiqued, even satirized, as Carl's attempt to impose his individual mark on the prairie, by sticking a red window-scraper in the snowbank where he has buried the ransom, appears ridiculous in the context of the seemingly endless fence line, the straight, featureless road in the background, the whiteness of the land itself. In this moment, Carl acknowledges the superficial stasis of his surroundings with his puny assertion of his individual desires, but part of what makes the scene satirical is the realization among the audience that his marking is in the snow, and will be buried by more snow, which will eventually melt, not only obliterating the marking but revealing the hidden treasure as well. The implication is that this landscape is one of continuous change (indeed, threaded through the narrative are references both visual and verbal to changing weather), and the human markings upon it that endure are ones that result from larger shifts in culture and social organization, such as the fence and the road. Hence the risible futility of Carl and his scraper: not a reprise of "man versus (vast, indifferent) nature," but rather an allegory of the pointlessness of individualism, of an atomized view of place and culture more generally.

For *Fargo*'s landscape is inscribable and decipherable under different ideological and hermeneutic circumstances—using different, localized forms of literacy. When Brainerd police chief Marge Gunderson (Frances McDormand) arrives on the scene of the kidnappers' murder of a state trooper and some innocent bystanders on the outskirts of town, she is able to quickly and accurately decipher the text of the crime-scape, its events and their implications. With her conclusion, that "the person we're looking for is not from Brainerd," she is not invoking a code of small-town nostalgia—"this couldn't happen here"—but rather, acknowledging that Brainerd as a place is permeable, is connected to other places, and is implicated in events on the move, connecting various places in material and social relationships of cause-and-effect. The implications of this moment perhaps help explain the inclusion of the rather cryptic scenes in which a high school classmate of Marge's, Mike Yanagita (Steve Park), tearfully tells her of his wife's death, and it is later revealed that

Interpreting the landscape: Marge Gunderson (Frances McDormand) in *Fargo* (1996). Image © CORBIS SYGMA.

Mike is delusional not only about the death but also about the fact that he was ever married. It is as if another movie inexplicably drifts through the middle of *Fargo*, but the inclusion of this incident underscores that in the social and cultural web of relationships, that is, the region, constructed in this film, multiple narratives intersect and influence one another, and lives connect in unpredictable but deliberate ways.

Brainerd in *Fargo* does not, in other words, figure as the "good place" exempt from the capriciousness of public life. But, on the other hand, it is not a place of otherworldly violence and horror, like *Pulp Fiction*'s inner city, or like the southern Appalachian landscape of *Deliverance*. Instead, Brainerd is a place where expected social roles are subtly reconfigured: the chief of police is not only a woman but a pregnant woman, whose husband Norm (John Carroll Lynch) is a nature painter—his ability to depict the local landscape an appropriate complement to his partner's ability to interpret it. This pairing is not merely a humorous inversion, however; Marge and her husband have a relationship marked by a healthy interdependency. He brings her food in a seemingly feminine-nurturing moment but also jump-starts her police prowler. Marge herself resists not only traditional female stereotypes but especially female cop stereotypes, as she is not depicted as having to sacrifice her personal life for her job.

But the challenge to conventional social order depicted in Marge and in Brainerd more generally is not utopian. The frequent depictions of these people coughing up phlegm, vomiting, eating (and eating and eating), reminds us that they have bodies as vulgar and demanding as anyone's, undermining the idea of the small town as idealized social space. Marge's pregnant body is even less convenient than most, and her need to sit down, her unwillingness to drink alcohol, and so forth, provide constant reminders of not only her gender but also, more generally, her bodily-ness. Her body also underscores the ways in which personal and public lives overlap and influence each other—especially in the scene in which Marge interrogates Jerry, noting her pregnancy, using it as a reason to take a seat, and generally manipulating the environment of the interrogation to her advantage.

Scenes like this emphasize that *Fargo* eschews separation and isolation as a matter of principle, but it is not without pointed contrasts, particularly between the unconventionality of Brainerd's social organization and the upper-middle-class conventionality of the Lundergaards down in "the Cities" (Minneapolis and Saint Paul). The Lundergaards' suburban home is the picture of "ordinary" Americana—the sort of setting that is included in *Pulp Fiction* in "The Bonnie Situation" only to illustrate the clash between the mannered stability of the world and the exigencies of the underworld. In *Fargo* the suburban home and family are the point of origin for the entire criminal conspiracy—it is inextricably linked to the violence of the plot as a space of both the causes of violence and their consequences.

Jerry's motive for the scheme he sets in motion, which involves kidnapping his own wife, then swindling his father-in-law out of the ransom money, derives from his insecurity as a traditional patriarch because of his reliance on his wife's father's fortune. The domestic interdependence we see in Brainerd is here transformed into relationships of domination, as Jerry is overruled and intimidated at every turn by his overbearing father-in-law, Wade Gustafson (Harve Presnell), whose fortune underwrites the Lundergaards' prosperity. Jerry, lacking the fiscal, hence psychological, authority to dominate his own family, hatches a plan that literally terrorizes his wife as it steals from her father, in order to give him the stake he needs to build a fortune of his own. He is trying to wheel-and-deal his way out of the emasculation that is perpetuated by his own investments, fiscal and emotional, in the value system that incapacitates him.

The opportunity for this plan, however, would not exist without the suburban, middle-class family's interconnection with the fates of other classes. Jerry recruits his kidnappers through a Native American ex-con mechanic at his workplace, his father-in-law's car dealership—showing that Jerry's world is at best only one degree removed from any putative "underworld," and his prosperous father-in-law no more than two. But the film makes a stronger statement than that, suggesting that there is in fact no practical distinction between Jerry's life and "the life," as *Pulp Fiction*'s criminals call their vocation. The first scene we see him in, he is striking a business deal with the kidnappers (who he is double-crossing just as he is duping his family); in the second scene he is closing the deal on a car sale, and swindling his customers there as well, while simultaneously fending off a finance company that he has cheated. "A deal's a deal," Jerry pleads later in the film, when Carl attempts to change their original arrangements, and the statement resonates through the scenes of his other business dealings, implying that the world of commerce and the world of crime are only different forms of acquisition, ethically and morally indistinguishable—all bent on using a rhetoric of fairness to conceal attempts to cheat. Carl himself is a reflection of Jerry, believing his willingness to kill for a deal has made him superior to the bartenders, prostitutes, and parking-ramp operators on whom he pours increasing verbal and physical abuse as "the deal" with Jerry spirals out of control.

This equivalence is particularly clear in the scenes in which Jerry approaches Wade for backing on "a real sweet deal" of a real-estate investment. In the course of the totally legal, if not necessarily amicable, conversation, Jerry finds himself not only failing to get the support he needs but also losing the deal itself. The swindle is not just part of "the life," it seems, but part of the world of mannered negotiation; the swindle is what provides Wade with his well-appointed office and its commanding views. A deal is a deal.

The appointments of Wade's office are worth a little closer scrutiny: why the Frederick Remington–style Wild West decor in this so deliberately midwestern setting? I suggest that this detail (and others, like the six-gun Wade wields in his confrontation with Carl) link the patriarchal, individualist capitalism reflected in Wade's financial success, and in Jerry and Carl's failure, to the expansionist mythology of Manifest Destiny and the United States' brutal conquest of North America itself. This is why *Fargo* has to be a midwestern story: it comes from the mythic heart of America, a place of visceral plenty revealed in smorgasbords and car lots linked by the interstate highway system roamed by killers like Carl and his monosyllabic accomplice Gaear Grimsrud (Peter Stormare), not to mention Howard Hawk Willis. But it is a plenty underwritten by the capitalist swindle that has left the prosperous inheritors of its landscape of consumption neurotically locked into contests of self-destructive acquisition, just as it has left so much of the actual landscape of the West an irradiated, postmilitary wasteland, as landscape critic Alexander Wilson suggests (278–82). Meanwhile, entirely too many of the few original inhabitants of the region (like Shep Proudfoot [Steven Reevis], the ex-con mechanic) are stuck scratching out a living on the boundaries between labor and the *Lumpenproletariat* of people like Howard Hawk Willis.

This historical underpinning, I suggest, allows the Coens the remarkable license of billing *Fargo* as a "true story" in a brief written statement at the beginning of the film—signaling at the very outset a distinct contrast to Tarantino's insistent *Fiction*. Though the story is not at all factual in a literal sense (and this move on the part of the Coens is often described as a hoax), the truth of *Fargo* lies in its commitment to social invention. *Fargo*'s tactics for place representation argue for a specific, historicized interpretation of the legacy of American history by producing in a mass medium the kind of "local" story that can resonate with individuals in their home communities. *Fargo* shows the cannibalistic effects of the capitalist era, the transformation of all human interaction into financial transaction, even in the sacralized domestic space of the middle-class home; it maps out the cascading failure of this ethic to produce livable landscapes across space and among different communities and kinds of communities. *Fargo* is not just a depiction of region, but a mode of representation that relies on having a strong sense of the interconnections of apparently separate localities. As Ethan Coen writes, "The world, however wide, has folds and wrinkles that bring distant places together in strange ways. The adage 'All politics is local' is really just a special case of the truism that all experience is personal. A corollary is that in some sense there is no exotica. Everything gets compared to your own experience. Paradoxically, what is closest to home can seem exotic" (35). The vacillation of this discussion, the reversibility of all of its formulations, can be taken to imply as well that if all politics is local, all locales, and all "personal experiences" of them, are political. And this politics, in the full sense of its roots in *polis*, the people of a community, is the strange force that brings these experiences together across regions in the larger contexts of nations and of the world, however wide.

In threading these statements through *Fargo*'s depiction of crime, the film makers have created a redefinition of region not as periphery, as frontier, but as a place where the physical effects of the struggles of history and the present are made manifest—the Midwest as the Middle of the West, where its cultural forces and crises converge. It is neither the anthropological leftovers nor the idyllic denouement of Anglo-American geographical, political, economic, and cultural expansion, but rather the contemporary embodiment of it. This is why a film described as part of a white-reactionary fantasy of "the rehabilitative or recuperative function performed by small towns" (Arthur 30) devotes as much screen time to depicting the postmodern architecture of "the Cities" as to Brainerd's lone prairie: not to indicate its separateness from the small town, but to emphasize its deep connectedness. One shot of Marge waiting at a fast-food drive-through as she leaves the Cities shows her framed by the landscape much as Jerry is by the strip-mall district seen through his office window. In Brainerd, they eat at Arby's, they recognize the bourgeois "quality" of a Radisson, they learn about interstate criminals by talking to the local prostitutes. Because of this overlap of the small-town culture of Brainerd with the urban and suburban life of the Cities, the alternative social order represented by Marge's person and household appears the result of negotiated resistance to patriarchal capitalism, not as the function of a rural ideal.

Fargo's treatment of the midwestern region points toward a more generalizable tactic for regional representations that carefully refuses to remove a region's alternative social order beyond the reach of the effects of violence, or invoke a conservative nostalgia for rural virtue, for the pastoral ideal. The pastoral genre, Raymond Williams argues (in *The Country and the City*), tends to erase social and historical conflicts from actual landscapes (18), much as *Pulp Fiction*'s urban dystopia isolates social violence from any real place. The resistance to pastoralism in *Fargo* is reflected in the fact that Wade Gustafson's emblems of western conquest have their exurban analogue, in the use of Paul Bunyan iconography. Ostensibly an emblem of Brainerd's civic pride, the Paul Bunyan statue on the outskirts of Brainerd, is consistently lit and shot from low angles, transforming the expansionist idol into a figure of crude, totemic horror. The statue's visual identification with Carl's accomplice, Gaear, completes the film's revision of popular memory of American expansionism. The statue is the only object or event in the film that seems to register with Gaear, who is otherwise a cipher, seemingly capable of acting deliberately, but not with deliberation; he stares at it fixedly each of the several times in the film he passes it. And the statue is a deliberate foreshadowing of Gaear's ax murder and subsequent wood-chipping of Carl. The identification is not ironic but direct: Gaear is Paul Bunyan, but he reveals folk-heroism to be a veneer concealing an existence of rootless wandering (hence Gaear's ethnically ambiguous name and accent), supported by extraction of resources from the landscape in the most crude and forceful fashion. Notably, this vision of lumberjacking is anticipated in the work of Benton MacKaye, who, as environmental historian Paul Sutter argues, departs from most conservationists before and since in his determination to engage with "the relationship between unsustainable resource extraction and the exploitation of labor" (557).

Gaear, like Bunyan, like Bunyan's trees, is an exploitable resource for the manipulative schemes of the ambitious—who now, in a pointed historical update, employ him as part of the service economy (kidnapper) rather than as a physical laborer (lumberjack). Gaear's indifference extends to accumulation (beyond grabbing whatever is at hand), as well as to destruction. However, he is a force that is impossible for his employers to control—*Fargo* argues that violence unleashed is not detached, containable, or retrievable. In a parable of the unsustainability of accumulation, each of the film's would-be plutocrats, its ambitious white men, is destroyed by the systemic violence they unleash (Gaear survives, of course, because he is the reserve force fueling the violence, and the film does not stage the kind of systemic overthrow necessary to prevent a similar incident in the future.) Carl, who swells with ego in the wake of killing, disintegrates bodily along with the scheme, becoming physically bloodier and bloodier, until he is pulped. Wade is gunned down by Carl, against the backdrop of the postmodern skyline of Minneapolis that his neo-gunslinging, the film implies, helped to construct. Jerry only perpetuates his emasculation, destroying his own family and becoming an embarrassing appendix to his own story. The scene of his arrest is tacked on after the reprise of the film's opening shot signals a kind of poetic closure. This move demotes Jerry to a constituent element of the narrative over which he thought he could exert authority, but also undoes the apparent seamlessness of the film's poetic closure. A narrative so driven by interconnection cannot close in this way—as *Pulp Fiction* does, uniting its disparate narrative strands in a set piece about redemption and a pastiche of enlightenment.

Indeed, *Fargo* is careful to reject "enlightenment," even in the midst of its mock-closure. Though its plot is suspenseful, there are no mysteries in *Fargo*, and hence no crypto-numinous moment of revelation. The scene that, within classical Hollywood technique, stages the revelation of the hidden comes when Marge delivers Gaear to the state authorities, who emerge from the driven snow just as Jerry's Cadillac did in the opening scene. But Marge can no more strike up a conversation with Gaear (who receives a final look at the Paul Bunyan statue during this same scene) than could Carl as the kidnappers rolled into Minneapolis, so all she is left with is her own lack of comprehension: "I just don't understand it," she repeats.

But just as *Pulp Fiction*'s moment of understanding is not really one, so *Fargo*'s apparent misapprehension is in fact a relatively cogent understanding: Marge correctly identifies "a little bit of money" as the cause of the seven deaths that result from the collapse of the conspiracy. It is an answer that is reductive, to be sure, but is nonetheless an opening onto the larger web of cause-and-effect that unites this human, social, economic landscape (not to mention an accurate reflection on the motives in the Willis case, where a little a bit of money that a set of credit cards made available motivated ghastly crimes). *Fargo* is careful to note in closing, however, that economic conflict is not the only form that human interaction can take. Within the unconventional, negotiated social space of her home, another narrative, interwoven intricately with the crime narrative of *Fargo*, leads out of this story and potentially into others: the film's closing line, "two more months" (until Marge's baby is born), demonstrates that eruptions of violence occur alongside relations of possibility forged out of the vernacular landscape by, in J. B. Jackson's memorable phrase, "hard work, stubborn hope, and mutual forbearance striving to be love" (xii).

Region and the Social Totality

The important thing about *Fargo* as an example of critical regionalist film is that it is not only the content of the film but also its structure and form that point toward a more sophisticated understanding of regional relationships. In other words, *Fargo* teaches us not just about the Midwest but about how to think about region in a way that can be revelatory for someone in another place, another region—someone confronted with a bizarre and bewildering murder that challenges local orthodoxies about the meaning of the local landscape, someone in Johnson City, thinking about the Willis case. In the way that an individual incident opens onto a broader network of social relations, both *Fargo* and the Howard Hawk Willis case can be considered examples of a genre Jameson describes as the "social detective" story, in which "the knower is part of the same social world as the known" (36) and the initiating incident "becomes the occasion for the indictment of a whole collectivity" (37). Too, both stage "the discovery that we are caught up in a collective network without knowing it, that people are already up much closer than we realized" (66). However, some important emendations to this classification need to be taken into account.

First is that in the nonfictional narrative there is no agent occupying the role of the detective as there is in the figure of Marge in *Fargo*, who "find[s] . . . herself occupying the intellectual's structural position by virtue of the premium placed on knowledge" (Jameson 38), who "transforms ... into a vehicle for judgments on society" (39). The consolidation of knowledge in Marge, however, and her presentation as a public figure, an officer of the community, points to her role as the film's pedagogue, whose function, allegorically, is as the representative of community and hence the site of identification for the audience. By providing the viewer with a figure of both intellectual and interpretive acuity, the agent of application of knowledge, but also a person deciphering and deducing previously unknown facts about the world, the subject of a learning process, the film breaks down the idea of a solitary pedagogue, the banking model's autonomous depositor. It is significant that even the authorship of this text is collaborative, unlike *Pulp Fiction*, with its wunderkind director. Because Marge is a site of multiple identities and identifications, "through dialogue, the teacher-of-the-students and the students-of-the-teacher cease to exist and a new term emerges: teacher-student with students-teachers" (Freire, *Pedagogy* 61)—a crucial movement of problem-posing education.

Breaking down the monolithic and monologic aspects of the banking model, creating sites where one can identify with both teacher and learner simultaneously, is essential to creating a cinematic place as a social invention that people can map across their own material places. Nonfictional stories such as the Willis case have no central figure, no social detective, no pedagogue-auteur. Investigators in several communities spread across two states had to reassemble not only a confusing and convoluted set of events and personal relationships, but even had to collaborate to reassemble the bodies of missing people. Each new piece of evidence has implied, but not revealed to any single individual, the full social dimensions of the event. Understanding the story is a collective undertaking that, in narrativization, almost invariably relies on the consolidation of these diverse perspectives in a single agent, a single knower (Jameson 38). As the author of my own iteration of this narrative, I have assumed the "structural position of intellectual," staging the revelations the story makes available, controlling the literate forms that reveal. However, I am serving in this text metonymically, rather than allegorically, as the regional citizen, the member of the community who must decode and justify the story in my own local circumstances. But like Marge, I too, as knower, am enmeshed in the same social world and representational practices as the known. As citizens and as readers and viewers of texts, each of us occupies at various times the structural position of intellectual; the media text, in its pedagogical function, acknowledges this fact and attempts therefore to shape our literate practice of that position.

More important, however, is the profound shift in the vision of social organization that the regional text makes available. Jameson's social detective and conspiracy films, among them, *Videodrome* (1983, dir. David Cronenberg), *The Parallax View* (1974, dir. Alan Pakula), and *All the President's Men* (1976, dir. Alan Pakula) all point toward a vertically integrated model of what Jameson terms the "social totality," a global cognitive map. The regional film, however, is more horizontal, meticulously detailing an area in relation to a larger project of connecting not the whole, but a meaningful selection of parts. Like Jameson's films, *Fargo* points toward connections and interconnections between and among social structures on a large scale, with the same "laterality" of levels, political, economic, cultural, social, and so forth. Too, *Fargo* features "a variety of landscapes within itself"—but not as a way of "documenting a model of social totality as conspiracy" (63). *Fargo* instead uses them to show the resources available at each and every "level" (revealed itself as an unsuitably hierarchical unit) that may be exploited by the conspirator (as in the collapse of public and private, legal and criminal in Jerry's deal making) or (as the negotiated, unconventional household of Marge and Norm suggests) reconfigured in ways that resist the hegemony/conspiracy. The local ceases to be a space to be exhausted by vertically superior orders of knowledge and power—at best a clue, an entry for the "hero as fall guy" of films like *Videodrome* and *The Parallax View* (27), who, like the citizen-viewer, learns only of his helplessness within structures of power—but meaningful only inasmuch as it leads up the cultural, political, economic ladder, in this case specifically defined in geographical terms, each rung a different place. In the regional film, localities become instead places of possibility as well as critique.

To do so, the regional film must explode the myth of what Jameson terms "spatial margins" that "connote a different set of political interests, that might euphemistically be styled 'grass roots.' These are the vigilante and paramilitary networks that flourish outside the urban centers, powered by narrow-minded moralisms of generally racist and gender varieties" (64). (In the southern Appalachian region, the quintessential American spatial margin, progressive grass-roots organizations like Save Our Cumberland Mountains, Kentuckians for the Commonwealth, and the Western North Carolina Alliance would be exasperated to find themselves caught up in this description.) This same homogenizing, undifferentiating view of regional life informs Paul Arthur's "Let Us Now Praise Famous Yokels," a critique of recent films set in small towns. His discussion, while accurate enough in its individual analyses of examples such as *Dadetown* and *Brother's Keeper*, plainly operates from the assumption that the "yokels" he digs at in his title, later specified as "fundamentalists, survivalists, and Freemen of various persuasions," while tellingly absent from nostalgic depictions he criticizes, in reality dominate regional life.

Fargo challenges this factually inaccurate and politically unhelpful presumption through a use of language that provides a thoroughgoing rebuff to the view of exurban literacy promoted in the films with which I began this chapter. For *Fargo* or for any film to create the conditions of possibility for a critical regionalist understanding of place, to serve as a social invention that encourages people to see local problems and priorities enmeshed in broader patterns of history, politics, and culture, it must at some basic level reject the premise that literacy is by its very nature a cosmopolitan and urbane cultural practice, and endorse instead the idea that valuable cultural productions and representational practices can not only exist but function in vital, even revelatory ways in exurban places. To conclude this chapter, then, I examine *Fargo* through the same lens of linguistic practices brought to bear on the "river trilogy" in the opening sections.

I note with interest that the Internet Movie Database lists among its keywords for *Fargo* "funny-accent"; certainly few films have foregrounded regional accents in such a deliberate, near-parodic way, and those that have almost invariably assign the funny accent to a comic, incompetent rube (with the notable exceptions of *Deliverance, Cape Fear,* and *Nell*). As with so much else in this film, however, careful attention shows the accent to be not a swipe at small-town life but a factor forging connections between different kinds of places across a regional landscape: everyone in the film talks this way, whether from the Cities or the small towns, and as the example of Mike Yanagita suggests, this accent even moves across races. But without this "funny accent" we would simply be watching a movie almost totally centered on white people; this emphasis on the way people talk is not only largely accurate (if overblown) but also a pointed revision to white identity on film. The film takes two highly normative cultural categories, whiteness and midwestern-ness (the latter generally assumed to be a geographical subclass of the former), both often presumed to be unmarked, the ordinary, and destabilizes them by highlighting issues of speech and language—highlighting the connection between literacy and community that I am arguing for here. Place and region inflect otherwise culturally unmarked identities—or if marked, only by presumptions of homogeneity—to let us know that we are not dealing with the "ordinary" but with a historically, geographically, materially specific population.

This move in itself is inconclusive, however—*Fargo* could still become a tale of rural harmony linguistically marked outside the working world, outside public life. This is why it is important to note that both urban and rural dwellers speak in similar accents, but use language in very different ways. I noted above that part of Marge's capability and effectiveness is her ability to read the landscape, her local literacy. This proficiency is reflected as well in her speech, which reflects the control and restraint, yet rhetorical skill in the form of sensitivity to specific situations of purpose and audience, as for example, when she interrogates Jerry, or Jerry's "contact" Shep. That this is a specifically local trait is depicted in other discussions, between Marge and Norm, or Marge and her deputy Lou (Bruce Bohne); it is particularly clear in a scene between Lou and Mr. Mohra (Bain Boehlke), a bartender who tips the police off to the whereabouts of Gaear and Carl. Without ado, Mr. Mohra immediately begins his tale the moment Lou arrives, relates the details without commentary, and stops succinctly at the end, adding only a utilitarian, "End of story."

Compare these habits with the incessant, often meaningless chatter of the film's most vacillating, manipulative characters, Jerry and Carl (and also to the nonstop, banal banter of virtually all of Tarantino's characters). Jerry's talking is nearly always duplicitous. As in the "dealing" described earlier, almost everything Jerry says is a misdirection or a manipulation or an outright lie. Carl, like Jerry, cannot remain quiet (his scene with Gaear in the car as they enter Minneapolis, when he cannot stop talking about his vow of total silence, underscores this fact in broad strokes), though his speech is even less purposeful than Jerry's, consisting mostly of bluster and swagger. The film's use of language is, in short, consistent with its critique of social and economic history: Carl and Jerry treat language the same way they treat money—as an end in itself, a commodity to be accumulated and expended in great heedless bursts. Here the idea of linguistic proficiency as mere mechanical facility with language, instead of a broader set of cultural competencies negotiated with a dominant culture in relation to local material conditions, is carefully undermined: those who use language most also use it least well.

Perhaps the film presents the taciturn, pragmatic approach to language and literacy as the more effective one in this particular place. But the film is careful to note, by making the brutal Gaear the film's most silent, non- or even antilinguistic character, that reserve is not in and of itself a positive virtue, but a tactic, whose ethical and useful value is highly contingent. Outright refusal to use language, to engage in public discourse, is in this character hand in glove with brutal violence.

The important strategy here for critical regionalist film is to develop modes of representation that acknowledge difference—especially as manifested in different uses of language and literacy—within a range of places that share connections with each other and to the broader cultural conflicts that inevitably shape the ways places are imagined and inhabited. This cultural form is democratic, a critical pedagogy, to the extent that it acknowledges, honors, and facilitates the needs and abilities of diverse populations to confront their distinctive, place-specific, material crises.

Fargo's overarching strategy toward achieving this goal is to foreground its own representationality. Unlike the banal and, in the end, unified and sealed system of self-reference in *Pulp Fiction*, *Fargo*'s irony calls attention to the process of construction, of itself as a made text, starting with that opening title card, generating a tension about truth and fiction, about the unnatural act of narration and the material impact of actual events, that animates the entire film. *Fargo* then sustains this gesture through a highly stylized mode of depiction that emphasizes that its shots, its places, are highly constructed, a style that alerts the viewer to the allegorical function of certain images—namely, the preternatural lighting of the Paul Bunyan statue or the image of Carl along the fence line that I discussed previously, or the achingly "composed" overhead shot of Jerry, having been humiliated by Wade, losing his composure in the snowbound parking lot. The almost Brechtian exaggeration of the Minnesota accents, too, is part of this effect, crucial to (though not in and of itself equal to) its problem-posing strategies. A traditional realist effect, an attempt to transparently impose the filmic depiction onto the material crises of actual places, is likely a less useful approach to the social invention of region than to foreground that the film itself is a literate form, one among many available for adoption, use, and reinvention within specific places.

The regional film as a potentially resistant social invention is, unfortunately, a relatively rare creature. Far more often one encounters regional life depicted in neutralizing or, worse, stigmatizing terms; the kind of democratic, literate pluralism that is the hallmark of the critical regionalist film as I define it here usually exists only as a counternarrative to be detected as the motivating force of representational regimes that aggressively centralize language and other cultural practices, through not only a banking-model mode of pedagogical address but through a pedagogical content that aggressively delimits and restrains possible modes of literate practice and cultural production. To better theorize what critical regionalist cultural production might look like, and what representational histories it might draw on, we must turn now to literature, and examine how constructions of place in American literary history have contributed to and challenged long-standing stereotypes and presuppositions about the political and cultural significance of regional spaces.

As the strange tale of Howard Hawk Willis makes clear, the need to understand and to represent local instances of violence as manifestations of broader historical patterns of conflict and violence can literally be a matter of life and death, a threat to actual bodies as well as a challenge to the body politic. The Willis trial has yet to take place; at this writing, this local story lacks a conclusion, stuck in a cycle of technicalities and delays. The case will likely be resolved one way or another, but the conclusion will be written and rewritten by the way the local events shape definitions of the city, of the region, and of its role in and relationship to broader landscapes. Critical regionalism seeks the tactics to make the ending to the story of the Willis case a useful one for the community, to find ways to understand conflict and crisis in the fullness of their imbeddedness in history, politics, and culture.

Jo Carson is an author, playwright, and storyteller from Johnson City, Tennessee, who, in the words of art critic Lucy Lippard, "knows her sight lines" (33). Working with oral histories, overheard conversations, local topography, and a blunt but revelatory wit, she not only creates genre-bending literary works that are at once portraits and landscapes, but she teaches others to do so as well, by performing her own work and by consulting with local theater and youth groups. Though she has traveled widely performing and consulting, she remains staunch in her assertions that her work is intimately tied to her place, to the city where she was raised and in which she lives today, and the culture and topography of its surroundings.

Sometimes her descriptions of this attachment can sound metaphysical: "Unless I can see these old mountains," she says, "some piece of heart is missing in me" (quoted in Lippard 33). Other times, though, she offers a much more materialist understanding of the relationship between the local landscape and her writing, as when she tells of the fact that she was given a house by her father after she spent many years caring for her Alzheimer's-stricken mother. Carson acknowledges that "the house has become a sort of safety net, a level of economic permission to take chances with my work and try things that may or may not be marketable but seem important to try" ("Good Questions" 78). What might seem like contradiction here is actually, I assert, something more like the untidiness of inquiry, a sometimes canny, sometimes cunning reluctance to exclude possibilities for new ways and means to examine her local landscape in its full cultural, political, material, and emotional complexity. Hence her deliberate refusal to be limited even by conventions of genre: "I don't really have a description for what I do as a writer/performer. I do have a tradition. I come from a nest of raconteurs who are not afraid of hard stories or the extremes of the human condition. I just take the process one step further: I write stuff down" ("Good Questions" 73).

A good example of what stuff Jo Carson writes down is 1989's *Stories I Ain't Told Nobody Yet*, a collection of fifty-four speeches (mostly monologues), by people in and around Johnson City. Most of these pieces are understatedly described in the preface as simply things the author has heard, but the book as a whole underscores the diverse and conflicted character of the region with its hybridized form. It is a slim volume that is difficult to classify: presented on the page like poetry, but plainspoken in its language to an extreme; specific in its attention to the details of vernacular speech and yet general in its refusal to identify its speakers in ways other than their speeches. Even its title is internally contradictory: because the book exists, the stories are already told—what does one do with a second reading of this book? In this aspect, as in many others, Carson's literary experiment evokes a set of questions. Indeed, there may not be a single word for exactly what Carson does, but perhaps you could describe Carson as a professional questioner, and an important part of her work is to make other people question as well. Her overarching question seems to be, How can literature use local materials to encourage people to learn how to think of their own places in terms of questions?

That is a critical regionalist question, and this chapter is less an attempt to answer those question than it is an effort to model a way of engaging with it. To do so, I examine historical examples of regional and national literatures, and try to discern the cultural roots of the problematic that Carson's work inhabits and engages with: the seeming incommensurability between dealing with questions of cultural politics on broad geographical scales and representing local sites in careful and attentive detail.

The history of regionalism features a persistent difficulty resolving apparently conflicting goals of both respecting local lifeways and subjecting them to a critique that reveals their implications in larger social structures and processes. I have rooted the model of critical regionalism I have developed thus far in a particular strand of thinking about the concept of region: a model that traces its genealogy back through the practice of architecture and planning to the transdisciplinary work of the Regional Planning Association of America (RPAA) and in particular its foremost thinker about exurban spaces, Benton MacKaye. It is my sense that in discussions of regionalism in both cultural criticism and popular discourse, something vital about the idea of region as articulated by this group of thinkers been lost: the integrative way they theorized and used the term to connote the relationship among different types of landforms, settlements, and patterns of material extraction, production, and circulation, and simultaneously to denote the generative interaction of different types of human endeavor. Culture, politics, economics, and environment are not, in this view, discrete spheres but they interact, overlap, and interrelate in ways that are formative of and specific to any given region.

However, it has persistently been the case over U.S. history that this way of approaching region, as correlative rather than disjunctive, has been thwarted. As I noted in chapter 1, the TVA, grandly conceived as a transformation of both the culture and infrastructure of its watershed region, quickly became a purely instrumental technology project, its efforts at a more nuanced understanding of and intervention in Appalachian cultures a minor sidelight. Benton MacKaye, who had joined the planning staff of the TVA with great optimism, came to realize his broadly integrative thinking was unwelcome. He was terminated in the same 1938 administrative revolution in the authority that also deposed idealistic director Arthur Morgan and set the entire project on a course toward becoming a publicly controlled energy corporation rather than a social invention for regional cultural and political change (L. Anderson 264–65).

The RPAA's broadly integrative vision of region was repudiated not only by the technocracy, in favor of a more narrow, instrumental model, but also by the literary world, in favor of a more romantic and ahistorical view. In 1931 Benton MacKaye, along with several RPAA colleagues including Clarence Stein and Lewis Mumford, attended a roundtable on regionalism at the University of Virginia, where the New York and New England intellectuals encountered their southern doppelgangers in the form of delegates from the Agrarian literary group, headed by John Crowe Ransom. The year before the Agrarians (under the nom de plume "Twelve Southerners") had published their manifesto of cultural politics, *I'll Take My Stand* (1930), a vocal rejection of northern industrialism and call for a return to pastoral southern lifeways disrupted by the Civil War and its aftermath, whose very title suggests a separatist principle for regional definition. MacKaye appeared on the program delivering a speech titled "Cultural Aspects of Regionalism," and while much of his talk dedicated itself to subjects dear to the Agrarians' hearts, the perils facing traditional rural cultures in an era of metropolitan and industrial expansion, he felt it necessary to deal also with material efforts to reconfigure rural landscapes, describing such social inventions as the Bronx Parkway and his own "Townless Highway" proposal. Perhaps regional antipathies doomed a sympathetic response from the Agrarians from the outset—Clarence Stein wrote later that, following two of the Agrarians to the podium, "Benton certainly looked and spoke like a Yankee" (quoted in L. Anderson 229). But surely more disturbing was his progressive, dynamic view of region and locale, the idea that a conscious and deliberate human effort could resist the strictures of tradition and reconfigure its more useful elements to reshape place and culture. According to historian Edward Spann, "the

Agrarians clung to their view that societies were formed by organic growth over time" and thus felt "rational planning and policy was a menace to the traditionalism they held dear" (129).

So for technocrats the idea of region as social invention seemed frivolous, and for literary regionalists social invention seemed a menace. The split between a rational, positivist version of region and one rooted in a more ineffable combination of landscape and culture (the same split I embodied in the museum and the map in chapter 1) has its roots deep in the formative period of region as a critical practice. This chapter examines how a similar split persists in different approaches to representing place and region in the fiction of this period. Novelists like John Steinbeck and John Dos Passos advocated for broad structural changes in U.S. culture and sought to develop new representational tactics that challenged readers' perceptions of the spatial, political, historical, and cultural relationships among local sites on broader landscapes. But like the TVA, they seemed unable to conceive of local spaces as valid or useful sites of cultural politics and production and, instead, created "landscape narratives" on a national scale, in which local cultures function as obstacles to change (much as the TVA did in its pro-development propaganda such as the film *Valley of the Tennessee* [1940]). Meanwhile, even the most progressive regional fiction (leaving aside the Agrarians, whom Lewis Mumford described as "slightly reactionary, still dreaming of the past instead of shaping a more integrated future"), such as James Still's *River of Earth* (1940), a novel born of the author's cultural work and political awakening in Appalachia, struggles with the seemingly incongruous goals of on the one hand depicting a vital local culture but on the other trying to connect the local scene to larger historical, political, and cultural conflicts.

Yet decades before the RPAA, the Agrarians, and the TVA all went their separate ways, the regional literature of the realist and local-color movements was already serving as a social invention, exerting rhetorical influence over the social construction of definitions and concepts of regions and catalyzing certain forms of social and political change. But socially inventive regional literatures were not (and are not) necessarily progressive in purpose and in effects. Take the example of John Fox Jr., whose Appalachian novels were among the most popular works of the local-color period and remain among the most popular representations of the Appalachian region (Batteau 64). The content of his works, especially his best-known novel, *The Trail of the Lonesome Pine* (1908), obsessively lionizes constructions of elite, nationalist white masculinity (D. Wilson 8). *Lonesome Pine* features as its hero a (white male) bluegrass aristocrat who, in order to clear the way for timber and mineral extraction, imposes martial law on an area of southwest Virginia; he enforces his edicts through vigilantism carried out by his fellow speculator elites and capital punishment of hillbilly ringleaders. Although this novel and Fox's work more generally allow for a somewhat more complex and fully realized portrait of its mountaineers than early writing about the region (Batteau 68), overall the work is unambiguous in its declared political positions. As Appalachian studies scholar Darlene Wilson has documented, Fox's fiction almost without exception represents a rationalization for economic exploitation of the region—an enterprise in which Fox and his family had considerable personal financial interest. More disturbingly, Fox's fiction is contextualized by a concerted attempt by absentee investors (like Fox's brother James) to unsettle the region and break local resistance to "modernization" through the creation of company towns, the renaming of existing towns, the movement of courthouses and other important public spaces, and the undermining of existing schools (25).

Far from a transculturating use of local materials in resistance to dominant culture, Fox's work reads as propaganda for a campaign of economic and legal crypto-colonialism, the effects of which are felt in the region today. Indeed, Fox's work, even as it declined in repute aesthetically, continued (and continues) to retain power as a source of specious information about the region. Fox created this power by establishing himself as a pseudoscientific "expert" on the region for the northeastern lecture circuit, despite the fact that his expertise was a mishmash of fiction, hearsay, and the popular white-supremacist "race theories" of writers like Henry Cabot Lodge (D. Wilson 24–26; Batteau 61; Mortensen, "Representations" 106–7). Fox's brand of "local color" is summarized neatly in Darlene Wilson's phrase, "the felicitous convergence of mythmaking and capital accumulation" (5).

Felicitous, that is, for Fox and his constituency, but disastrous for the southern Appalachian region. When regional fiction is identified as exploitative, the "exploitation" is typically better described as "excess." Take, for example, this proclamation by literary critic Floyd Watkins, in which allegations of gothic sensationalism, parochialism, and aesthetic failure are jumbled together: "The local colorist creates an exaggerated nature to emphasize the strangeness of his characters and their remoteness; his descriptions of ugliness in nature are melodramatic; the beauties of nature appear in a polysyllabic vocabulary and saccharine imagery" (109). However, the material implications of how a region is imagined and represented can be more profound than mere offenses to refined literary tastes. Fox's work represents a maleficent kind of social invention for an ideological purpose, whose exploitation manifests itself not simply in purple prose or an unseemly attention to the crude and vulgar, but in sponsoring the cultural preconditions for material relations of injustice and economic oppression.

The deep irony of Fox's fiction and public lectures is that they portray the mountain region as a place at best resistant and at worst hostile to change, even as they contributed powerfully to a version of the region that justified a dramatic rewriting of the landscape of the region, its politics, economics, social order, and cultural practices. But Fox and his oeuvre are not alone in this irony: it is part of the same intellectual history, which postulates region and cultural innovation as incompatible, that later split MacKaye from both the Agrarians and the TVA. Critical regionalism engages with such ironies by examining the conflicts and interactions that shape representations of identities in the context of a particular physical location, in order to connect these local interactions, by orders of geographical, cultural, and historical magnitude, to broader patterns of history and society. This task requires an admixture of strategies and approaches, appropriated into tactics designed with the problems and priorities of the locale in question specifically in mind. As literary historian Richard Brodhead writes, "Literary difference . . . is neither a pseudoreality nor an automatic consequence of social identity but something effected through the mediations of literary-cultural situations" (11). While regional fiction has received increasing critical attention from scholars exploring social construction of various kinds of identity politics, gender, race, class, or sexuality, critical regionalism asks how and to what extent any or all of these factors combine and converge in a particular site, how broader patterns of difference shape and are shaped by local landscapes. As with my interpretation of popular film, what I am calling for here can be summed up as reading the text through the place, rather than seeing the place through the text.

Art critic Lucy Lippard describes a similar project in the visual arts in her introduction to *The Lure of the Local*:

> Of all the art that purports to be *about* place, very little can truly be said to be *of* place. . . . I am concerned here only with that which is directly tied to place—with examining the ways art can help us focus on existing places, how their topography and every detail reflects and generates memory and a certain kind of knowledge about nature and culture. (20)

Later she raises an important set of questions that place-specific art engages with:

A Critical Regionalist Literature

What kind of reciprocal art . . . might help the struggles against destructive practices fueled by greed and shortsightedness? Stimulate people's own ideas about what they would like to see in their environments and empower them to make changes? Connect very different neighboring communities? (286)

Lippard's questions point toward a disposition toward the critical analysis of representations similar to that of chapter 3, as they imply that images of place can be approached not only from the standpoint of reading the place through the lens of the representations, but that texts and images might also be read through the lens of the problems and priorities of particular places. Thus texts that are not necessarily about a given place may yet contribute to the ways that the place is perceived and portrayed by the people who inhabit that place, because they offer tactics for comprehending and representing that place and the particular admixture of historical, cultural, political, and economic forces that converge there. The remainder of this chapter, then, analyzes several examples of the cultural politics of place and region in U.S. literature, first in innovative national epics from the era to which critical regionalism traces its intellectual history, John Dos Passos's *U.S.A.* trilogy (completed with the 1933 publication of *The Big Money*) and John Steinbeck's 1939 *Grapes of Wrath*. Then James Still's lesser-known 1940 Appalachian novel *River of Earth*, in many ways a more conventional (if less canonical) effort of regional fiction, provides an example of a contemporaneous attempt to portray a local, exurban space as a vital and dynamic intersection of larger patterns of cultural conflict.

The purpose of these critical regionalist readings is not, however, to evaluate these particular works, to adjudicate whether or not they should enter some regionalist canon. Rather, they provide examples for thinking more broadly about the tactics for literary production, and cultural production more generally, that writers who seek to respond to Lippard's challenge might follow. How can writers make reciprocal, socially inventive versions of places that challenge their readers to perceive and represent their own places in new, more complex, and more volitional ways, and teach them that their local circumstances and the broader range of places to which those surroundings connect can be changed—perhaps even for the better? What resources do these forebears have to offer to the critical regionalist writer of today, and what formal and conceptual changes need to be made to move beyond their limitations? To see how questions like these might be taken up, the chapter closes with a closer look at Jo Carson, and her *Stories I Ain't Told Nobody Yet* (1989). Carson's mix of oral history, poetry, social criticism, and public performance bends genres and literary conventions and creates a vision and a version of place and region that sponsors a consideration of how a regional literature could bridge the gap that separated conceptions of regionalism in its heyday during the period between the world wars. Carson's particular place is Johnson City, Tennessee, the geographical center of this book —not a coincidence, since finding ways to trace a path from east Tennessee to *U.S.A.* (by way of the Steinbeck's Dust Bowl and Still's coalfields) is the kind of connectivity critical regionalism is all about. How can we find the representational trail that links Johnson City to national epics and historical regionalisms into one vast landscape narrative?

Discerning Local Colors

The routes exist, but you have to look closely to begin to be able to think of how to create an Appalachian reading of Dos Passos's and Steinbeck's national epics. The emerging history of financial and resource exploitation of the Appalachian region, for which Fox was in the cultural vanguard, had produced conflicts that at least partially revised the role of the Appalachian region in the national imagination during the period in which Dos Passos and Steinbeck constructed their version of the national landscape. Strife fueled by labor unrest transformed Appalachia into an icon for the regional imbalances, the violence of uneven economic development, beginning in 1912 with the Paint Creek and Cabin Creek (Kentucky) strikes, culminating in the Battle of Blair Mountain (West Virginia) in 1931 and the "Bloody Harlan" (Kentucky) conflicts of the 1930s. Although these struggles subsided somewhat during and after World War II, the coalfields of the region saw a period of intense violence in the struggles of coal miners for basic human rights and economic justice that are still unresolved today (Batteau 102–26, J. Williams 266–72). While some writers and journalists of the day persisted in portraying the unrest, like Fox, as growing out of traditions of feuding and moonshining and the general barbarism of the population, the experience of the coalfields energized public discourse about industrial oppression (Batteau 102–3).

In this context John Dos Passos attempted to use his craft to stage an intervention in the cultural politics of the region, taking an active hand in the cultural transformation of Appalachian identity. On 4 through 7 November 1931, he joined a group of writers led by Theodore Dreiser, under the rubric of the communist-affiliated National Committee for the Defense of Political Prisoners, in a fact-finding mission to Harlan and Bell counties, gathering information to be reported in a collection of essays called *Harlan Miners Speak* and a series of articles in national periodicals. One of Dos Passos's contributions to this public intellectual project, an article titled "Harlan: Working under the Gun" in the *New Republic* (2 December 1931), uses the region to illustrate "how completely the 'American standard of living' . . . has collapsed." But he also recognizes the constructedness of the region's image in relation to similar problems in other areas of the country: "The fact that the exploited class in Harlan County is of old American pre-Revolutionary stock . . . will perhaps win them more sympathy from the average American than he would waste on the wops and bohunks he is accustomed to see get the dirty end of the stick in labor troubles" (62).

In statements like this one, Dos Passos subscribes, to a certain extent, to popular mythology about the region in his ungrounded assumptions about the regional population's genealogy. But he clearly understands it as mythology—as an image of Appalachia that has a certain tactical, political, rhetorical power in popular discourse of labor strife and social justice (anticipating the use of Appalachia as the "white face of poverty" decades later during the Great Society period of the 1960s). The power of white Appalachia is to confront the rest of white America with the failure and collapse of its ideals, the price of its advancements and successes, with the contradictory mythology that makes wage slaves of people who are central to the nation's patriotic belief in itself, people that supposedly "still speak the language of Patrick Henry and Daniel Boone and Andrew Jackson and conserve the pioneer traditions of the Revolutionary War and of the conquest of the West" ("Harlan" 62). This paradox within American mythology, which Dos Passos found to hold Appalachia in a death grip, is an irony that feeds the more sardonic traits of *U.S.A.* (though the nostalgia for white male, nationalist, and triumphalist history shaping his thinking here foreshadows Dos Passos's later turn to a libertarian-individualist conservatism).

Indeed, Dos Passos's Appalachian experiences fueled the project of *U.S.A.* as a whole. Dos Passos accords the historical experience of Harlan, and his personal observation of it, a very significant place in the structure of the trilogy as a whole, as he describes and meditates on his visit to Kentucky in the novel's fifty-first and final installment of the autobiographical, prose poem "Camera Eye" (one of a variety of writing tactics the novel employs in various sections). If the Camera Eye sections are the story of an individual's journey to political consciousness and an understanding of structures of privilege and power in American culture (Pizer, *Naturalism* 62), then Harlan has a certain pride of place as the culmination of the speaker's confrontation with "the full political and personal implications" (Pizer, *Dos Passos* 51) of his commitment to radical democracy. Indeed, as Donald Pizer points out, in terms of Dos Passos's biography the Camera Eye ends as the author is preparing to write *U.S.A.*—thus the Harlan experience is the political epiphany that the author takes with him into the composition of the novel, the rhetorical occasion for his cultural production (*Naturalism* 63).

This mythological-but-rhetorical understanding of Appalachia is one that Steinbeck shares. The plight of Appalachian workers and families in labor struggles underpins Steinbeck's depiction of his Okies—Appalachian people are the Okies' forebears and at times their comrades-in-arms. When Tom Joad first returns to his family from jail, this important establishing scene includes a reference to the family's (and more generally the Okies') ties to the mythology of Appalachia in a telling reference to feuding. Grampa greets Tom by saying, "An' ol' Turnbull, stinkin' skunk, braggin' how he'll shoot ya when ya come out. Says he got Hatfield blood. Well, I sent word to him. I says, 'Don't mess around with no Joad. Maybe I got McCoy blood for all I know' " (102).

A later, more direct discussion of Appalachian people establishes them, as in Dos Passos's article, as a people at the center of political struggle, a people who present the possibility of alternative interpretations of and responses to political conditions—in sum a kind of critical regionalist construction. This mention takes the form of an anecdote providing the denouement of perhaps the only incident in the novel in which collective resistance to oppression is both attempted and achieved, as the settlers in the government camp nonviolently eject agitators from their dance. It is a telling detail that this story of Appalachian people is told by a Native American—another of the novel's links between varied historical collective struggles. Black Hat's story of the actions of "mountain men" in a labor struggle in Akron, Ohio, provides the men of the camp a point of reference for their own victory:

> Well, sir—it was las' March, an' one Sunday five thousan' of them mountain men had a turkey shoot outside a town. Five thousan' of 'em jes' marched through town with their rifles. An' they had their turkey shoot, an' then they marched back. An' that's all they done. Well, sir, they ain't been no trouble sence then. These here citizens committees give back the pick handles, an' the storekeepers keep the stores, an' nobody been clubbed or tarred an' feathered, an' nobody been killed. (444)

This story represents a complicated and contradictory use of nationalist mythology similar to Dos Passos's "Working under the Gun." Here the pioneer tradition, embodied in the turkey shoot, becomes not a theater of individualistic conquest, but a rallying point for collective action, a tool for social change. While still clearly a masculinist and militaristic heritage, the mythology of frontier heroism is put to a very different use here than it is in nationalist narratives of the "winning of the west." Pioneer masculinity that once served the nationalist project is still alive and well but now serves to immunize the project of labor organization against Red-baiting and the threat of middle-class vigilantism. This subversive project (qualified in its radicalism, like Dos Passos's historiography, by its unreflective admiration of masculine displays of power) allows, perhaps requires, this story to be related by a Native American. History has brought together the tools and the victims of conquest in a shared struggle of class and culture.

Steinbeck's reference to the labor struggles of Appalachian people is somewhat more optimistic than Dos Passos's—pioneer mythology provides an image of muted hope as opposed to a bitter irony—but both picture the region and its people as an important site of broader struggles for justice, and an important source of rhetorical power in those struggles. Both Dos Passos and Steinbeck are involved in the reconfiguration of the mythological aspects of Appalachian identity in an alternative cultural politics. The way both of them use Appalachian motifs suggests a tacit understanding of region as an interconnective figure: in both these cases the image of the region is deployed specifically to tie local, historical instances of political and cultural strife to larger discussions and debates, to integrate them into broader landscapes. As we shall see, however, this acknowledgment of the potential rhetorical power of place and of region has limits within the politics and logics of their landscape narratives; for both authors, displacement and rootlessness offer more powerful oppositional tropes.

"The Letters at the End of an Address
When You Are Away from Home"

John Dos Passos's epic trilogy *U.S.A.* offers powerful resources for critical regionalist cultural production: in both form and content, it is dedicated to illuminating the cultural patterns and connections that thread a broad and variegated landscape into a complex skein of cultural and political connections. Dos Passos challenges readers to rethink the nature and degree of interconnection among disparate places through a series of fictional narrative strands organized around individual characters, each of which is autonomous but each of which overlaps with other characters. But these individual narratives are even more broadly contextualized

by intercalary sections: "Newsreels," collages of popular culture fragments, songs, stories, headlines; blank-verse biographies, often quite
caustic in the satire, of the era's prominent figures from Thorstein Veblen
to Henry Ford, from J. P. Morgan to Isadora Duncan; and the aforementioned "Camera Eye," prose poems that implicate the author's own biography in the political landscape he evokes.

The trilogy as a whole is bookended by the "U.S.A." and "Vag" sections
—a prologue and epilogue that echo themes and styles of the other sections
but are relatively autonomous. These prose-poem vignettes illustrate a
lone man, a vag, out on the road, often on the bum, a metonymic figure for
the ceaseless migration for most of the trilogy's principles and the speaker
of the Camera Eye, all of whom drift along through their rising and falling
fortunes from town to town amid the kinetic cultural life, dramatized in
the jump-cutting Newsreels, of a nation growing in political power and
complexity. The Vag is not just a stand-in for the rest of the novel, an
allegorical figure; he is also a point of reference, a kind of chorus that
disrupts the teleology of the trilogy, suggesting that the actions that compose the space between his two appearances are part of a larger continuum
of continuing movement and migration. Both are written in a restless
present tense, in panoramic, Whitmanesque catalogs of place-names,
practices, sounds, events, phrases:

> [U.S.A.:] It was not in the long walks through jostling crowds at night
> that he felt less alone, or in the training camp in Allentown, or in the
> day on the docks in Seattle, or in the reek of Washington City hot
> boyhood summer nights, or in the meal on Market Street, or in the
> swim off the red rocks at San Diego, or in the bed full of fleas in New
> Orleans . . . or in the smokers of limited expresstrains, or walking
> across country, or riding up the dry mountain canyons. . . . (*The 42nd
> Parallel* vi)

> [Vag:] The young man waits on the side of the road; . . . thumb moves
> in a small arc as a car tears hissing past. . . . Head swims, belly tightens,
> wants crawl over his skin like ants:
> went to school, books said opportunity, ads promised speed, own
> your own home, shine bigger than your neighbor, the radiocrooner
> whispered girls, ghosts of platinum girls coaxed from the screen . . .
> waits with swimming head, needs knot the belly, idle hands numb,
> beside the speeding traffic. (*The Big Money* 555–56)

Even when stationary, this archetypal figure remains in motion: skin
crawling, head swimming, belly knotting, thumb swinging. The waiting

note on which the trilogy ends is not a patient one—it is a pause in the ceaseless movement, but not a respite. Various commentators have interpreted this novel's nomadicism in different ways: from a celebration of liberal individualism (Butler) to a jaded picaresque satire (Fichtelberg), but no one has questioned the fact that human motion across the landscape is, on a very basic level, what *U.S.A.* is about from the outset.

As these passages show, this movement is an ambivalent experience at best. The Vag is a figure of privation, of unprovided material need and unsatisfied sexual desire, and as the second excerpt shows, these are not separate conditions, but linked not only in the body but in cultural institutions as well: schooling, advertising, media. The connection between bodily desire and cultural institutions is central to this novel, for it is through this connection that the complex of desires assumes political force, naturalizing the institutions by making them seem the inevitable extension of trying to satisfy basic physical needs. Thus these many desires, played out in detail in the lives of the trilogy's dozen principle recurring characters, are both fed by and feed this restless movement. Whether these desires are venal or idealistic in any specific instance, rootlessness is a common denominator.

But in the case of the trilogy's radicals, movement takes on specific political meanings. This complex of desires, and its impact on political action, plays out particularly clearly in the case of Mac, who, along with Mary French and Ben Compton, is part of the radical minority among the novel's twelve principals. As not only the first radical but the first main character the reader encounters, his story sets a pattern for later strands. Mac's first section commences with a brief cultural geography of his hometown of Middletown, Connecticut, including the ethnic divisions of the proletarian neighborhoods; the shops, homes, and factories; the sights, smells, and practices that shape space into place. But very quickly the scene shifts as the family flees debt following the death of Mac's mother, and before Mac's story ends he has spent time in Connecticut, Illinois, Michigan, British Columbia, Washington, California, Nevada, Texas, and Mexico.

Along the way his life is marked by twin impulses: the first to settle down and get married, the second to dedicate his life to the labor struggles he encounters at almost every stop on his journey. The potential for developing a strong sense of political purpose distinguishes Mac's character and his travels from *1919*'s drifter, Joe Williams; many of Mac's wanderings are in search of revolutionary action (as in his trip to Goldfield, Nevada, and his later migration to Mexico), whereas Joe follows the course dictated by work and his persistent bad luck. Mac's tense relationship between inhabiting and migrating comes to a head near the center of his story, as he is forced to choose between his political leanings and the domestic demands of his girlfriend, then wife, Maisie. Maisie is a woman intent on joining the growing middle-class, with a casual obliviousness to political struggles: "He tried to get her to read pamphlets on socialism, but she laughed and looked up at him with her big intimate blue eyes and said it was too deep for her. She liked to go to the theater and eat in restaurants where the linen was starched and there were waiters in dress suits" (*The 42nd Parallel* 81).

Unfortunately, Mac's growing interest in Maisie, sustained by his desire to "love her up," develops about the same time as the Goldfield, Nevada, miners' strikes, and as Maisie makes it clear that he must keep his job and marry her, his choice is between her and political work. Mac, characteristically trying to have it both ways, sleeps with her and promises to marry her, in a scene that clearly insinuates that her sudden sexual availability is an attempt to keep him—then he slips away, realizing "he was selling out" (83). Once in Goldfield, receiving a letter from Maisie telling him she is pregnant and stating unambiguously, "you must come right back," his fellow Wobbly Fred Hoff makes the political equivalence of settling down equally clear:

> "A man's first duty's to the workin' class," said Fred Hoff.
>
> "As soon as the kid's born an' she can go back to work I'll come back. But you know how it is, Fred. I can't pay the hospital expenses on seventeen-fifty a week."
>
> "You oughta been more careful."
>
> "But hell, Fred, I'm made of flesh and blood like everybody else. For crissake, what do you want us to be, tin saints?"
>
> "A wobbly oughtn't to have any wife or children, not until after the revolution." (*The 42nd Parallel* 93)

While the dogmatic Fred Hoff is not the most sympathetic character, his lesson, that domestic stability produces political stasis, is repeatedly and vividly illustrated in Mac's narrative. Mac's first political work, producing and distributing radical handbills in his Uncle Tim's printshop, is quashed by the collusion of local businesses (resulting in Uncle Tim being berated by his wife, foreshadowing Mac's later problems). His political education, foreshadowing Ben Compton's (*1919* 424–29), comes during his subsequent wanderings, where he meets itinerant radicals at many stops. When he finally returns to California from Goldfield and marries Maisie, his married life is a political reeducation: "Whenever there was any of the wobbly crowd in town . . . he never could do much for fear Maisie would find out about it. Whenever she found *The Appeal to Reason* or any other radical paper round the house she'd burn it up . . . it kept them apart almost as though he was going out with some other woman" (*The 42nd Parallel* 105). The tie between "settledness" and capitalism becomes absolutely clear as Maisie's brother Bill, a real-estate speculator, tries to rope Mac into an investment scheme: " 'Suppose a feller didn't want to get rich . . . you know what Gene Debs said, "I want to rise with the ranks, not from the ranks,"' said Mac. Maisie and Bill laughed. 'When a guy talks like that he's ripe for the nuthouse, take it from me,' said Bill" (*The 42nd Parallel* 108). Mac's ambivalence to wealth is interpreted as treason against family (" 'I'd think you'd be more grateful to Bill,' snapped Maisie" [*The 42nd Parallel* 109]), and eventually plays its part in the inevitable collapse of the marriage, which sends Mac to Mexico in pursuit of revolution. Given the pattern of Mac's experience with Maisie, and the pattern his life develops in this segment of his story, it is unsurprising to see him in Mexico City once again reluctantly but inevitably depoliticizing his life and work to accommodate another family, this time with a subservient but middle-class Mexican woman who believes "peons are ignorant savages fit only to be ruled with a whip" (*The 42nd Parallel* 277).

Beyond its misogyny, this treatment of domesticity is part of the novel's persistent critique of the artificial pieties of the family structure that limits both its women and its men—though it is discomfiting how shallow, conniving, and vain Dos Passos's women characters are as a rule. The story of "Daughter," however, describes the restless yearning of a woman, Anne Elizabeth Trent, with energy, intelligence, and charisma; but as her unimaginative nickname indicates, she is severely constrained in her possible lives by home and family (values again linked to financial acquisitiveness through Daughter's lawyer father). When she crosses paths with political organizer Ben Compton in New York City, she has the stirrings of a political conscience, attacking a policeman as he clubs a demonstrator, but her family obligations truncate this change in her. As soon as she is released from jail, she receives telegrams from her family commanding her first to remain silent, then to "COME ON HOME AT ONCE" (*1919* 282). This summons home reshapes her, redirects back to a more "proper" quest for a husband, which ends in her death after bourgeois Dick Savage gets her pregnant, then spurns her.

Part of the political value of wanderlust in this novel is that it breaks down the stifling ties of family, which the novel suggests is a purely hegemonic, middle-class institution. Because it is the only social structure in the novel associated with remaining in place, indeed, a structure that forces otherwise mobile characters to stop moving, family structure is by default the only persistent factor in this novel that constructs the experience of place. *U.S.A.* is, in the eponymous introduction, "the letters at the end of an address when you are away from home" (*The 42nd Parallel* vi), but as Daughter's and Mac's experiences indicate, the letters those letters are written on are not good news but an attempt to limit or control you, by putting you back in your place.

The View from the Road

Grapes of Wrath, the Joad family's journey from its Dust Bowl homestead to itinerant farm-working California, juxtaposes family and mobility, conservative stasis and radical possibility in a similar fashion, though for Steinbeck the diametric opposition of the terms is even more extreme. Like Dos Passos, Steinbeck has an ambivalent view of displacement, as both a symptom of strife but also as a cultural disruption presenting the possibility for the formation of alternative forms of social and political organization. Composing his novel almost ten years after Dos Passos began his trilogy, perhaps Steinbeck was able to take displacement, particularly the nomadicism caused by the Great Depression, as more of a given, more of an inevitability than a likelihood. Focusing exclusively on one journey of a single displaced family, rather than the migratory patterns of an entire nation, Steinbeck assumes, and intensifies, what Dos Passos argues: that sustained, dedicated inhabitation of a specific place is not just an undesirable option, but rather not an option at all, in an increasingly capitalistic and unjust America.

Even in Steinbeck's depiction of Appalachian people, place is what has already been lost rather than a source of identity or a crucial site of cultural work. Steinbeck's "mountain men" are in Akron, not in Appalachia; though their pioneering identity clings to them still, they have migrated to midwestern cities following Industrial Age jobs. Only the Appalachian people are mentioned, not the Appalachian landscape.

Of course, the Joads' place has already been lost at the novel's outset, too—another parallelism subtly linking the Appalachian region to this novel. Like *U.S.A.*, *The Grapes of Wrath* begins with a lone man on the move, a Vag, though here he is on the way home, or so he thinks. His home—Tom Joad's home—is gone; local culture has shifted in his absence in a profound an elemental way. Drawing out the metaphorical equivalence of violent weather patterns and large-scale changes in landscape and culture contained in the title of *The 42nd Parallel*, *The Grapes of Wrath*'s first chapter is an allegorical, archetypal description of the origins of the

Dust Bowl. Dos Passos's introductory vignette "U.S.A." is in some ways a similar maneuver, connecting the events of the body of the novel, necessarily individualized, in a broader context. But in that first sketch of the Vag, the emphasis is on social interaction, on cities and towns, language and practices. Steinbeck, on the other hand, begins with displacement as a natural fact, a force of nature against which humans appear insignificant, and language becomes an exercise in futility, an attempt to leave a lasting mark on dust: the chapter concludes, "The men sat in the doorways of their houses; their hands were busy with sticks and little rocks. The men sat still—thinking—figuring" (*The Grapes of Wrath* 7).

Like the waiting Vag at the end of *U.S.A.*, the "still" men are not stationary—how could they be with the land literally flying about them on the wind? Steinbeck begins where Dos Passos concludes: like the Vag at the end of Dos Passos's trilogy, these men are pausing, gathering the strength to take the only available option, migration. There is no other tenable course of action, as Tom's encounter with the allegorically named Muley Graves, so-called for his stubborn fatalism, at Tom's former home place makes perfectly clear. Muley's metaphysical attachment to the land defies the economic determinism setting all others out on the road, but to no particular end. Chastised by preacher Casy for letting his family leave without him, his only explanation for staying put is " 'I couldn'. . . . Somepin jus' wouldn' let me" (62). Muley is aware that his own place constructions—a nostalgia that confuses the site of an incident with the social interaction comprising the incident itself—is futile. He admits to Casy and Tom, "I'd tell myself, 'I'm looking after things so when all the folks come back it'll be all right.' But I knowed that wan't true. There ain't nothin' to look after. The folks ain't never comin' back. I'm just wanderin' aroun' like a damn ol' graveyard ghos' " (65). Muley's ghostly state—he repeats that description three times—puns on his last name but also underscores how his blind commitment to place has separated him from the world of social interaction, from public life. He is, for all practical purposes, dead to the world. He has become part of the depopulated terrain as surely as if he lay in a grave. Only Casy, who has already made a transition from a mystical to a strongly social world view, recognizes Muley's problem is neither supernatural nor metaphysical: "You're lonely —but you ain't touched," he tells him (66).

The undead Muley foreshadows the death of Grampa almost immediately after the Joads' departure from their home; he simply does not survive the separation from the land. Though his death is the first in a series of tragedies for the Joad family, it is also the first crack in the "natural" order of its former life, the beginning of the reconfiguration of

the family structure by which the Joads have all unquestioningly organized their relationships. Grampa's scatalogical habits—when we first see
him his fly is open (100)—and his visceral desires, such as his oft-stated
desire to eat fruit straight off the trees and vines in California, "and squash
'em on my face an' let 'em run offen my chin" (107), present him as the
atavistic "natural man." Muley has regressed to Grampa's anachronistic,
bestial relationship to the land; his humanity has become ghostly, but he
lives on physically first as a wolf and then a weasel (73).

Grampa's organic relationship to the world around him is ultimately
fatal (as we may speculate Muley's is, as well), and it anticipates the first
serious insurrection in the Joad patriarchy, when Ma uses the threat of
force to overrule Pa, ironically about Tom splitting off from the family's
expedition to repair a car (216–18). A site-specific creature, Grampa cannot be transplanted, and the death of the natural patriarch underscores
that the family structure cannot survive transportation, either (not even
the family's transportation can survive transportation—the truck, which
becomes both literally and symbolically their home, is eventually destroyed). Significantly, Grampa has to be drugged to be induced to leave,
and he never recovers from this act of insubordination, the deposition of
the figurehead.

In another echo of Dos Passos, the naturalization of the family structure, and its focus, through the character of Grampa, on a very particular
location, suggests that family order is the most basic and predictable
structure to the experience of place. But even before the death of Grampa
broadly signals the collapse of this organic structure, the novel dramatizes the waning of this patriarchal order. Though patriarchy and hierarchy are performed all through the novel in quite literal ways, as in the
ordering of seating on a wagon or the division of labor in a specific job
(124–25), the family, even in the early phases of the novel, is depicted in
the voice of the omniscient narrator as an organization more socially
than biologically constructed. Casy, serving as usual as the novel's seer,
watches the Joads assuming their "natural" roles and assigning certain
roles to him as well, and the narrator notes that "he knew the government
of families" (132).

This political description of family life is apt, as the family acquires a
new kind of political significance on the road, as a reactionary construction, blocking the ability of the Joads to act effectively on behalf of
their class and in terms of larger units of social organization. The road,
the act of going, therefore assumes, just as it did in Dos Passos, an
essential political and critical status. The physical act of displacement
might be carried out by agents of faceless corporations, against which

one can take no personal revenge, as in chapter 5's exchange between a caterpillar driver and the tenant farmer, who wants to know "Who can we shoot?" But the act of displacement itself has a political side effect that the capitalist did not anticipate: by disrupting the naturalized social structures that are (Steinbeck suggests) a side effect of place construction, displacement affords a view of the constructedness of these institutions. As such it becomes the facilitator of unrealized forms of collective organization and action.

These new forms, however, even when they are described in familial terms, are diametrically opposed to the traditional patriarchal family structure, which disintegrates around the Joads with the attrition of one member after another. Ma must use violence, or the threat of it, against her husband, to assume her evolving role as the Joads' logical and ethical center, and even after she overcomes external control, she must free herself of now-vestigial family loyalties to feed the starving children in the Bakersfield camp.

In this instance Ma shows she has learned to "build the new society in the ruins of the old," as she redirects her maternal responsibilities to the good of community instead of family. When the Joads reach the government camp of Weedpatch, they discover this appropriation and redirection of traditional duties happening on a large scale, as the socialist utopia is managed on a daily basis by the Ladies' Committees. Their welcoming visit to the Joads is prepared for by Ma with mock epic intensity, and although their lengthy discussion of the operation of the bathhouses and washtubs is presented in a gently satirical light, the role women have in the public life of this alternative community is clearly invigorated; if not feminist, it is a significant challenge to the rigidly gendered familial roles that structure life in Oklahoma.

The formation of these new collectives is summarized in an interchapter that is literally at the heart of the novel, number seventeen of thirty, covering pages 249–58 of 581:

> In the evening a strange thing happened: the twenty families became one family, the children were the children of all. The loss of home became one loss, and the golden time in the West became one dream. And it might be that a sick child threw despair into the hearts of twenty families, of a hundred people; that a birth there in a tent kept a hundred people quiet and awestruck through the night and filled a hundred people with the birth-joy in the morning. (250)

That most essential of domestic scenarios, the birth of a child, becomes a public act, and as Steinbeck uses this event to open on to the whole range of cultural practices in the pages that follow, all revised and reconfigured in their newly collectivized dimensions, it is clear a new and potentially productive—or, more appropriately, generative—social structure is emerging. Moments like these give *The Grapes of Wrath* an air of muted hopefulness noted by many critics, and often noted for its absence in the deeply, often bitterly ironic *U.S.A.*. But even though Steinbeck is more willing to strike a prophetic (even didactic) tone where Dos Passos prefers to wither, these opportunities for resistance to the oppressive forces of American culture are founded on the irony that it is a certain capitulation to capitalism, in the cession of control over place-formation, that underpins these possibilities. Interchapter 17 begins with departure, as "the cars of the migrant people crawled out of the side roads onto the great cross-country highway, and they took the migrant way to the west" (249), but it also ends with departure:

> The tents came down. There was a rush to go. And when the sun arose, the camping place was vacant, only a little litter left by the people. And the camping place was ready for a new world in a new night.
>
> But along the highway the cars of the migrant people crawled out like bugs, and the narrow concrete miles stretched ahead. (257–58)

"The Billiondollar Speedup"

There is no place for place, it seems, in the visions of progressive, alternative social worlds that inform these sweeping political novels. In these novels of restless, agitated, and agitating movement, place is stopping, giving up, selling out. In this respect the two novels echo John Fox Jr.'s specious theory of Appalachian settlement as he explains that residents of the region were the descendants of would-be pioneers who broke an axle on their way west.

Dos Passos's restless Americans, especially those with radical leanings, are never accorded any enduring place attachments; indeed, commitment to a specific place is satirized when a young J. W. Moorhouse, already showing the inclination toward shallow promotion that will shape his career, writes saccharine ditties about his home state: "Oh, show me the state where the peaches bloom / where maids are fair . . . It's Delaware" (*The 42nd Parallel* 161). The one figure of the trilogy for whom inhabitation presents the possibility of radical political and cultural change is Frank Lloyd Wright, profiled in a biographical section called "ARCHITECT." Wright, who was also praised by Lewis Mumford as "our greatest regional architect" (quoted in Spann 122), understands that "building a building is building the lives of the workers and the dwellers in that building," and he therefore tries "to draft plans that demand for their fulfillment a new life. . . . His blueprints, as once Walt Whitman's words, stir the young men" (*The Big Money* 440). But even this possibility is frustrated by the American status quo; in conclusion, and close on the heels of the expressed hopeful assessments, Wright is in sum the modern manifestation of the prophet "not without honor except in his own country" (*The Big Money* 440). The conservative power of place thwarts his radical vision. Interestingly, this biography comes immediately after Newsreel LXIII, which is structured around the Appalachian equivalent of Moorhouse's Delaware anthems, a song about feuding in the Tennessee mountains—one of those cultural representations that thwarts action and depoliticizes strife in regional settings (Blee and Billings 133–34).

Even when good places are established, when cultural space for social change is opened up through collective resistance, the gesture is not sustainable: the Joads (and, given their allegorical status, other Okies as well) cannot dwell in Weedpatch but have to move on to find work, leading them to the wage slavery of the Hooper Ranch. The socialist utopia is only a stopoff. Indeed, the conclusion of the novel seems quite pessimistic about the possibility of even a transitory sense of community, as the boxcar encampment, which is the Joads' best living conditions of the entire novel outside of the Weedpatch camp, is destroyed not by political and economic oppression but by a flood. The description of the flood itself is structured by the narrative of Pa's failed effort to achieve the same kind of collective awareness that Ma and Tom have attained, as he mobilizes the men of the camp to build a floodwall, only to see it washed away (559–69). The one time the Joads and their fellow refugees are able to attempt a solution to a problem other than flight, other than displacement ("If them fellas won't dig, then we'll all hafta go," declares Pa [559]), they are foiled by the land itself. With the flood at the end and the drought at the beginning framing the narrative as a whole, ultimate agency and responsibility for the tragedy of *The Grapes of Wrath* is transferred to nature itself—unlike *U.S.A.*, where the Vag frames the novel's problems as profoundly social. How can a good place be possible in a hostile universe? How can you understand how your place relates to others when the terrain itself is in turmoil?

In the novel's concluding image, the Joads' daughter, Rosasharn, nurses a starving man, an action that also nurses the possibility of human compassion, suggesting that resources for care can yet be found in reconfigured relationships. As in interchapter 17's image of the birth of the child to all the camp, here family structures are challenged and redefined

A Critical Regionalist Literature

on their most basic level, symbolized in the loss at last of even the truck, with its family-ordering seating arrangement and gendered distribution of the work of maintenance and driving. But because the novel, like *U.S.A.*, equates the experience of place with the family structures it persistently challenges and undermines, this hopeful moment also cements the novel's theory of the inherently reactionary status of durable commitments to place and in so doing stymies the possibilities for a critical sense of regionalism to emerge.

This concluding move is prepared by Tom's final, principled split with the family in *Grapes of Wrath*—an absolute precondition of his new dedication to radical political praxis. The poetically chanted "wherever" of Tom's famous final soliloquy (537)—"wherever they's a fight so hungry people can eat. . . . Wherever they's a cop beatin' up a guy"—is an endorsement of the novel's underlying theory, that resistance to oppression can only be undertaken through an individualistic, nomadic activism anchored geographically only by individual incidents of violence and injustice. Inhabitation—in Tom's words, "when our folks eat the stuff they raise an live in the houses they build"—is the end condition of social change, and not a vital site of political and cultural strife. Place is only possible on the other side of the struggle.

Of course, these two novels are not placeless; as an emergent quality of social life, of human interaction, place cannot be destroyed, only transformed. As Delores Hayden points out, what is usually referred to as "place destruction" or placelessness is usually more like a bad place (18). What these novels envision is rather an America in which place is controlled almost completely by dominant interests and paradigms, by Dos Passos's "POWER SUPERPOWER," which expresses itself in domineering corporations and rigid family structures. And that control is never really contested, but taken as a first principle, an underlying assumption, before political and cultural change can begin.

This concession is a curious one for two such combative novels to make, especially since large-scale changes in the geographical shape of American culture and the arrangement of political, financial, and cultural power within that culture structure the content of both of these works. Displacement and movement in these novels is not random but purposeful—even though it is often involuntary or (more so in *U.S.A.*) seemingly unconscious on the part of the character in motion.

The title of *The 42nd Parallel* seems to describe something chaotic, a winter storm; but more specifically it is the movement of those storms, in a predictable direction: east. Similarly, most of the characters in the novel, if not already born in the Northeast, move there eventually, especially if they are one of the characters—Moorhouse, Savage, Stoddard, Hutchins, Janey Williams—who come to take more and more significant roles in the regulation of public discourse through Moorhouse's conservative, influence-peddling advertising firm. As Mac's world of localized public spheres and political struggles—his Uncle's printshop, the Goldfield strike—is dominated, neutralized, he moves to the south and west, until he disappears before the first volume concludes—the only principal character in *The 42nd Parallel* to do so. His kind, and the directions in which they are moving, do not survive into the new era that emerges in the trilogy. The restlessness of *The 42nd Parallel* comes to rest in New York City, which is the dominant setting of *The Big Money* (Pizer, *Naturalism* 40). The action, the cultural and economic power, comes to be centered on that city (much as it is in real life) by way of the First World War and the transportation of many of the novel's principles to France— a pattern of movement connected to national crisis, a symptom of the consolidation of a national culture in the United States. In sum, *U.S.A.* shows how American culture emerges in the period between world wars to have a strong, metropolitan center to its public life, as the energy spent in the internal migrations of *The 42nd Parallel* are channeled through the war effort into a stable, centered structure.

The one character who grows in power, in cultural authority, and, as inevitably happens in *U.S.A.*, in dissipation and cynicism is Margo Dowling—and significantly, she migrates in the opposite direction from the novel's other social climbers. Appearing only in *The Big Money*, the trilogy's novel of geographical consolidation, she begins her narrative in New York City but ends up moving west, stopping finally in Hollywood, the rise of which complements on the West Coast the growing centrality of New York in the East, and presages the emergence of Los Angeles as the United States' second center.

Within this historical development the entire narrative of *The Grapes of Wrath* resides: the resettlement of people and power in American culture that is the modern history of California and the West. The mythological dimensions of the Joads' odyssey is so widely recognized it verges on cliché, but perhaps it is best recognized as a founding myth, a creation myth of California. While *U.S.A.* moves in labyrinthine but inexorable fashion toward New York, *The Grapes of Wrath* is a direct migration to California, augmenting Margo Dowling's story of the rising cultural power of Los Angeles with a narrative of the human costs of California's growing influence, of the establishment of the reserve labor force necessary to the incredible expansion of that region in this century.

This counterpoint—between the migration of the powerful and the forced march of the powerless—is dramatized in miniature in *U.S.A.*'s concluding section, "Vag." Unlike *U.S.A.*'s eponymous opening section, in which the narrative perspective remains firmly rooted in Vag's perception, in "Vag" an intrusive subnarrative creates a counterpoint to the aimless wanderer: "the transcontinental passenger" who, freed from the rigors of the road in favor of cushy air travel, ". . . thinks contracts, profits, vacationtrips, mighty continent between Atlantic and Pacific, power, wires humming dollars, cities jammed, hills empty, the indiantrail leading to the wagonroad, the macadamed pike, the concrete skyway; trains, planes: history the billiondollar speedup" (*The Big Money* 555). This is the grand planning perspective de Certeau describes as that of a "voyeur-god" (93): a vision of a displaced, passive nation that is enforced a few paragraphs earlier at street level, in the railroad bull's coarse words to the Vag: "Git the hell out, scram! Know what's good for you, you'll make yourself scarce" (554).

The passenger's vision of networks and roadways reveals plainly the essential role place plays in the operations of power: it is the grid, the matrix, the source. And motion—described here as the hills emptying into the cities—is what keeps the power flowing. Even if, as a side effect, some resistance (here in the form of the Vag) is encountered, it can be circumvented, rerouted; indeed, the transcontinental passenger passes straight over the head of the Vag, oblivious to his very existence. Though I argued at the beginning of chapter 2 that roads, power grids, and the like are crucial elements of a critical regionalist landscape narrative, here they are used not to connect local sites to broader cultural struggles, but to suggest the ways that the evolution of the modern landscape disconnected people from local concerns and channeled all their energies into a centralized antiregion, an increasingly stable metropolis. It is a vision of something like the opposite of critical regionalism, the RPAA's worst nightmare: instead of a diverse, complex, multicentered landscape, the cultural landscape harnesses all experience in the yoke of a single, monolithic way of life.

Despite the progressive intent of the novels, however, this conclusion is in the end oddly similar to the parochialism of the Agrarians, merely absent their nostalgia. The power of place in negation, in the form of displacement, is absolutely central to the politics of American culture and geography that animates these novels. But displacement is the one social institution that goes largely uncontested in either one.

"This Mighty River of Earth"

This critical regionalist reading of *U.S.A.* and *The Grapes of Wrath* indicates the limits of their vision of social change, limits that do not, in and of themselves, undermine the ethical commitments of these authors and their works. They dramatize, often polemically, not only the injustices and determinisms that arise from the economic, political, and social structures of American culture but also the naturalization of these disparities in personal and familial relationships, in structures of inhabitation and desire. But the critique of these structures in Dos Passos and Steinbeck is founded on a tautology, one that becomes clear if these novels are read alongside a text that frames the experience of place from a different perspective, reading from the local site outward, rather than the literal top-down perspective of the transcontinental passengers and vags of *U.S.A.* and *The Grapes of Wrath*.

A critical regionalism must recognize that representations of place are always partial and perspectival and that a more intellectually valid and complete understanding of place is derived not by surveying the relative accuracy of any one text but by understanding the varied and competing representations that create among themselves a dynamic and evolving mosaic of social construction that composes the larger identity of a place. Alongside these political novels of displacement, we can read a contemporaneous novel addressing structural problems of injustice in dramatizations of economic and cultural struggle that are firmly emplaced, a novel that explores the possibility of devising alternative social structures using a commitment to a specific place as a central resource. A fiction of inhabitation, read alongside fictions of migration, need not countermand or subvert the political vision of its counterparts, but instead can supply a broadened perspective on and range of possible tactics for social invention. *U.S.A.* and *The Grapes of Wrath* contribute to this project by offering a critique of place through negation—a necessary voice in thwarting the nostalgia and sentimentality that is attached to the concept of place. James Still's *River of Earth*, I suggest, augments this negative critique with an unsentimentalized dramatization of the possibilities for a specific place. Just as important for this critique, it is an Appalachian place, in which economic oppression exerts an intense determinism. Nonetheless, a commitment to inhabitation forged out of a working relationship to the land and to other people—not to some mystified, metaphysical "sense" of place—augments the cultural and material resources that people use to counter unjust forces and pressures.

More than the content and perspective of the narrative leads me to place Still's novel alongside Dos Passos and Steinbeck. I have already discussed the importance of Appalachia in the political imagination of both Dos Passos and Steinbeck during the period in which these novels were composed and published. This connection between the two of them also ties them to Still, a native of Alabama, whose literary preoccupation with Appalachia grew out of political interest in and sympathies with the plight of the region in the Coalfield Wars and the Great Depression (Olson 95). Echoing Dos Passos's experiences in Harlan, Still later said, "It was my first sight of people starving in America. In America!" ("August" 136). Unlike Dos Passos, however, Still's response was to become permanently a cultural worker in the region, as librarian at the Hindman Settlement School from 1932 to 1939 (a period coincidentally bracketed by the completion of *U.S.A.* in 1933 and the publication of *The Grapes of Wrath* in 1939), an occasional teacher in universities in the region thereafter, and a writer and farmer in and around Knott County, Kentucky, to the present day. *River of Earth* was completed in a log farmhouse on Troublesome Creek still in Still's possession (Turner 12).

This is not to suggest that the nativity of the author determines whether a specific text offers resources for imagining alternative futures for a specific place; after all, the settlement school movement (as David Whisnant argues in *All That Is Native and Fine*) has a problematic history as a cultural intervention in regional life. However, Still's biography presents a habit of mind reflected in his own social and cultural practices that clearly informs his text. His work as a novelist in some ways parallels his work as a librarian: in both roles he works to provide access for the people of eastern Kentucky to literary discourses that have often been spatially and culturally removed from that region—appropriating literature to the region rather than vice versa. This approach sponsors a social invention of region in *River of Earth*, in which inhabitation can, though by no means always does, present the possibility of appropriation to alternative political uses, and in which place, rather than being conceded a priori to conservative interests and cultural forms, is a vital site of conflict and change.

The title of the book itself is an example of this appropriation and reconfiguration. The fact that the phrase "river of earth" is drawn from Psalm 114 could connote, perhaps, a stereotype of religious conservatism and a general cultural entrenchment. Instead, while it evokes the religious history of Appalachia, the image of the landscape as fluid, mutable, in motion undercuts any idea of this landscape—even the Appalachian mountains themselves—as an immutable haven from change. The southeast Kentucky setting of this novel, in which the family of Brack and

Alpha Baldridge drift from subsistence farm to coal camp and back again in an attempt to eke out their survival, is a dynamic, transforming landscape deeply implicated in the broader operations of American culture. When the title appears in the narrative itself, in the sermon delivered by Brother Sim Mobberly (who "was borned in a ridge-pocket" and "never seed the sun-ball withouten heisting [his] chin" [76]), it is part of a question, which in its very form denotes ambivalence, and his query frames the experience of the landscape, its conflicts and opportunities, in specifically social, not transcendental terms: "Oh, my children, where air we going on this mighty river of earth, a-borning, begetting, and a-dying —the living and the dead riding the waters? Where air it sweeping us? . . ." (76; ellipsis in original).

This formulation, thematically central to the novel and rhetorically addressed directly to the reader, implicates the reader in the crises of the novel. But it also performs a very important function in relation to *The Grapes of Wrath* and *U.S.A.*: it breaks down the tautological relationship of motion and stasis that charges place and inhabitation with a conservative valence. In this context *River of Earth* can stage a critique of many of the same cultural institutions as *The Grapes of Wrath* and *U.S.A.*, but carry out this critique within a specific place. *River of Earth* is not an Agrarian novel; though it is wistful about the effects of industrialization on the yeoman father, it does not look backwards to find models of social organization like the yeoman farm family that have been lost to modernization. Instead *River of Earth* focuses a subtle but consistently withering critique on current conditions. As literary critic Martha Turner argues, the novel takes the position that "a dream of permanence may remain unattainable in an area characterized by motion" (15). Indeed, family structures, duties, and roles are under scrutiny here much as they are in Dos Passos and Steinbeck.

The complicated and ambivalent nature of family ties in this novel is established at the very outset, as "Two of Father's cousins, Harl and Tibb Logan, came with the closing of the mines and did not go away" (3). Unlike the "fambly" (as the Joads put it) of *The Grapes of Wrath*, which, at least until Ma's political transformation, automatically demands loyalty and mutual support, here family takes on an unpleasant resonance, on the first page of the novel—not simply out of selfishness, but because family bonds do not automatically resolve problems of need, and family members are not automatically deserving of aid, even in this firmly emplaced narrative. " 'It's all we can do to keep bread in the children's mouths,' Mother told Father. 'Even if they are your blood kin, we can't feed them much longer' " (3).

In this light the direct equivalencies of family structures and the process of inhabitation, the naturalization of family structures as the terms of enduring emplacement, are no longer tenable as assumptions and are even less so as the chapter ends with a remarkably contradictory incident. Proclaiming that "We've got to tie ourselves up in such a knot nobody else can get in" (9), Alpha sets fire to their own house and moves the immediate family into the smokehouse, a space too small for the cousins, and now Brack's Uncle Samp as well, to continue to live with them. This action comes in direct defiance of Brack who has declared that "My folks eat when we eat . . . and as long as we eat" (8), making it clear that she is rebelling against the patriarchal family structure as well as the presumptuous obligations of kinship structures that deprive women and children in order to satisfy men. But the destruction of the home, this violence on domestic stability, is not carried out in the name or under the auspices of displacement and movement, which in *The Grapes of Wrath* and *U.S.A.* are the conditions that facilitate the kind of awareness Alpha demonstrates in this incident. Rather, Alpha takes her drastic measures in the name of facilitating their continued inhabitation, which demands ridding their household of patriarchal freeloaders.

This opening incident sets up family as a flexible and multivalent social structure, more adaptable and transformable—as well as resistible—than we see it in the other two novels. That we see it through the eyes of a narrator who, early in the novel, reaches his seventh birthday, is itself an underscoring of that fact: the child-narrator is acquiring knowledge of his own roles and of other's expectations, but rather than assuming his place within a fixed hierarchy like that of *The Grapes of Wrath*, we see the child influenced consciously or unconsciously by a variety of figures and models. Not only are there alternatives to his own father, in the shiftless but ultimately gentle Uncle Samp and the ne'er-do-well Uncle Jolly, but the narrator learns the most about his family's history and his own place in it from his maternal grandmother, with whom he spends the central portion of the book, helping her while Uncle Jolly is in prison.

What he learns from her is not a nostalgic reverence for the good old days, however. She tells him of her disappointment in his mother's choice of husbands, of missed opportunities for greater material wealth, and of the kind of agrarian life-style that generates rural nostalgia: "Married a coal digger, a mole-feller, grubbing his bread underground . . . allus I'd wanted her to choose one who lived on the land, growing his own victuals, raising sheep and cattle, beholden to nobody" (130). She tells him of historical conflicts that generate enmity within the mountain communities, of old debts of revenge that, as it turns out, she is secretly repaying.

Grandma's campaign of fence cutting against her neighbor reveals her to be not a passive feminine vessel of ancient wisdom but an active agent within the strife growing out of conflicting interpretations of history and community standards. Her conflicts are not limited clan feuds, either, but are found within her own family as well: she complains bitterly of her neglect at the hands of her remaining family: "Never they come to see their mommy. Old, and thrown away now. No good to fotch and carry for a soul" (130).

The body of wisdom, legend, and lore she confers on the narrator depicts patterns of inhabitation affected by class, gender, age; economic exploitation, poor health care, uneven development; but also work, hope, and collective action. It is a very important point that the narrator receives this knowledge from a woman, and not only that but a maternal relative. The child is moving toward the world of men; by the end of the novel, an anonymous man has told him that he will be a coal miner, insisting on the primacy of environmental and social factors, on place's conservative determinisms: "You can't git above your raising. Born in a camp and cut teeth on a tipple. Hit's like metal agin lodestone. Can't tear loose. Whate'er you're aiming to be, you'll end snagging jackrock" (227). But at this central moment of the boy's awakening to the world (and the physical and narratological center of the novel), he learns about the history of his family and community from a woman's perspective. An important and recurring conflict of the other two sections are Brack's and Alpha's strongly gendered, widely variant, often incompatible priorities and values about place, a conflict that is never fully resolved (Turner 15). But the central section carefully allows a woman's voice to dissect a male-dominated social world.

Grandmother's stories thus cement a view of a locale that is complex and conflicted throughout the novel. Democracy is practiced but problematically; Uncle Jolly lands in jail in part due to the need for the judge to get reelected. " 'I seen Les Honeycutt talking to Judge Mauldin,' Logg [the jailer] said. 'I figger he's trying to get you sent back to [the state prison at] Frankfort. Les's folks can swing nigh every vote on Jones Fork, and the judge knows it' " (162). Schooling occurs sporadically, tied always to the economic health of the community and thus the operation of the mines; but schooling is itself a kind of tyranny that ceases when it runs up against the greater tyranny of patriarchal codes of honor: the schoolmaster is murdered by the father of a student he has beaten (97). Religion, in the form of Brother Sim Mobberly, offers not bromides and escapism but the troubling, not-so-rhetorical questions about the changing landscape offered up in the sermon from which the book takes its title. Like the family structure, the cultural institutions that shape the public life of the community are not monolithic in any respect but deeply implicated in the conflicts that shape individual identities and the character and politics of the community as a collective.

Life for the family is also shaped by interrelationships between its community and the broader culture: not only in the unspoken ways in which uneven industrial development of the southern Appalachians is the field of attitude and reference for the entire novel, but also within the novel itself. Characters are subject to a broader system of law, as Uncle Jolly (as in the quote from Logg) experiences more than once in the book; the availability of work and income depends upon fluctuations of supply and demand far from their own community: " 'They're wanting coal on the big lakes,' Father said. 'It'll be going over the waters to some foreign country land' " (67). In other words, Still's Appalachians are connected to the very same problems that *U.S.A.* tackles on a cosmopolitan scale, and *The Grapes of Wrath* sometimes even on a cosmological (at least meteorological) scale.

Still's novel, then, locates broad cultural conflicts in terms of a specific place, interpreted as a significant site of negotiation and struggle, and argues that, while the terms of inhabitation have changed, it remains a politically viable goal. Formally, however, the book represents much less of a challenge to readers, lacking either Dos Passos's forays into experimental collages and prose poetry or even Steinbeck's intercalary chapters, linking the Joads' personal travails to a broader portrait of a population. *River of Earth*'s at times stilted dialect links it to the most traditional forms of regional fiction under the tutelage of William Dean Howells. Still's relative conventionality as a writer suggests that despite the unconventionality of his political thought, the challenge of developing new representational tactics, new regional landscapes, is an especially troubling one. The emerging pattern among *River of Earth*, *U.S.A.*, and *The Grapes of Wrath* suggests that the schism encountered by MacKaye in the views of both the TVA and the Agrarians persists in the era's literatures of place.

Read together, this cluster of works addresses the challenge of inhabitation in many respects: the unequal relationships that inevitably structure communities at every level under capitalism; the material consequences of that inequality for the less powerful and the powerless; the broad, national, centralized structures that regulate place construction. Dos Passos describes the circulation of power and of the powerless in broad national and transnational terms, with the recurring thread of cultural texts that shape and color individual experiences. Steinbeck focuses the lens on a single displaced subculture, and the transformations that a population with strong historical place connections undergoes when those connections are disrupted. And Still adds to this emerging sketch of the politics of culture a portrait of a subculture tenaciously clinging to place, not for its purity or metaphysics but out of a detailed, site-specific, working relationship to the landscape.

"Tales of the Unrecognized"

As a social invention of region, a kind of curriculum in the politics and power of place, this cluster of texts is necessarily incomplete, as indeed any selection of readings would be. Because of the structures of injustice that characterized the cultural conditions under which these novels were produced, the experiences and perspectives of gays and people of color especially are neglected here. The different gendered experiences of the American landscape appear only secondhand, through the eyes of men. But they provide a basis for an inquiry into these problems of identity, which have emerged in a very deliberate way in much contemporary writing, in the context of careful attention to the historical endurance and transformation of local forms of cultural conflict, and a sense of the history of representations of cultural strife.

Historical perspective on conflict is absolutely central to critical regionalism, not just an awareness of the past but a sense of how its dynamics are intricately connected to the democratic struggles of today, how the languages used to confront oppression continue to shape the public discourse of today. Confronting the limits and liabilities of past visions of social change is an integral part of using cultural texts to imagine alternative futures for the places we inhabit. But as bell hooks writes, "critical interrogation is not the same as dismissal" (*Teaching* 49). In the weak formulation of identity politics, a dismissive, proscriptive subtext emerges: neglect of one particular strand of identity provides a basis for devaluing or dismissing the text in question. But place is multivocal, and no voice, however hopeful, can say all things that need saying at once. In hooks's words, "To have work that promotes one's liberation is such a powerful gift that it does not matter so much if the gift is flawed" (*Teaching* 50). Considering examples from across the spectrum of the representational history of a region in terms of how their definitions of the region compare and contrast, and using their juxtaposition and interaction to expose the strengths and limitations of the resources for change they make available, and addressing them to the specific problems of specific communities, the practice of critical regionalism can create powerful meta-texts, new social inventions.

But if these modernist texts taken together gesture, at least, toward what a more fully critical regionalist literature might be like, they also preserve the split between respect for the rhetorical and political value of local cultures in Still's fiction and the development of a thorough critique of the material relationships among different places in Dos Passos and Steinbeck, that same fissure in regionalism MacKaye attempted to bridge in his comments to the Agrarians in 1931. In other words, while the analysis here has been critically regionalist in its motives and tactics, the novels under consideration are not works of critical regionalist literature themselves—*River of Earth* is an exceptionally perceptive example of a fairly traditional regionalism, whereas *The Grapes of Wrath* and *U.S.A.* are experimental examples of the national epic. If critical regionalism is not just about cultural critique but also about cultural production, then what would a work that responds to the challenges posed by *The Grapes of Wrath*, *U.S.A.*, and *River of Earth* look like? What kind of work engages with national and global politics from a firmly emplaced perspective, engaging in formal experimentation that challenges readers to reconceive their understanding of the structure and dynamics of their own places' relationships to broader patterns of conflict and change, while respecting the political complexity, intellectual validity, and cultural generativity of the local scene? What kind of work can bridge the gaps of regionalism's historical articulations and point to critical forms of regional literary cultural practice?

The purpose, then, is not just to advocate for the inclusion or exclusion of an individual author or work from a literary tradition, but to discern and define representational practices that can reveal ties between historical and contemporary struggles, locating the problems and the discourses of community in a context that confronts these struggles tactically, mediating but also drawing energy from the tension between national and local cultures. For literary production, region can be a rhetorical figure used to engage local conflicts and crises on terms that link them to a broad, structural critique of American culture by reclaiming a too-often politically uncontested category, the geographical margins, as a network of sites of significant and dynamic cultural and political activity. As a literary reclamation project, what is being reclaimed here is not specific texts or authors but a set of tactics for cultural production, as texts are read not to evaluate their contents but to see what approaches in them are useful for the creation of new texts, critical regionalist texts that can build on or redirect the representational histories of places and regions in ways that foreground their implication in larger patterns of historical, political, and cultural conflict and change.

A Critical Regionalist Literature

Anchoring this politicized social invention of region in the daily life of specific communities, on the other hand, might involve attention to cultural texts that have as yet escaped the notice, much less the scrutiny or value, of literary intellectuals, of traditional standards of aesthetics or "taste." Lucy Lippard makes a similar point about the visual arts: "Little attention is paid by anybody . . . to the vernacular artists who have burst out of the usual and sometimes even out of acceptable decorative conventions. A good many vernacular artworks are just figures with no ground which seem to deny their place in place. . . . Self-taught art . . . is an exercise in rehabilitation and restoration, an assertion of existence and of the importance of one community, one place" (192). These community-specific texts, engaged on terms that connect them to broader histories and patterns of representation by investigating their regionality, could invigorate both the public life of communities and regions as well as the prevailing definitions of culture, localizing, multicentering, and democratizing practices of cultural production and reception. For one potential example, we can return to Johnson City, and the work of Jo Carson.

Stories I Ain't Told Nobody Yet by Jo Carson is literally an exercise in vernacular art in the fullness of the paradoxical nature of that term: it presents, in the self-consciously literary format of "found poetry," examples of local, vernacular speech. Perhaps we should not be surprised that a text from such an oxymoronic genre is able so effectively to deal with the seemingly paradoxical challenge of writing about place in ways that create a rich cultural and political landscape narrative by emphasizing not local distinctiveness or exceptionalism but an intricate pattern of relationships among the terrain, built environment, social structures, and cultural practices of a network of places. In *Stories*, Carson addresses the problems of place and movement, of hegemony and resistance, of tradition and change in my home community Johnson City that we have seen in broad (if successively narrower) ways in *U.S.A.*, *The Grapes of Wrath*, and *River of Earth*. Interrogating this work along the same lines as I have handled these earlier novels, the rest of this chapter asks how and what representational tactics this text makes available for inhabitants of this Appalachian city to envision their future as part of the region, the nation, and the world, in new and alternative ways—but in ways that also draw on the representational and rhetorical history of the place and region to which it is committed. *Stories* continues the tradition of vigorous political representation and critique of place found in Still, Dos Passos, and Steinbeck, but attempts to bridge the gap between formal and intellectual innovation and commitment to place that marks the relationship of these works. Carson attempts to demonstrate the transformative potential of commitment to place while deploying the kinds of representational experiments necessary to creating and portraying regional connections.

I mentioned at the beginning of this chapter the book's internally contradictory title. To a degree, Carson is being arch and playful, but the ironies of the title also serve an important purpose, to connect the stories to broader concerns: these are materials that are not normally art, materials that are, to reverse Lucy Lippard's formulation about vernacular art that I quoted earlier, all ground and no figures. These are voices often speaking but rarely heard, telling what de Certeau calls "tales of the unrecognized" (68).

This radical contextualization is acknowledged by the author in a brief preface (xi): "The pieces all come from people. I never sat at my desk and made them up. I heard the heart of each of them somewhere. A grocery store line. A beauty shop. The emergency room. A neighbor across the clothesline to another neighbor." In this sense *Stories* recalls *U.S.A.* in its stubborn insistence on using ordinary language rather than attempting the extraordinary with language; Carson pursues Dos Passos's declaration that "mostly U.S.A. is the speech of the people," but reinvents its scope, changes its orientation from epic sweep—"the people"—to individual people attempting to describe their life worlds. But this is not to say her stories are of strictly parochial interest; indeed, the initial sentences of her preface open the work to multiple emplacements: "What follows are monologues and dialogues collected from east Tennessee and the Appalachian region. They are not exclusive to the region. I made a woman angry once: she swore I got them from east Texas and just said east Tennessee. She was from east Texas."

Though Carson can be evasive about her own priorities here—for example, the inconclusive statement of intent in the preface: "My intent has been to remain true to the speakers' thoughts and rhythms of speech and anything else that can be kept somehow in chosen words"—she is unambiguous about her own position as cultural worker: "I did sit at my desk to reconstruct what I heard, so it was not that I hauled out notebooks on the spot and copied down people's words. The pieces are distillations. Some of these conversations took longer than others. Some took longer to write than others; one or two took years." This act of disclosure is important, because (as we have seen) emplaced works can be vexed by problems of authenticity and agenda. As Carson acknowledges her craft of constructing common speech (and is acknowledged for it: "My aunt introduced me for a while saying, 'Be careful what you say; she writes things down'"), she is simultaneously revealing that her work, while interrogating and reconsidering the status of common, regional speech, and attaching to it a new value, is work, produced by an active, interpretive agent in a specific place and time. In short she acknowledges that this is work, that it is made, has undergone interpretation, and is offered for further interpretation. This note on craft makes the circumstances of the text's creation available to the reader, empowering that reader to work further with the text, to work it into her or his own discourse of community and region and place—as the east Texas woman did, but (perhaps) without the anger.

This disclosure means that Carson's agenda here, and she has one, is not obfuscated by claims to a privileged speaking position or appeals to exceptional cultural authority. Rather, this book is an argument by a stakeholder in a place to her peers, about the values and practices that will facilitate the survival and growth of the community and region as a people through collective action in a context of mutual respect. Appropriately, however, the book is arranged to have the reader first hear the voices and experiences Carson has collected here before suddenly having to confront a shift in the tone and purpose of the text in a section entitled "Observations." The first entry in "Observations" (number 16 overall) is a manifesto, cataloging the aggregation of negative stereotypes about the region: "Mountain people / can't read, / can't write, / don't wear shoes. / don't have teeth, / don't use soap, / and don't talk plain." The catalog continues: child- and dog-beating, dirt farming, poverty, shacks, stills, shotguns, foodstamps, cars on blocks in the yard, and the page concludes with a rhetorical question, but a suasive one: "Right?"

Then, on the next page: "Well, let me tell you: / I am from here, I'm not like that, and I am damn tired of being told that I am." This is a remarkable moment in this book not for aesthetic reasons but for its use of the apparatus. In a work so centered on orality, here the author manipulates the reader through the use of the printed page—a self-conscious acknowledgment of the mediation of this work that thwarts any claim that Carson is trying to evoke some essentialized version of a folk culture or an authentic vernacular to a necessarily conservative effect, the sort of claim that can be lodged against more conventional, dialect-laden varieties of regionalism. Significantly, this tactical use of the apparatus of the book comes in a monologue that is a brash denunciation of stereotypes; the sudden retort to the reader is all the more blunt and confrontational for its concealment; the speaker turns on the reader even as the reader turns the page.

This passage is polemical, but it raises the problem that many of the book's monologues and dialogues address more subtly: that regions and communities are, whatever presumptions are made, more diverse and vital than they are generally presumed to be. The social invention of region that these monologues collectively construct is not a monolithically nostalgic or oppressive place of stable social structures but a complex matrix of voices, practices, experiences that change over time. It is not something that is sensed; Carson seems to share Lippard's conviction that " 'A sense of place' has become not just a cliché but a kind of intellectual property, a way for nonbelongers to belong, momentarily" (33). This book refuses to pretend to provide readers touristic access to that commodified version of place. Instead, as the many strands of place converge and intertwine in the juxtaposition of the monologues, "ownership" of the book's Appalachian east Tennessee is dispersed, as the region is something that is built, witnessed, and attested, as the orality of this text underscores. But it is also something threatened, undermined, contested, challenged; voices of anxiety and uncertainty resonate throughout this book, in voices like that of the scientist, speaking in number 33, who senses his warnings have fallen on deaf ears not with an illiterate or ignorant citizenry but with an oblivious and indifferent group of businesses and industries.

If Carson's version of the region is something socially constructed, and hence contingent, susceptible to change by its constituents, this is despite the powerful, deterministic forces that shape the lives of the speakers—vivid in 31, which proclaims, "Don't talk to me about no options; I'm poor. / . . . I get to choose / between pinto beans or navy beans at the grocery store, / between rats and roaches where I live, / between the used coats at the Salvation Army." The opening entry, an elegy, concludes, "What can be said of Willis / can be said of everybody: / he made it through this world / the best way he knew how" (3), a theme reprised near the book's conclusion, in selection 46: "a person does / what they have to do" (81). But these statements, in the context of the book as a whole, do not translate into automatic approval of the necessary. This book's determinisms are not archetypal, paradigmatic, or metaphysical in any way; rather, they are the endless variations of obstructions and deprivations that grow out of gender difference (number 29's graphic confrontation of domestic violence), racism (number 21 especially), and, probably most importantly, class and, more broadly, unequal economic relations. Money, buying, acquisition, and barter appear in the vast majority of entries. An entire section is dedicated to work.

Another section, significant in light of my analysis of *River of Earth*, *U.S.A.*, and *The Grapes of Wrath*, is given over to "Relationships." That word, broadly conceived, could apply to the entire book, in which human interaction shapes memory, politics, culture, and the lived experience of the landscape. But specifically, family structures, as in *River of Earth*, are places in which negotiation, debate, and outright conflict can structure experience as much as filial piety or patriarchial totalitarianism. Indeed, the final entry is the lament of a neglected elder, echoing *River of Earth*'s Granny as she tells her absent children, "I've got whole lives of stories that belong to you. / I could fill you up with stories, / stories I ain't told nobody yet, / stories with your name, your blood in them. / Ain't nobody gonna hear them if you don't / and you ain't gonna hear them unless you get back home" (93).

There is a surprisingly complex range of definitions of place at work in these almost-final lines of the book. Place is discourse, the story itself, and rhetoric, what the story does. Place is performance, the act of telling the story, and reception, the act of hearing the story. Place, as it is, is past and present, and it is dependent on human intervention to have a future. This fusion creates a kind of discursive region, a broad and textured zone in which knowledge of a specific place is created through its circulation among these various discursive realms. By including in the apparatus of this cultural work mechanisms by which this work can encourage others to adapt Carson's tactics to their own repertoire of representational strategies, the work functions as a social invention designed to facilitate the work of reshaping the understanding of the place in ways that point toward a more democratic culture.

In fact, such a stubbornly hopeful book ends on a cautionary note: "When I am dead it will not matter / how hard you press your ear to the ground" (93). Yet this is an appropriate moment given the book's larger stance. If place is a function of human interactions in a specific landscape, maintaining one's place as a good place, as a place worth living in, demands dedication to doing the critical, dialogic cultural work that a place of possibility requires. Without it, the land itself has no meaning; listening to it without listening to the people who inhabit it is a fruitless gesture.

Which raises a final, important point about this unusual but modest book: that it is not just a text emulating orality, but a text for an oral performance: "I have used these pieces in performance for several years. Doing them always seems to call up other stories. 'You need to meet my cousin, he's got this dog. . . .' It's the thing I love best about them" (xii). This text is intended as a manifestly public and dialogic experience, creating a kind of pedagogical scene in which people are encouraged to create their own representations of place in response to Carson's own. In so doing *Stories* functions as a social invention, with particular emphasis on the sociality. Its partisan attachments to place and descriptions of collective struggles for better places are intended to be presented to groups of people as much as to a lone, silent reader; this is a book about talking intended to inspire discussion. This aspect of the larger cultural work transpiring here endorses the book itself as a purposeful object, its ideas and voices dedicated to a goal, enmeshing the text itself in a broader range of interactions that clearly the book tries to position within a project of social and economic justice and environmental responsibility. Or, as Jo Carson has herself remarked (in a comment that echoes, intentionally or not, Frederic Jameson's formulation that "History is what hurts"), "I write out of what I feel . . . it is important to say out loud, and I holler as loud as this messenger knows how about the things that hurt" ("Good Questions" 75).

In sum, the experience of reading the text leaves you with the question, "what is to be done?" Which is also the question with which I wish to conclude this chapter. I have declared at the outset that my goals here lie outside of the debates about canon formation and reformation, instead insisting that bringing works together in contingent, tactical formations geared toward the problems of particular places can achieve some useful task. I do not want to overstate this point. The material effects of the kinds of injustices described in all of the texts I present here are too severe for me to believe that recommending a good book is the beginning and end of political action.

But I believe that culture is an important part of the life of a society in which to intervene to facilitate material and physical change. Jo Carson says, of "my own country" and our shared home of east Tennessee, that "this is the geography that fits my imagination or that my imagination has been shaped to fit" ("Good Questions" 75). Johnson City, Appalachia, and indeed each reader's or listener's place, Carson argues, are geographies imaginations can shape, given the texts and the tactics that can help people get to that cultural work.

Lippard sums up this project in the visual arts:

> The challenge is to establish more bonds radiating out from the art "community"—to marginalized artists, to participant communities and audiences, allowing the art idea to become, finally, part of the social multicenter rather than an elite enclave, sheltered and hidden from public view or illegibly representing privileged tastes in public view. The ideal should be an accessible core of meaning to which participants are attracted from all sides of art and life. (286)

Jo Carson is one person using the resources she has to pursue this project: among her own writing projects, she travels as a consultant to local performance groups, assisting them with the writing of plays and stories designed to help them mobilize local oral histories within multifaceted dramatic, literary, and documentary projects—in short, helping them devise tactics for local representation, much as she did in *Stories I Ain't Told Nobody Yet*. The site of the literary pedagogy I envision need not be a classroom: how can the project of searching for and circulating these texts be made more public? How, for example, could Carson's representational tactics help people in places like Bumpass Cove (see chapter 2) comprehend and communicate the experience of their community in crisis? Or provide that vernacular language of planning that would sponsor social action for a more just set of regional relationships?

There is only one Jo Carson, and I mean that both as a compliment and as a way of raising one final problem in this chapter. Carson actively works to transmit the means of her art to people in many places, and the tactics for adapting it to their own local circumstances. But as she acknowledges when she recognizes the role owning a house free and clear plays in making her work possible, the option to become a full-time independent cultural worker is not open to very many people. While her work offers many clues as to what a critical regionalist literature might look like and what it might do, her career can hardly be taken as a model for the apparatus to circulate her knowledge.

Moreover, if critical regionalism requires people to take careful stock of their own locatedness within the social, political, and cultural structures of their homes, communities, regions, then its practitioners must do the same. If you are reading this book, you are very likely an academic. Academia as a subculture cherishes a powerful ideology of place, one that divorces "the university" from "the community," sunders "town" and "gown." Academics are often encouraged to think of themselves as in place, perhaps, but not of place—not only by their professional culture but by popular culture as well, where the contrast between "college" and "the real world" is a commonplace. An academic practice that attains to some broader public significance must engage with this problem first and foremost: there is no reason to turn one's back on colleges and universities as places that could play a vital role in the invigoration of local public life and the production of cultural forms that envision regional relationships between local struggles and other spaces and places. But to serve this purpose, colleges and universities must reorient their institutional constructions of space as surely as cultural criticism must change its aesthetic and political conceptualizations, a problem with which I will now engage. If we are to consider how critical regionalism could work to achieve its loftiest goal, teaching people how to reconceive their own local spaces in terms that comprehend their social construction, understand the rhetorical force of social inventions of place, and recognize the possibilities for social action to change them, we must turn to schooling and to questions of a critical regionalist pedagogy.

In January 1999, the *Chronicle of Higher Education*'s "Ms. Mentor" (a kind of academic "Dear Abby" written by Emily Toth, a professor of English at Louisiana State) fielded complaints from junior faculty in a column called "What to Do When You've Been Exiled to the Provinces." One bitter respondent alleges a deterministic relationship between the landscape and its people: "I've taught for four years at a small liberal-arts school where the students are as dreary and flat as the local landscape. I want to quit. Even teaching part time in New York would get me back to civilization." Others also candidly disdain their adopted homes; one writer complains about, of all things, friendly colleagues: "My husband and I, new faculty members at Rural U., have seemingly been adopted as best friends by another faculty couple who seem a bit conservative by our New York standards."

Ms. Mentor characterizes these complaints as "the yearning and moaning" of "latter-day Romantic poets" who "imagine themselves as brilliant flowers, wasting their sweetness on the desert air," but on closer inspection it appears that even as she criticizes them, she accepts the same construction of marginal places as her novitiates. In fragments around the edges of her answers, Ms. Mentor suggests that her correspondents could construct their relationship to their places differently and discern connections rather than obstructions to their work: "Think," she suggests, " 'What can I learn here that's valuable and challenging?' " And she also encourages her advisees to recognize in their provincial places greater political and social complexity than they might suppose—she notes, albeit within parentheses, that "there are more African-American elected officials in Mississippi than in New York." Mostly, though, she summarizes her advice in a quote from Lenny Bruce: " 'Time to grow up and sell out.' " If you want to be in New York City, she tells them, be prepared to adjunct, and otherwise, consider leaving the field, unless you "enthusiastically hie . . . to potato bowls and farm festivals and tractor pulls."

Purely in terms of professional goals, narrowly defined, her advice is no doubt sage and savvy. But, curiously, neither Ms. Mentor (who, the author note indicates, "never leaves her ivory tower") nor her petitioners contemplate the possibility that, as cultural workers in these far-flung yet vitally conflicted areas, these young intellectuals could actually work with local conditions to apply their powerful training to social change. However, doing so would require defying the element of their profession's conventional wisdom that insists on the disconnection between universities and their values and the communities and regions of which they are a part. To think about how to do that, Ms. Mentor's advisees—not to mention the academics who work at institutions like Johnson City's own East Tennessee State University—might look instead to a more recent *Chronicle* piece by Louise Blum, a professor of English at Mansfield University in Mansfield, Pennsylvania, titled "Lesbian, a Mother and Tenured in God's Country."

Blum's autobiographical story of working at a regional university and living in a small town initially, at least, confirms the professional authority of Ms. Mentor's view of regional places as intractable. Blum at first could have been one of Ms. Mentor's correspondents, asserting "I assumed I'd be gone in a year, packing my bags and heading off to a real life, in some other, more civilized part of the country." She also documents the professional lore, that consensus view that urbanity is the only possible mind-set for an intellectual: "A tenured professor advised me in Iowa City as I prepared to leave: 'Just don't let them give you tenure.'" The provincial character of the place even limits her ability to do her intellectual work: "We were five hours from any major city, which on the initial phone call had been suggested as a good thing (as in: only five hours to New York! Philadelphia! Toronto!). . . . There was nothing to do after work but go home and write, and there didn't seem to be much to write about."

Yet, in this stereotypically regional community, seemingly so free from the dynamics of conflict and change that shape more vital places, Blum encounters conflict and change nevertheless, as she confronts, then embraces her lesbianism. Her committed relationship to a local woman, a student at the university (though not a student of Blum's), not only changes her personal and political life but also her sense of the shape and meaning of the local landscape: "She [Blum's lover] introduced me to the area, taking me beneath the surface impressions. A chain of hills called the Endless Mountains circled our town, hiding the sun from our view, seeding our sky with clouds, and giving our town a strange dark beauty." What Blum has discovered is that the deterministic relationship between place and people that caused the writer to Ms. Mentor to complain that "the students are as flat and dreary as the local landscape" works more than one way. When one finds motive and opportunity to understand the particular shapes that change takes in a specific landscape, from sexual politics to qualities of light, people and places that once seemed fatally featureless become textured, multifaceted, complex—worthy of intellectual inquiry and involvement.

However, Blum recognizes that uncritical celebration of a place—enthusiastically hie-ing to tractor pulls and so forth—is not the only alternative to fatalistic dismissal. While she gains a new appreciation of this place in its own right, she also actively engages in changing those aspects of it that limit social and cultural possibilities and veil the political dynamics of the community. Through her institutional work in pedagogy, she promotes these changes in curriculum development, in changing the culture of the institution, and in her own work as a writer. She participates in the development of a women's studies minor and designs the university's first course in gay and lesbian literature. She expands the kinds of writing she asks for from her students and pays a new kind of attention to the writing that they do, gaining new insights into their local circumstances and how she might usefully engage with that experience to get more insightful, incisive work from them. She shares her own writing with her students, inviting them into her own composing processes and giving them new prominence in the content of her writing. Working outside the curriculum itself, she sponsors the formation of a gay and lesbian student group. Through all these activities she not only comes to know herself better, but she begins to realize that part of what made the place seem so flat and featureless to her was that her cosmopolitan, academic understanding of regional relationships could not account for the way her students experienced the landscape, "how rural the hometowns of these kids could be, [how] Mansfield, with its stoplight and its brand new Wal-Mart, could take on a nearly cosmopolitan air."

And slowly but surely, Blum's campus and community began to change as well—but not into some progressive or cosmopolitan utopia. Even as she begins to sense new beauty and complexity in the local landscape, she encounters new kinds and degrees of conflict as well. When Blum becomes pregnant, she also becomes the target of a hate-flier campaign. She complains to her institution's president to no avail, but having worked to develop political, cultural, and social connections in her community, she is able to find the resources to see different possibilities for her place. For example, despite her new and potentially dangerous visibility, she supports a lesbian student's determination to perform her poetry at an open mike night. As her student receives a standing ovation, Blum describes her feeling of emplacedness in a landscape metaphor: "I felt like a tree in the middle of a forest, surrounded by my community." Blum's encounter with cultural and political conflict in her community, seen through the lens of her more nuanced understanding of her place, makes her feel more deeply connected to a landscape she once loathed, rather than more alienated.

Though Blum would not be likely to use this term, I call what she has done critical regionalism. She has rejected a received definition of an exurban place that describes it as cut off from broader patterns of historical, cultural, and political conflict and change. In its place she has forged a version of the place that discerns, in whatever unlikely or obscure(d) forms, the particular shapes that cultural conflict can take, seeing the place and its people as implicated in important struggles. And she has engaged with those conflicts, not only through activist organizing, but through the creative use of specifically local materials to construct the mechanisms to encourage others to recognize and adopt the representational tactics for understanding their local scene in terms of its interconnection to, rather than disconnection from, larger cultural and political landscapes.

That she did so at, through, and despite the university is particularly significant, given that dominant values in academic culture—the same ones we see in Ms. Mentor and her advisees—led her to a dismissive stance toward her surroundings in the first place. In each chapter, I have begun by considering the cultural, political, and intellectual obstacles to the practice of critical regionalism as a necessary step toward envisioning its possibilities. There is one considerable challenge that remains to be addressed here, however. A critic of place must, I assert, include in that critique not simply an awareness but a deliberate recognition of his or her own locatedness—not just in terms of identity but in terms of the material and cultural landscape and the regional interconnections in which the writer is enmeshed. As I, and practically all of my readership, are academics, this study must include some consideration of how colleges and universities shape the particular relationships of academics to their local and regional places.

While institutions of higher learning are, like almost all places, variegated and diverse spaces with complicated relationships to their surroundings, they are also (as both Ms. Mentor and Louise Blum make clear) strongly influenced by cultural values and practices that, like so many of the landscapes, films, and texts examined in this study, insist on disconnections between local spaces and broader historical patterns of conflict and change. While academics are encouraged to see their surrounding communities, especially if they are exurban spaces, as isolated, unproductive sites, they are at the same time encouraged to see themselves as disconnected not only from the particular places in which they are located but from the concept of place altogether. Instead of being a part of any given place, we instead see ourselves (and are seen by others) as part of a placeless free flow of ideas. How can we begin to strongly assert the interconnectedness of any place, much less create critical regions, if we deny the vital implication of our own most immediate surroundings, the campus landscapes in which we think, write, and teach?

The question is not rhetorical, in the vernacular sense of the word, and the stakes in answering that question are the very effectiveness of the practice of critical regionalism as both cultural critique and cultural production. In this chapter, then, I examine the social constructions that enforce a view of colleges and universities as separate from the problems and priorities of local communities. These constructions must be confronted in order to understand how the cultural practices of academic life—not only research and writing but hiring, labor, and social structures and procedures as well—can be more meaningfully attuned to the project of describing the regional forces that intersect in local spaces. Critical regionalism must challenge the entrenched hierarchies of academic life that reward those who become increasingly distant from local populations—from "regional" institutions that serve local populations, for example, but also within institutions, from teaching introductory courses that bring academics into contact with broader cross sections of the population than graduate seminars. To transform a critique of the social constructions of place that inhere in the institutional culture into a set of principles for cultural production requires envisioning the representational practices that could make academic work more effective as social action. But this project also demands considering how the university itself could be a social invention, making critical regionalist representational tactics available for people to describe and depict their local spaces in terms of their implication in broader patterns of conflict and change.

This chapter, therefore, uses a critique of some of the theories of and assumptions about place implicit in academic literacies, in order to begin to describe the guiding principles and challenges for a critical regionalist pedagogy in higher education. The focus on pedagogy rather than method is deliberate; what I discuss here are theoretical considerations to undergird decisions about what to teach and how to teach it, not specific techniques for doing so. This chapter is not about what to do on Monday morning, but what to think about on Saturday and Sunday. It would be paradoxical, at least, to offer a prepackaged set of tips or tricks for critical regionalist teaching, since the details of any such project must be determined in a generative relationship to the local landscape and the particular admixture of broader forces that converge there. Instead, I draw on my own experiences and my particular location as an academic with training in English and professional experience as a writer and teacher in the humanities, drawing together examples from the migration from institution to institution that has been a necessary part of my career, as it has for most academics, and centering my pedagogy on the teaching of writing.

College writing instruction is not just an example tied to my own biography but, I assert, a particularly important site for a critical regionalist pedagogy. Not only is first-year writing typically a universal requirement, and therefore an opportunity to shape the representational practices of a broad cross section of an institution's students; it is also a course whose content is intended to apply across disciplines. But first-year writing is also, like the regional sites I have examined throughout this study, often conceived of and depicted as a space marginal to the real work of cultural production, a mere "service" course detached from the vital, dynamic, and conflicted work of other, more powerful parts of university hierarchies. In this chapter, then, I think about how the reclamation of the seemingly inert spaces of the geographical margin can be carried out via the reclamation of the seemingly inert spaces of writing, how the first-year writing classroom can be a social invention that helps students understand and argue for their places in intellectually richer and politically and culturally more generative ways. Perhaps, too, we can come to understand the "provinces" of our professional terrain as spaces in which we can (as Blum's example suggests) come to learn something useful about the places we academics inhabit. A new understanding of the university landscape as a part of broader regional relationships can be an integral step toward working collaboratively with others, to better envision and represent regional landscapes in fuller complexity, and thus become not desert flowers but an integral and vital part of larger landscapes.

Getting Local, Going Public

Near the end of his life, critical teacher and theorist Paulo Freire addressed the problem that "education takes place in a given space, to which, customarily, little or no attention is paid"; this heedlessness, he argues, neglects the crucial fact that "care for space reveals a willingness to fight for it and an understanding of its importance. It also reveals that a conscious body refuses and resists fatalist indifference, the idea that nothing can be done" (*Letters* 123).

If space is a resource for struggle and for hope, why, then, do intellectuals give so little attention to it? Freire attributes this indifference to a syndrome he calls " 'mental bureaucratism' about the task to be accomplished in the space" (*Letters* 123), a compartmentalization of intellectual work from its material contexts, the ability to separate the mind from the body, or at least to dramatize this separation in the disjunction between one's scholarship and one's institution, community, and region. When academic intellectuals disconnect their scholarship from the place it occurs, we literally alienate (in the more literal sense of being put off one's land) our ideas, our writings, and, to the extent that our personalities and personas are invested in our literate practices, ourselves.

An awareness of place in political and cultural critique, on the other hand, claims local ground, the immediate surroundings, as the starting point for change, moving from reflection to action by making the local a site of vigorous cultural struggle. As Freire writes, "[T]he university [must] have its original context as the starting point of action. Or, in other words, the university must speak its context in order to be able to unspeak it. . . . The university that is foreign to its context does not speak it, does not pronounce it. It speaks a distant context, alien, thus it cannot unspeak one or the other" (*Letters* 133). Yet in the United States, the university is almost always populated by people from somewhere else, who often look somewhere else not only for their research interests but also for their values, intellectual stimulation, and emotional satisfaction. University life and its values, broadly conceived, are oriented toward and dedicated to a cosmopolitan ideal, even (perhaps especially) when the university in question is physically and culturally far from the urban centers (recall Blum's lament about being "only" five hours from the nearest urban centers). But that allegiance is one of those facts of academic life that is both omnipresent and largely unspoken.

For practitioners of cultural studies and progressive critique—not just critical regionalism, but especially critical regionalism—to make good on vows that "its practice does matter, that its own intellectual work is supposed to—can—make a difference" (Nelson et al. 6), we must engage with the distinctive shapes conflicts take as they play out in specific sites on particular landscapes. In this call for a recentering, a multicentering of critical scholarship, I am, I hope, augmenting calls for increased public relevance and public accountability for academic work, and thus pursuing the goal proposed for cultural studies scholarship by cultural critic Lawrence Grossberg when he calls for "a different model of intellectual politics": "a more flexible, more pragmatic, more modest, and more contextual model of the political function of the intellectual, connecting to, constructing, and reconstructing its conjunctural constituency" (8). Peter Mortensen issues a similar call specifically to his fellow literacy researchers but adds cautionary terms that have implications for critical regionalism as well:

[O]ne finds repeated again and again the assertion that our work—our teaching, researching, and theorizing—can clarify and even improve the prospects of literacy in democratic culture. If we really believe this, then we must acknowledge our obligation to air that work in the most expansive, inclusive forums possible. . . . in failing to do so, we consign ourselves to mere spectatorship in national, regional—and, most importantly, local—struggles over what counts as literacy and who should have opportunities to attain it. ("Going" 183)

Mortensen urges that we reflect on the situatedness of academic cultural work, its overlap with other political, cultural, and material social relations—the role it can and cannot play as a social invention shaping social construction of the relationship between local problems and priorities and broader patterns of historical, political, and cultural conflict and change. But the rhetorical tactics for enacting academic discourse as a social invention would not involve mere simplification, "making intellectually dishonest concessions to audiences not attuned to nuanced argumentation" (Mortensen, "Going" 195). Instead, locating critique in site-specific conflicts in order to reveal the larger forces that converge there demands a confrontation with a new set of complications and problematics: "[W]ith conditions here [in Kentucky, where Mortensen worked] and elsewhere even more complicated than I have described them, it is going to be difficult for any academic figure to cultivate *local* ground in order to address a *local* audience" (194; emphasis in original).

How might greater local applicability and public participation increase the effectiveness of colleges and universities as social inventions, facilitating social action by arguing for a richly interconnected, socially constructed model of region? How could universities and colleges in regional places, institutions like East Tennessee State, help people achieve the kind of nuanced understanding of their daily experience that Jo Carson encourages in her writing and cultural work, and be the kind of far-reaching apparatus for distribution of these representational practices that Carson lacks? How could the university supply the same kind of resources for cultural production that it offered the people of Bumpass Cove in the form of scientific and medical advice? How could East Tennessee State help its students better understand the historical contradictions of the landscape that surrounds them, or better respond to the theories of place and region in global media culture? By making connections between our progressive, political, theoretical knowledge and specific instances of cultural struggle at particular sites on the landscape, in short, by giving greater attention not only in scholarly research and cultural critique but in institutional culture and pedagogy to matters of place, we might begin to find an answer to those questions.

Without attention to place, academic intellectuals are not connecting to, much less reconstructing, our "conjunctural constituencies." To reconceive colleges and universities as critical regionalist social inventions is to pursue cultural critic Henry Giroux's call for a more public academy, "vital to the moral life of the nation and open to working people and communities that are often viewed as marginal to such institutions" (Giroux, quoted in Mortensen, "Going" 195). But Mortensen issues a very important caveat, which is at the heart of the issues I wish to speak to: "If . . . teacher-researchers are to stand as public intellectuals, they may indeed wish to speak to the vitality of literacy for the 'moral life of the nation,' but they must also speak to the ethical concerns of the local—the community, the commonwealth, the region. Else they risk making generalizations that may be as attractive and forceful as they are baseless and misleading" (195). Mortensen's telescoping definition of "local"—connecting community to commonwealth to region—is a critical regionalist one: an integrative, relational, dynamic approach. That Mortensen specifically addresses *composition* teacher-researchers is, however, a useful tactic. The composition course is often the only course all students are required to take; too, it is often among the first courses students encounter. This placement within academic institutions means that composition not only reaches a broad cross section of future college graduates, but also those students who for whatever reasons never complete college degrees. The composition classroom, and, more generally, the core curriculum, has often been characterized as a "contact zone" between the university and broader publics (Pratt, Miller), but I would like to call particular attention here to composition's status as one of the most public sites within higher learning, in order to tactically rethink its vexed (and often vexing), traditional status as the "gateway" to academic literacies.

By understanding how their institutional existence is continuous with, not disconnected from, the communities beyond their campuses, academic intellectuals can construct a landscape upon which they can act in their capacities as citizens of these communities to address localized social problems and cultural conflicts, in order to connect local struggles to broader cultural, historical, and geographical patterns of strife. This critical regionalist project demands a reconception of scholarship in terms that embrace a broad spectrum of academic literate practices, teaching and service as well as research writing, and requires revaluing these activities to recognize the ways they have an impact on the problems and priorities of local communities as well as more cosmopolitan, disciplinary debates. This work must be preceded by reflection upon the ways in which the geographical margins, the "provinces" where most academics live and work—an inhabitation that must be thought of as more than mere "exile"—are vital and conflicted points on the cultural landscape. Their connections to other places are multiple: political, economic, and social; material and discursive. A critical regionalism can serve as a rhetoric to identify and act upon these interconnections.

Soldiers of the Revolution

Too often, however, academic life is informed by the kind of denigrating assumptions that local cultural practices, rooted in and definitive of specific landscapes outside of the metropolitan cultural centers, serve only reactionary conservative ends. Too often "regional" (as in "a regional university in the South") is used in place of "backwards" or "second-rate" or "dull." As I have suggested in the other chapters of this book, confronting these kinds of stratifying, disconnecting assumptions is a necessary, preliminary movement for critical regionalism. Jane Smiley's *Moo* (1995), a novel of life at an anonymous land-grant state university somewhere in the American Midwest, is a work that both confronts and, to some extent, reflects the fact that we operate too often on the principle that local knowledges and literacies are by nature incompatible with academic intellectual practice, suggesting that Louise Blum's advisers and Ms. Mentor's advisees are not anomalies.

Indeed, the novel's very title evokes the vexed relationship between the university, its faculty, and the surrounding community and region that is emphasized throughout the work. Her fictional "Moo U.," the generic midwestern "cow college," is populated by academics "exiled to the provinces," living in fear of the ways their location far from the urban cultural centers of the coasts are dulling their professional ambitions, their political commitments, their intellectual acuity. Cecelia Sanchez in Romance Languages confronts her disconnection from her ethnic heritage; literature professor Margaret Bell feels her theoretical approaches to race drifting involuntarily toward conservatism; creative writer Timothy Monahan begins to sense the price of his detachment from the New York literary elite.

The narrative is fueled by the irony, however, that, despite the myopia of the faculty, the campus and the lands beyond are embroiled in political conflicts and crises with far-reaching interconnections and implications, inextricably binding their academic literacies to local public discourse. Lionel Gift, a prestigious economics professor, files a consulting report for a vast multinational corporation that rationalizes and recommends the ecological rape of Costa Rica, and his plan reverberates through the public and private lives of the university community. The chain reactions and counteractions his scheme sets off embroil the campus in controversy, feeding the already acrimonious office politics, awakening some almost dormant radical tendencies among some of the faculty, and posing material threats to the grants and travel funds of others by poisoning the university's relationship with the megacorporation and its ally, the statehouse.

Smiley carefully highlights the rhetorical and discursive practices of university life, and their interconnections to other literate forms, as she successfully adapts and combines tactics from Steinbeck and Dos Passos, building interchapters out of memoranda, minutes, and reports; newspaper clippings and columns; and even, in a pivotal moment in the novel, a Costa Rican news report documenting the final collapse of the Gift scheme, written completely in Spanish. This tactic dramatizes in the novel's form the specific yet often ephemeral connections that link the local to the national and global in patterns that are rightly viewed as regional. It also demands of the reader a recognition of and flexibility with the multiple forms and languages of representational practices that impact the circulation and meaning of academic discourses. But Smiley gives attention to the languages the university cannot or will not master as well.

Beyond the faculty's and administration's intramural sparring is a community landscape marked by political struggles that also shape the university's material and cultural life, in unacknowledged but substantial ways. Loren Stroop, a local farmer, develops a paranoid but not ungrounded theory of the power of agribusiness as he perfects a mysterious machine, constantly wary of the agents of "the FBI, the CIA, and the big ag businesses, all of whom, he knew, wanted to get him out of the way before he perfected and marketed his invention, which was going to revolutionize American agriculture" (84). Stroop's introductory chapter is tellingly entitled "A Soldier of the Revolution"; his political intervention comes at the level of the land itself, which he hopes to radically reshape. Stroop is drawn into the story by way of his touchingly naive belief in the historical mission of the land grant school, "his university, founded under the Morrill Act to help him" (86), to advance society by making applied knowledge available to the public, to open the work of the disciplines for the improvement of the community.

The university, however, in the person of the extension dean, Nils Harstad, alternately ignores and condescends to Loren Stroop until the farmer is felled by a stroke, literally robbing him of the voice he already could not make heard in academia. And Stroop's writings, in the form of a set of plans for his machine, prove equally incomprehensible to the university. Stroop is acutely aware of the formal incompatibility of his cultural practices with the technical and specialized languages of agronomy: "[T]he plans, so carefully put together, were drawn wrong. Nils Harstad not only wouldn't understand them, he would be repelled by them, since they were stained here and there, soiled here and there, continued here and there on the back of the sheet" (106). But when he dies, Stroop's plans wend their way through a maze of coincidences and into the possession of the university. And when they are finally translated, the farmer's text rescues the university from the financial pinch precipitated by the political fallout from Gift's foiled scheme. But in selling Stroop's visionary machine, the university also realizes Stroop's worst nightmare: his invention falls squarely into the hands of his dread adversary, the big ag companies, who, it proves, exercise far more influence over the actions of the university than any sense of its historical, democratizing mission. Thus the translation of local literacies into academic practice, which the university proves to have the critical tools to carry out, fails in the end to serve the resistant and transformative ends envisioned by Stroop. Instead it is rechanneled into narrowly conceived institutional goals that serve only to entrench capitalist hegemony with the university's support and approval—and to the university's profound economic benefit.

This subplot is the most sustained development of a perception that the university is adversarial to and subversive of local community life that circulates through the novel. It is cafeteria worker Marly Hellmich, however, who really puts her finger on the problem. Marly is a part of the population who reach the "gateway" to academic literacy only to be turned away. When her freshman comp teacher writes on the board that "Critical thinking is to liberal education as faith is to religion," Marly, who comes from a fundamentalist household, decides that "the wiser course" is "to cast her lot with faith and forget about liberal education . . . she felt much better for it, while at the same time noting the irony that her unskilled labor was worth more to the university than it was to any of the other employers in town" (24). In this one intellectual stroke (which, ironically, displays something of the critical thinking her instructor assumes she lacks), she recognizes a number of things: first, that academic literacies are, in the view of the academics who teach them, wholly incompatible with her local ways of knowing; second, that the only way to resolve this conflict is renunciation of one form or another—hybridization or integration of literacies is not being offered as a possibility. And third, this academic decision, however one decides to resolve it, takes place in a network of social and economic relationships that bind the university to community life regardless of its differences in intellectual practices.

However, Marly's understanding of the university's relationship to the community should for all academics be most disturbing, implying as it does that academic literacies, far from having a transformative power, are an isolated and ultimately unimportant set of practices that can be cheerfully ignored. Marly's father sees the university as simply an inconvenient spot on the local map, a quizzical spot on the local landscape, "a set of one way streets in the middle of town that sometimes were confusing, and always snarled traffic." But watching the flow of the academy through her line in the Union, she comes to realize that the relationship between the town and gown is not even antagonistic, just indifferent: "[S]he didn't see the people she had served over the years as participants in a secular humanist conspiracy. . . . The secular humanists and critical thinkers didn't really offend her, maybe not as much as they should have. It was easier, once you were among them, to accept and even enjoy their flow" (27).

Moo leaves one to wonder whether the university has the resilience or the resources to respond to this crisis of irrelevance. The novel's most overtly political figure, the horticulture department's Chairman X, does focus on the local landscape as his field of intervention. But by novel's end he has not only been deposed as chair of his department, but also married, ending his and his partner's attempt to maintain an alternative family structure. The wedding is an ambivalent element of the novel's theme, but it is also an ironic element of the novel's form. The last chapter, titled "Some Weddings," provides the book with an intentionally classical comic form, narrating a period of disorder and reversal brought to a close by the uniting of men and women in natural, domestic harmony.

Is Smiley duplicating, in a way, the political problematics of her novel as she overlays a classically structured plot onto this vernacular landscape? Her allegiances to sophisticated, canonical forms enact an assertion of an academic literacy over a broader community. What would a narrative form generated by interaction with the public discourse of a specific, local community look like? (More like the work of Jo Carson?) The question is not even entertained here, as Smiley chooses instead to contain the local culture in an academicized (if not historically academic) discursive form.

This decision, like the ones made by the characters in the novel that blind them to localized representational tactics and the political conflicts these practices give shape to, is part of a pattern of disconnections that opens the university to the attacks of populist demagogues. When academics fail even to attempt to address the fact that theirs is one among multiple literacies that shape public life, and fail to work to provide access to academic literacies for people of varied types and histories of literate practices, the public stature of academic literacy is diminished. As public, political work, cultural criticism has as often as not posted a record of resounding failure: pleas for tolerance and respect in public discourse are ridiculed as "political correctness," the Ebonics debacle wins national derision for the proposition that children be taught standard English in the context of their home languages, and, more recently, the conservative assault on providing broad public access to higher education successfully ends open admissions in the CUNY system, the very site where this experiment in democratic higher education began. An insular, devalued academy loses the opportunity to apply or integrate the knowledge it produces, because it is vulnerable to attack by whatever interests seek to defend the status quo.

An Academic Literacy Crisis

For Paulo Friere, "the importance of pedagogical space" is "the first basic principle of education" for Freire (*Letters* 127), yet academics seem so much to have their eyes always cast elsewhere, their voices not speaking or unspeaking their contexts but speaking of distant matters in languages that locally are not intelligible and seldom even audible. But this too is a kind of regional relationship—or perhaps an antiregional relationship, a syndrome that frustrates comprehension and thwarts formation of broader spatial, discursive connections.

So it appeared at East Tennessee State when, in the winter and spring of 1992 (where I was in my first teaching job at the time), the local "old boy network" conspired to install its own homegrown candidate into the presidency of ETSU, generating several weeks of popular outcry from both faculty and local residents. A state representative, a city councilman, and an assortment of business leaders backed the presidential candidacy of Jack Campbell, the president of Walters State Community College in nearby Morristown, Tennessee, an ETSU graduate and a Johnson City hometown boy. When Campbell was eliminated in early rounds of the university's national search, Campbell's supporters both turned to the community, to exert the influence of public opinion on the search process, and began proceedings in the Tennessee legislature not only to force Campbell's name onto the list of finalists, but also to reshape the board of regents' selection and approval process to allow a more direct role for the governor and his political appointees. In effect, the traditional academic procedures for evaluating credentials would become an optional part of an overtly political process (S. Watson 1; Houk, "Campbell" 6).

This blatant attempt to bring the university under the control of local cronyism relied on a public campaign designed to increase perceptions of an academy divided from its home community, an attack on the academy based on a roughshod critique of place. Lynn Lawson, the Republican state senator sponsoring the selection-process overhaul legislation, laid the blame for the controversy on "academic elitism" and alleged that "campus politics are far worse than any played in the state Legislature" (Houk, "Threat" 3). State representative Zane Whitson, sponsor of the bill to force Campbell on the nominee slate, more bluntly replied to expressions of anxiety by faculty and administration about such matters as the impact of the controversy on national accreditation, saying their concerns were "just a bunch of baloney . . . incorrect and misleading" (Houk, "Threat" 3). Whitson further played a populist strategy by portraying academics as people who "want to choose their own boss" (Weston 1)—clearly hoping to rally the working classes against the university's relatively democratic workplace culture.

The trump card for stirring up local indignation, however, was to emphasize Campbell's down-home pedigree. Local business leader C. B. Kinch asserted that a hillbilly was necessary to lead hillbillies (quoted in Granger), and another local luminary, John A. Jones, contended that Campbell "walks the walk and talks the talk" of his upper east Tennessee home (quoted in Logan). Campbell's supporters' localist rhetoric revealed an understanding of cultural conflict to which the university seemed by comparison almost completely oblivious. The Campbell coalition recognized a disjuncture between the literate practices of academic life, specifically, in this case, the reading and writing of individual qualifications and institutional values in a job search. Why wouldn't you want someone who knows the locality to run such an important local institution? How could these professors place loyalty to abstractions like "fresh perspectives" and the authority of "outsider" institutions like accreditation boards and the AAUP over "one of our own?" The clear implication was that academics must not be "our own" either; they must represent a colony from somewhere else, speaking its own language exclusively to itself. By focusing on one aspect of academic literate practices that, out of context and beyond academia, seems counterintuitive, these reactionaries were able to intensify a line of difference within the broader public discourse of the community, the traditional slippage between the duties and desires of town and gown, and make it appear to be an outright fissure.

On the other hand, this crisis also presented an opportunity to members of the faculty, the professional community of ETSU—a teachable moment. And, as one might hope, given their advanced training in writing and rational persuasion, some members of the university community took their case directly to the community at large. Unfortunately, the rhetoric of faculty replies sometimes served mostly to reaffirm the argument that Johnson City's academics inhabited a separate world. Notable, for example, is the rhetorical maneuver of the signatures of certain faculty letters to the editor, which included not only the name and the institutional affiliation but also some assertion of credentials: "David G. Logan, Professor of Art;" "George L. Granger, Ph.D." These faculty replies to local opponents were not so much a defense of academic literacies as an assertion of their incompatibility with local rhetorics, as when David Logan asserts that Campbell's ability to talk the local talk (a tellingly literate turn of phrase) "indicates a weakness of Campbell's candidacy. Perhaps Mr. Jones sees in Dr. Campbell someone with whom he can be comfortable. But in higher education we don't need to be comforted. We need to be challenged." Logan's vaguely contemptuous attitude, communicated in his refusal to even contemplate that local anxieties might have some significant basis, receives a clearer expression in Granger's letter. Granger describes Campbell as "Morristown's Principal for grades 13 and 14"—a remark that quite precisely echoes Freire's claim that "it is unfair and blind for a university to serve only the elite of its context, to offer it excellence, while doing nothing to improve the standards of basic education. . . . Yet, almost always, the university avoids its role by stating that a university is not a high school" (*Letters* 133).

By contrast, while English professor Anne LeCroy (a frequent local letter writer on matters of university-community relations) makes her institutional loyalties clear in the body of her letter, in her signature, "Anne LeCroy, Johnson City," she asserts her membership in the broader community as the basis for her response. And her letter suggests that the university is not isolated and insular, but a vital and accessible cultural site within the community, when she writes that "some of the legislators —and commentators—[should have] come to campus (incognito, if need be) over the past months. I believe they would have seen classes meeting, the library actively helping students and faculty with their research, labs functioning efficiently and the business of the University going its daily round." This rhetorical tactic suggests that not only could community members not formally affiliated with the university come there and feel welcome, even blend in with the crowd, but also that the activities of the university are recognizable and comprehensible, a "daily round" analogous to lives beyond the campus boundaries.

But LeCroy's tactics are the exception to the rule, and even her thoughtful missive ends by blaming "external agitators" for the controversy—reinscribing the insider-outsider dynamic her adversaries exploited to set off the whole dispute. The focus of the academic critique of Campbell and his backers consistently rested on the would-be president's shortcomings within academic formations of quality and value, his lack of scholarly publications and classroom teaching experience. But the academic writers made little, if any, attempt to translate these academic literacies of evaluation and credentialing into a public language, to teach the practice of academia dialogically to practitioners of different forms of representation and interpretation. It's worth noting that the University Archive from which I retrieved these letters did not preserve those written by local people not formally affiliated with the university.

None of the academics bothered to explain why, in academia, nativity is not part of the definition of value, or to teach the community the values academia attaches to migrancy in the production of knowledge. Not surprisingly, no one even contemplated challenging the academy's own hierarchies and practices by asking whether it is right for academics to consider local skills not only not a virtue but, in many cases (as David Logan suggests), a liability outright. No one stopped to consider for a moment that there might be some substance, however slight, or distorted by its use by the old boy network, to the critique of academic literacy circulating in public discourse. As composition and rhetoric scholar John Trimbur has argued, crises about literacy are not simply shams or frauds; though they may be expressed in terms that are unreflective, unverifiable, ahistorical, counterfactual, prejudicial, or ill-conceived, literacy crises manifest serious and deeply held social anxieties that demand serious ethical address, and they have material implications and consequences. They are, Trimbur writes, "attempts to resolve in imaginary ways actual tensions, anxieties, and contradictions" ("Literacy" 281).

What many of ETSU's academic intellectuals (many of the letter writers, at least) failed to realize, then, was that their community was in a kind of academic literacy crisis. The local politicos and "old boys" certainly precipitated, in a meddling and maleficent way, the crisis that entangled and derailed the presidential search. But without the existing tension, the popular perception of a disjunction, between the university and community, they could not have done so. And, as if to confirm the local imaginary, many academics failed on this occasion to either speak or unspeak their university's context, to answer the anxious questions about the pedagogy of academic practices that the crisis brought to light. Why does the academy consider migration so central to the production of knowledge that, through the structure of its job search procedures, it insists almost unfailingly on the essential virtue of uprooting individuals, so that faculties are seldom ever composed of people who have enduring historical and political commitments to the specific places they inhabit? And certainly no one paused (in any public way) to consider that the crisis had a bright side: that the university and its ways of knowing were suddenly at the center of public debate. What opportunities for involving broader publics in academic literacies were missed on this occasion? Were lost by deploying rhetorical strategies that retained the sense of the university, even one as geographically specific as East Tennessee State, as a place apart?

Of Cows, Colleges, and Commuters

However much the culture of academia studiously ignores the fact, local cultures interpenetrate the campus in ways that leave visible, material traces. In East Tennessee State's gallery and museum, a quaintly neoclassical, that is, generically academic building named after a Republican senator, if you walk down into the basement you find a log cabin and a small and now itself antique display (it has remained largely unchanged since I was a child) of pioneer tools, weapons, and crafts, a very standard roster: a Conestoga wagon, a massive loom, a moonshine still, a plow, a crosscut saw, and so forth. For me, this room encapsulates some of the perhaps less flattering aspects of university culture's posture toward other aspects of local culture: its proprietary claims, its occlusion and neglect of the dynamics of regional life. Here the local landscape, including the university's 600 acres of former East Tennessee farmland, is oddly revised to become the exotic. Yet one might also derive a slightly different interpretation: that here in the symbolic heart of the university's dedication to high culture (as represented in the art galleries above), local culture has a persistent, visible presence, underpinning the more cosmopolitan cultural performances upstairs.

This moment on the landscape of the campus both underscores and undercuts the illusory autonomy of academic literacies in the discourse of the community. And it is only the tip of the iceberg, just one contradiction in the university's role in a community landscape already conflicted in its identity as an "Appalachian city." ETSU is an institution built on former cow pastures in 1911 as the State Normal School, its early land-

Construction of Gilbreath Hall, East Tennessee State University, circa 1911. From University Photographic Archives, courtesy of Archives and Special Collections, East Tennessee State University, Johnson City.

scape literalizing the idea of the "cow college," as the Georgian architecture of Gilbreath Hall overlooked a muddy cattle wade. The institution literally grew out of the evolving, once-agrarian landscape of the region, thoroughly enmeshed in its histories and futures, while simultaneously part of the broader and itself highly contradictory project of the establishment of normal schools and the extension of educational access nationwide (F. Williams).

The landscape of the university and its surroundings encodes these historical contradictions in ways that likely sustain local controversies about the university—but could animate and engage with them. Even its earliest layout represents a visual reinforcement of the university's urban loyalties. Despite being constructed on farmland literally on the edge of town, straddling Johnson City's western corporation line, and despite being dedicated to producing teachers for the state's rural schools, all the university's earliest buildings were built facing resolutely toward the city. Likewise, in the University Archives, there are no surviving photos depicting the university from the farmlands to the west; the vocabulary for representing the university visually is defined by the perspective of the town. However, the university did, at that time, have a high degree of physical continuity with the town that played host to it. A panoramic photograph of the campus at its opening in 1911 depicts the way the university landscape linked wooded hillsides with the former pastures

Critical Regionalism and the University

State Normal School's first cohort of students, 1912. Note streetcar arriving at Gilbreath Hall in background. From University Photographic Archives, courtesy of Archives and Special Collections, East Tennessee State University, Johnson City.

with the foundry—one of the young city's most important and earliest industries (Lee 50)—and beyond it the mixed-income neighborhoods of the town itself. The institution was physically as well as intellectually a meeting place of a wide range of local cultures, the conjunction of a variety of landscapes.

It is significant, then, that industry, agriculture, and residential neighborhoods have all withdrawn from the vicinity of the university campus in the intervening years. Throughout the 1940s the university acquired the farmland adjoining the campus to the west, beyond the town; Mary Lyle, the last resident of that land, relinquished her property in 1961. Campus development became a significant local industry in itself, as the university accounted for 40 percent of the city's major construction projects from 1947 to 1963 (Lee 262). Industry and residential neighbors endured somewhat longer, but the 1970s saw the construction of University Parkway, a wide thoroughfare that severed the campus from the middle-class residential neighborhoods to the east, and during the 1980s the construction of State of Franklin Road insulated the campus from the industries to the north and, to the northwest, obliterated one of the city's oldest working-class neighborhoods, the Y-section (so-called for its location in the fork of the railroad tracks). The foundry was a pivotal institution in the history of industry in the community, the site where iron ore mined in places like Bumpass Cove around the turn of the twentieth century was refined into steel, a business once hailed as transforming Johnson City into "the Pittsburgh of the South." It (along with the oil

Critical Regionalism and the University

company next door to it) has become a student parking lot. Now five-lane arterials block pedestrian approaches to the campus from the two sides, the north and east, that face most of Johnson City. The evolving landscape of the borders of town and gown dramatizes the split between the campus and community that the reactionary pols exploited so deftly.

However, these new roads also have a somewhat different implication, one reflected in the concurrent growth of parking lots in and around the campus—a particularly vivid difference between the 1915 campus layouts and the physical plant of today. While the traditional, conservative landscape aesthetic dictates that the imposition of concrete upon grassy lawns may be distressing, to say the least, the need for roads and parking lots leading to campus also suggests a growing role for the university not just in the city but across the region—a growing need for access. These roads do not represent an ideal form for that access to take—this landscape demands inquiry, for example, into why the area's streetcar system, which ran literally to the front door of the first academic building, Gilbreath Hall, no longer exists. But here at least the environmental costs of American car culture have the return of enhancing both the university's institutional mission of providing higher education for the region and enhancing the ability of regional people to come to the campus. Whatever its mixed messages, the physical space of the campus, seen in terms of its relationship to the community and the region, reveals a culturally complex and conflicted site, a place that, carefully assessed, could shed new light on the connections among segments and interests in this community.

One of the most important things that conflicts like the Jack Campbell affair obscures is the myriad ways ETSU, its students, faculty, and administration, have long engaged with those connections. Recall that in chapter 2, it was environmental health specialists from ETSU who helped Bumpass Cove citizens bolster their public arguments about their toxic waste crisis. Today, that tradition has not only continued but expanded, as initiatives across the university and its medical school focus on issues of regional public health and medical care. In the humanities, ETSU's faculty have long represented an important stakeholder in the development of Appalachian Studies, and the university not only offers regional studies courses across the curriculum but is home the Center for Appalachian Studies and Services. The center has for more than two decades served as an important interface between the campus and its region, making its mission both supporting the work of academic researchers and making this work available to a larger public. Ironically, the campus characterized by political power brokers as hopelessly cut off from its surroundings is also the institutional home of the production of the

Encyclopedia of Appalachia, a 1,800-page reference work dedicated to consolidating a body of scholarly knowledge about the region in a form accessible to and useful for school children and university academics alike.

This intellectual and physical landscape's liminality, its mediation between city and country, between high and low cultures, academic and vernacular landscapes, affords a point of entry into a variety of cultural conflicts. It provokes consideration, for example, of how the origin of many regional universities as institutions centered on undergraduate teaching, and more specifically the teaching of teachers, contribute to and intensify the "cow college" stereotype. The history of regional universities —and more generally of the "state universities" (as opposed to the "universities of . . .")—is linked inextricably to the history of teaching teachers in America, which has from the outset been a deeply conflicted and contradictory enterprise. As historian of education Jurgen Herbst documents, normal schools, which became teachers colleges, which in turn became (usually regional) state colleges and universities, represented a rare opportunity for access to advanced education for rural, working-class, and female students in America. As such they formed an indispensable part of the project of public education. Supporters of the Normal School movement in the 1830s such as the Boston-based American Institute of Instruction hoped that "state-supported normal schools would usher in a new age in which the school would find its place at the center of society's concerns" (Herbst 60).

Even this aspect of the public university's mission is problematic, however; the extension of opportunity it offered was motivated as much by the desire of early nineteenth-century Whigs to indoctrinate and assimilate the lower classes, rather than to empower them, to quell dissent rather than to invigorate public life, and to create a filtering mechanism whereby exceptional and elite students could take their place atop a quiescent social structure (Herbst 13–21, 54–56). As Herbst observes, "A philosophy of common schooling could and did go hand in hand with a conservative social philosophy" (55). In this sense the normal school movement was born of an older variety of the same kind of contradiction Allen Witt sees in the origins of junior and community colleges: "Populists wanted to provide access to higher education for the masses, whereas elitists hoped to purify higher education by providing separate institutions for the teaching of lower-division students" (quoted in Lewiecki-Wilson and Sommers 444). Perhaps if he saw the mission of his own institution as an earlier historical iteration of the same kind of socializing mission as the community college movement, ETSU's David Logan would have been less quick in his rebuke of "Morristown's Grades 13 and 14."

But at the same time, from their earliest days the faculty and administrations of the normal schools and their descendants have complained about the quality of their students, have attempted to reject their institutional mission of democratizing education, and have looked to distant, elite universities for models of their mission rather than to the communities they were conceived and dedicated to serve. Herbst notes that before the normal school movement expanded beyond its places of origin in Massachusetts, its earliest teachers would complain that their students were "not an impressive lot" (83), and "would strive to imitate their colleagues in the colleges. . . . The desire to become like academy and college teachers . . . would come to be a constant theme of normal school instructors" (63).

This deflection of enthusiasm and ambition away from the place-centered aspects of the historical mission of the normal school movement is cunningly self-perpetuating—inducing the neglect of local conditions that sustains neglect of local conditions. Institutions like ETSU would be better equipped to fend off populist sedition of the kind I have documented here if the academy in the United States were not shaped by a de-contextualized, monolithic system of professional priorities and rewards. As Richard Ohmann (among others) has long maintained, the supposedly free exercise of critical inquiry, the practice of academic literacies, occurs within social processes of standards and evaluation that reproduce structures of class and restrict "free collaborative exercise" (23–25).

My point here is to undermine the idea of "academic exceptionalism," that our work is somehow exempted from the physical, material relationships that structure other work and workers, an illusion encouraged by the inattention to place that university culture encourages. When oriented too exclusively toward the abstract, disciplinary institutional structures of the academy, academic intellectuals, in their myopia about the materiality of their intellectual activities, can fail to seize the opportunities for cultural work that are made available by the contradictions and conflicts that animate the existence of home communities like Johnson City, and can thus find themselves the objects rather than the agents of the ongoing processes of social change that surround them. Local conflicts, the kind that are encoded in the landscape of sites like East Tennessee State, can animate and energize academic literacy by posing constant challenges to academic practice, and by opening to scrutiny the existing relationships and continuities between academy and community.

These conflicts engulf not only the landscape of the campus itself but engage other sites in the community as well, reflecting the articulation of local and academic cultures and literacies. The neighborhood where I grew up, an enclave of faculty all hired during the baby-boom expansion of ETSU in the mid-sixties, was known locally by the nickname of Scholar Holler—a hybridized turn of phrase that locates academic work and workers in the local landscape whether they will or no. (The subdivision is more formally known by the name Seminole Woods, and all its streets are named for native tribes of Alabama, Georgia, and Florida—like most of the residents, the street names were brought in from elsewhere.) But most significantly, hiding in plain sight, the student body of this predominantly commuter campus brings local cultures and localized literacies flowing onto the campus every single day.

Place, Institution, Discipline

Perhaps this last fact in particular produces the defensive, insular reactions of many academics in this setting to local lifeways. Within university reward structures, this kind of local constituency is not usually a badge of pride—note, for example, the tradition of celebrating in admissions brochures the geographical distribution of the student body. ETSU, for example, celebrates its geographical diversity on its Web site even as it identifies its primary constituency as Appalachian: "While ETSU's more than 11,000 students include individuals from over 65 countries, the majority of our student population comes from Northeast Tennessee, Southwest Virginia, and Western North Carolina, the heart of the Appalachian region" ("Our Students"). Assertions in this context that a university is a place apart are an assertion of status in professional peerages, an attempt to identify up, to the high end of the Carnegie classifications, and although that typology is not supposed to be a hierarchy, everyone in the profession knows which end that is.

The late Ernest Boyer's special report for the Carnegie Foundation for the Advancement of Teaching, *Scholarship Reconsidered*, marshals a range of statistics that have documented the grip of a single set of standards of excellence, centered primarily on publication, that blankets academe without reference to the specific institution or even the type of institution. I will only briefly note here that the problem is not recent: as long ago as 1958—just as the baby boom generation prepared to swell the enrollments and the faculties of regional universities nationwide—surveys of young faculty found that most felt they were evaluated on the basis of research while their primary job duties involved teaching (11).

But this syndrome has also been accelerating: in 1989, 43 percent of faculty at teaching-centered regional comprehensive universities (a category distinct, in the Carnegie classifications, from doctoral-granting and research universities in its primary mission of undergraduate instruction) answered "Strongly Agree" to the statement "In my department it is difficult for a person to achieve tenure if he or she does not publish." In 1969, only 6 percent voiced strong agreement (12). Boyer notes that this narrowing of "the standards used to measure academic prestige" comes at a time when the baby boom and the GI Bill, among other factors, were moving the nation toward a mass rather than an elite system of higher education: "[A]t the very time America's higher education institutions were becoming more open and inclusive, the culture of the professoriate was becoming more hierarchical and restrictive" (12–13).

My call for reevaluating the priorities of academic cultural practices is familiar to scholars of composition studies, who have long demanded a reassessment of the values assigned to different kinds of work within the English discipline and have attempted to reclaim the devalued sites and practices of our departmental lives, especially those centered on teaching, and specifically teaching writing. As Boyer's statistics suggest, the problem of institutional hierarchies duplicates many of the structures of value and of power that professionally marginalize composition classrooms and, more broadly, teaching as a professional activity—the two problems exacerbate each other. Prestige declines institutionally at the same rate as teaching increases as part of the average faculty member's normal workload, just as professional prestige and material support declines the closer one gets to teaching local populations in institutional classrooms.

Composition studies has been one of the few areas of research to take issue with the exploitation of the part-time and non-tenure-track faculty who teach these introductory courses—and who, significantly, are not hired through the displacing national job search system but generally from local pools of labor. Thus the part-timer's ties to the community, her local status, is part and parcel of her preterit status in the academic community. Often, this lack of a place in academic life is material, not metaphorical, manifested in a lack of office space, a parking permit, full access to libraries, gyms, and other facilities; these indignities come on top of being denied "a place at the table" in department business, even when it pertains to the writing programs that could not meet their obligations without their part-time staff. (With a total of six years of adjunct teaching experience at four different institutions, I write from experience.) A project of reclaiming the value of local literacies and local perspectives must also, then, be linked to reappraising and better compensating the work of adjuncts, whose "dual citizenship" could be perceived not as a weakness but as a special qualification for work in the contact zone between academy and community. As it stands, however, these especially public academic workers, providers of the broadest public access to academic literacy, have their lack of institutional and disciplinary value communicated to them in the daily life of departments—especially on payday.

Of course, regional campuses tend to rely substantially on adjunct labor because they have so many introductory courses to staff, courses tenure-line faculty are sometimes reluctant to teach, so the labor problems of departments become part of the larger syndrome of institutional hierarchies. Too many adjuncts, too much access, reflects badly on a school. When our profession tends to devalue institutions whose mission is specifically and historically defined in terms of increasing access to academic literacies, not only in its own confines but by training others to encourage access to academic literacies, it is time for a serious reappraisal of our attitudes about access. When the production of knowledge becomes a complete insider's game, then it is academics, not the hillbilly locals, who are being parochial. Why do so many progressive intellectuals endorse academic Reaganomics—a trickle-down intellectual economy?

However, Boyer's call for academics to confront the fact that "campus priorities frequently are more imitative than distinctive" and ask "how . . . each of the nation's colleges and universities [can] define, with clarity, its own special purposes" (2) is belied by his reaffirmation of the Carnegie classifications. He clearly intends these categories to emphasize the difference between institutional missions, but it inescapably becomes a peerage, because it remains an abstract, institutional frame of reference, with no attention to or reflection upon the specific material circumstances of the campuses that fall into its typology.

Boyer attempts to recast systems like the Carnegie classifications, which have had the historical function of ranking and classifying institutions in relation to each other, as a means for celebrating the diversity of institutional missions—a cause that seems incomplete in its reformative rather than transformative approach, and naive in its reliance on the abandonment of professional self-interest on the part of faculty and administrators. Instead, the argument Cynthia Lewiecki-Wilson and Jeff Sommers make for the professionally marginal space of open-admissions writing instruction needs to be made more generally for institutions on the professional verge: that they be seen "not as a low-level site merely for the application of knowledge, but as an intellectually productive and transformative site of disciplinary practice" (459). Unlike Boyer, whose interests lie almost completely in the institutional realm, Lewiecki-Wilson and Sommers emphasize the friction between academics' institutional role as teachers and their disciplinary priorities as writers and researchers. A transformative project must intervene on the landscapes of specific campuses and their communities, at the sites where these two parallel, often competing aspects of professional practice conjoin.

In other words, in theory, we can separate teaching and research, institution and discipline, but in the classroom, in the physical space in which we practice academic literacies, these distinctions are not so distinct. Even if the relationship is not convivial, even when, for example, we resent the time teaching demands as a distraction from research and writing, different aspects of professional practice overlap and influence one another. The classroom is the space where this struggle to define and develop academic practice takes place in front of a public audience. And the writing classroom, in particular, is where the process of defining and transmitting academic literacies is intentionally foregrounded, where the teacher's ongoing process of definition initiates similar struggles in new populations. Letters to the editor, while important, seem almost paltry as a means of intervention in local public discourses when compared to the opportunity to shape and expand the literate practices of a substantial cross section of the population. But viewing the problem of place as one of professional practice, either as an internal adjustment in institutional values to be carried out by faculty and administrators or as a disciplinary matter to be resolved by researchers and scholars in journals and professional meetings, only reinscribes the very boundaries this line of inquiry is attempting to problematize and undermine. This transformation must be carried out by students and teachers who, working collaboratively, learn new methods for using academic literacies to interrogate the problems and priorities of their own communities, who can bring the connective, integrative, critical skills that academic literacies comprise to energize the local public discourses in which they are involved, and situate those places in broader patterns of historical, cultural, and material struggle.

The teacher who engages students on this basis, with these goals, must then necessarily learn from the students about local conflicts and local forms of knowledge and culture—in short, must acquire from students local literacies in order to pursue this project. The writing classroom, that primary site of interface between academic communities and local populations, is thus transformed into a vital site of literate practice for all involved. Composition, as Susan Miller has argued, can appropriate its disciplinary liminality as a resource for cultural intervention; how much more so might this be possible when that liminal space is poised on the edge of a campus that is itself the edge of the larger structure of academia —if, that is, academic intellectuals are willing and able to reclaim the supposedly tranquil or inert places of the geographical and cultural margins as vital sites of intervention, and the too-often burdensome practice of teaching as a powerful medium for that project?

I am not, by any means, suggesting that universities engage in some kind of populist acclamation, uncritically celebrating the local at the expense of broader concerns, or abandoning intellectual rigor and expansive scholarly investigation in favor of devoting themselves purely to raising basic community literacy. As Freire writes in response to similar objections:

> No progressive educator should ever reduce the democratization of the university to simplifying the treatment of knowledge. . . . Rather the distance between the university (or what is done in it) and the popular classes should be shortened without losing rigor and seriousness, without neglecting the duty of teaching and researching. In order for that to happen, the university must, if it hasn't yet, increasingly become a creation of [its] city and expand its influence over the whole city. (*Letters* 133)

The educator should, as she enlists students through the transmission of advanced, academic literacies to the project of a critical, regionalist examination of the places they inhabit and participate in, also be enlisted to the project of critiquing her own places, learning to transform and recreate universities as creations of and agents of democratic recreation for their communities and regions.

Critical regionalist pedagogies can more fully integrate these issues with the history of the specific communities and institutions, can more deliberately choose specific conflicts and create texts that stage more purposeful, tactical interventions. Critical regionalist writing should not only enhance the landscape for the benefit of its current and future students but also challenge academic practice to have a transformative impact on local social structures and greater relevance to local struggles for justice and care.

Bull City and Beyond

Although I have focused in this chapter on a regional comprehensive university, I do not mean to suggest or imply that the task of forging regional connections between campuses and broader landscapes is a project specifically intended for such institutions. Indeed, it may be equally important to pursue this pedagogical project at institutions that have even less of a sense of mission to their surroundings because their students come from elsewhere, or universities that, by virtue of their status as "research" institutions, have even stronger allegiances to a geographically decontextualized model of the circulation of knowledge.

Much of this manuscript has been revised at a desk in an office at Duke University, in the somewhat faded tobacco and textile-mill city of Durham, North Carolina, in the heart of the Carolina Piedmont where industry flourished in the late nineteenth and early twentieth centuries. A highly selective research university, Duke draws both students and faculty from across the globe and occupies an enviable position in the peerage of higher education in the United States. Not coincidentally, I think, students (and to some extent faculty) strongly subscribe to an ideology about the city and their institution's role in it that casts the university as an island of culture and knowledge surrounded by the alternately dull and scary postindustrial ruins of town. The landscape of campus affirms to students their separate, exclusive status (and the preterit nature of the "townies") and encourages increasing myopia toward the community: entering first-year students live on a campus surrounded by a low wall, which symbolically, if not practically, discourages movement into the former mill town neighborhoods adjacent to them. The vestiges of the former company town of West Durham, once owned by Benjamin Duke, lingers on the campus borders as a kind of shadow campus: like Duke, a centrally planned landscape designed to inculcate personal propriety and social control but, unlike Duke, designed to create workers, not leaders. No one was supposed to graduate from the mill town. But after their first year, Duke students migrate toward the gothic core of the university's West Campus, surrounded by an Olmsted Brothers–designed berm of woods and gardens that transform the urban surroundings into pastoral ones.

As this manuscript goes to press, Durham finds itself embroiled in one of the most serious challenges to town-and-gown relationships in its history, as members of the varsity lacrosse team face sexual assault and kidnapping charges after a rowdy party in an off-campus house known by neighborhood residents as a trouble spot. The victim was a student from the historically black North Carolina Central University and single mother, who was working as a stripper. She claims three men raped and sodomized her in a bathroom after she abruptly ended her performance, fearing the crowd was turning violent and losing control. Suddenly, Duke's town-and-gown relations have become the object of international scrutiny, and the incident has been widely characterized as a "perfect

1920s aerial photograph of Trinity College, now the East Campus of Duke University, Durham, N.C. The photo looks north; Trinity Park, a neighborhood developed by the Duke family, is visible to the east; a Duke Tobacco factory is partially visible to the south. Courtesy of Duke University Archives.

storm," the convergence of historical forces of race, class, gender, and sexuality touching down in the Carolina Piedmont like a tornado. The case is unfolding literally as I write this, with two Duke students indicted by a grand jury and arrested, and both prosecution and defense using the media exposure to advance their theories: "Sex, Lies, and Duke," shouts the cover of the *Newsweek* (1 May 2006) in my mailbox; with new developments in the story emerging every day, it would be premature for me to offer any assertions about the case at this time. But one thing is clear: the vexed history of the cultural and political fissures between the university and its surroundings, the manifest differences between the campus and the "real world," have never appeared more stark.

I argue, however, that it is every bit as important in a milieu such as this to encourage students (not to mention colleagues) to see their surroundings as intricately interwoven with the history, politics, and culture of local and regional landscapes, by helping them recognize the ways their own cultural practices can often work to obscure those connections. The first-year writing course I designed and taught in the spring semesters of 2003 and 2004 in response to this particular local situation, "Bull

City and Beyond," asked students to practice critical regionalism (though I do not necessarily describe it to them as such) to challenge social constructions in the local landscape and in student lore. They studied that barrier wall, how it shapes their perceptions of more ephemeral, discursive relationships between town and gown. They collected student lore about the town, a project we called the "Durham Stories," in which students gave their peers a prompt, asking them simply to "briefly relate in writing a story about Durham: the city itself, the people who live there, its government, landscape, institutions, etc." and to give their authorization for the anonymous reproduction of their work. Quoted material from student responses is included exactly as the author wrote it, unless otherwise noted, and the complete texts of the Durham Stories cited here (by year and number) are included in the appendix.

Analyzing the narratives, we paid careful attention to the attitudes about local and regional cultures that discourage or obscure perceptions of the city of Durham and the Carolina Piedmont as a space of vital cultural production, conflict, and change. And in following up the study of the Durham Stories with research into local and regional history, they searched for connections between the history of their university, its setting, and the broader region, and they identified points of commonality, interaction, even antagonism that bind the institution and the larger place in a shared set of problems and priorities, contact and consequences. In other words, I asked my students to do with their own folklore what I have done elsewhere in this volume: to begin the search for lines of interconnection, articulation, and affiliation between local sites of cultural conflict and broader social, historical, and political landscapes in the very practices of representation that most strongly insist on disconnection and isolation.

As the Durham Stories suggest, and as you might expect, the contrasts between the Duke campus and its surroundings are sharp. As one student melodramatically writes, "While Duke is the epitome of order and structure; impressive and imposing and looming under Gothic architecture, Durham wildly flails about itself, unsure and despondent" (2004 #47). Duke's landscape of prestige and upward mobility is juxtaposed with an urban landscape marked by the processes of contemporary deindustrialization and all of that syndrome's symptomatic social problems and conflicts, and the students know this, writing frequently of the empty or readapted industrial buildings near campus.

Encounters with panhandlers form a genre of Durham Stories in themselves. I find it emblematic of the larger sociopolitical and cultural trend the stories represent, not to mention more than a little disturbing, that despite daily interactions with university staff and faculty, local shop-keepers, and campus neighbors, all of whom are Durham residents, it is the panhandler (many of whom, we might assume, are transients) who is so often presented as Durham's representative citizen. These racially charged tales inspire both fear and a degree of self-examination, as in this eighteen-year-old female student's contribution:

> Six of us hurried across the fields by East Campus in the direction of 9th Street. The late September weather encouraged jackets at night, none of which us girls were wearing because they would cover our carefully picked outfits. A laughing and loud group, we passed by Whole Foods and the Cycle Shop with purses and boys in tow. Our group had become incohesive and we were walking and chatting in twos staggered down the block. I was walking with Mark and we could see our friends ahead stop to speak to a dark figure in the unlit parking area across from Cosmic. As I approached I could see he was a middle-aged black man in worn clothes arguing with two of my friends. He just wanted a little money for food. I have encountered many situations similar to this in New York and Washington and have always walked by without acknowledgement. This is not because I believe they will take my money and buy drugs or alcohol. I simply feel that there are places where people can go to seek help and that by handing them money it is only prolonging there willingness to remain pan-handlers. This particular gentleman was not leaving us alone and we were all beginning to get uncomfortable. The guys we were with told us to keep walking. They said they would handle it. Although I didn't think anything would happen, it still made me nervous to leave them with this man in an unlit area. Halfway down Main Street they caught up with us. Mark said they had given him a couple dollars so that he would leave them alone. Everyone had been in a party mood and it was hard to just shake it off and go dance it up knowing that this man was still on the street begging for money. Less than a block from East Campus—full of students pursuing an excellent education, many from wealthy families and comfortable homes—was a man with nothing. I have so much more than this man, yet I did not want to help him. Is it the job of people more fortunate than others to hand out dollar charity? Or is it that man's responsibility to take care of himself and pursue a life off the street? On that September evening, I had decided that is was not my responsibility. (2004 #56)

Finding themselves in the midst of these complexities, burdened with a lurking sense that they bear more than just a positional relationship to these broader social problems, Duke students have responded by creating and circulating a powerful landscape metaphor about their campus. They call it "the Bubble," and it is a term no doubt familiar to many of my readers; it seems to be a popular way of describing the pastoral refuge of a stereotypical college campus in many places, another trope that works to exempt the academy from the local scene. At Duke, however, the Bubble has an especially hermetic, even defensive, quality. Students warn each other and are warned by campus security during first-year orientation not to leave the Bubble. The result is a peculiar, patchwork cognitive map of the area, highly detailed on campus and in the vicinity of student-friendly sites, such as expensive restaurants, bars, shopping malls, and the airport, but a menacing void in most of the areas adjacent to campus. As one student observed, "Beyond the university lie so many unknowns lurking, ready to pounce on you if you let your guard down all but a minute" (2004 #3).

The unintelligibility of the city's landscape contrasts with the university's hyper-legibility, a landscape in which every building is named and, indeed, virtually every tree, flowerbed, and park bench features a name and a date explaining who donated that item when. Another subgenre of the Durham Stories, by contrast, features tales of getting lost in the city, facing dangers (real or imagined) before successfully returning to the Bubble:

> One of the first things I learned when I came to Duke was that it really wasnt the best idea to bring a car to school. The roads in the area are confusing as hell and the neighborhoods around Duke have uncomfortably high crime rates. This combination led to an interesting experience of mine.
>
> It was only about 3 weeks into fall semester when three guys and myself went out to buy beer for a party. As was the norm for the first few weeks, I was lost almost immediately. Soon we were no where close to anything that seemed familiar or the least bit comforting. After about 20 minutes of driving around aimlessly in the ghettos somewhere around east campus we decided to bag it and ask for directions. So we went into some food mart at a gas station and bought the beer (which was ridiculously expensive: $15 for an 18 of nattie [Natural Light] . . . thats a *expletive* crime if you ask me).
>
> When we asked the clerk for directions, there was no response. We asked again, slowly, and still nothing. The worker was either mute or lacking the ability to speak english. . . . vive la difference. So anyways, we hopped back in the car for more aimless driving, but there was one

problem: my car's alternator was (messed) up and the car began to die. I was like, "well this is great guys, we are all going to be robbed, beaten, and murdered." In the end, my car was able to suck it up and we made it back to East Campus—a true diamond in the rough. (2003 #31)

The dividing line between the knowable and the unknown is the three-foot-high wall that surrounds East Campus, where first-year students reside. "Duke and Durham seem like two separate entities. Duke is its own town in its self. The stone walls that encircle East Campus seem to echo the separation of city and university in a physical sense," a student writes (2004 #55). While clearly, given its dimensions, it is of little practical efficacy as a defensive emplacement, it marks for students a point of transition from safety to danger, from comfort to anxiety. "You notice after only a few weeks that a four foot wall separates old money from no money. It's a really sad, ironic, juxtaposition" (2004 #5), says one student; another, more critically, notes that "thousands of 18 year olds, sold on the virtues of education and career advancement, arrive at Duke and immediately recoil in aversion to the world around. It is a clash of cultures. From the beginning they are warned of the dangers which lurk just north of the East Campus wall" (2003 #43). Indeed, a legend still circulates on campus claiming that the wall is in fact ten feet tall, by order of the bequest of Washington Duke, but college officials had seven of its feet buried beneath the ground for aesthetic reasons. Though the facts of this story are all wrong, that students want to believe that the wall is three times as tall as it appears is significant in its own right (Wharton 330).

Studying the wall itself, however, my students have discerned that in practice it has multiple meanings. An edge of this sort, demarking two distinct districts, can be a border, but it can also be a seam, joining districts together. The wall divides town from gown, but it also provides a sort of liminal space where the two meet. A series of openings in the wall, for example, provide townspeople access to a jogging trail within the wall, popular with pushers of baby strollers and walkers of dogs. But the wall also provides a space where less convivial town-and-gown relations are laid bare—by the network of emergency phones which line the jogging trail, or the security details that were parked at each passage through the wall after a series of robberies on campus in the fall of 2003.

In any event, the social space of the wall is marked by reminders of the multiple, variable relationships between the campus and its host city. The history of Durham and of Duke's role in the community belies the Bubble's mythology of disconnection, and a study of the history of Durham, the Carolina Piedmont, and the South supplies students with powerful tools to interrogate these dominant discourses. Given that Duke has become such a major economic and political force in the community—the university and its medical centers are the county's largest employer and economic engine—it is perhaps not surprising that the history of the institution and the town have been closely intertwined.

Indeed, the neighborhood immediately to the west of the campus where first-year students live was developed by the Duke family in conjunction with the construction of the campus in 1892. To the east, Benjamin Duke, the Duke family's major advocate for support of the college and university, built Erwin Mill, a textile factory with a large mill town, which opened the same year, 1893, as the Durham campus of Trinity College, which would become Duke University in 1928 (J. Anderson 212). I asked students to reflect on the fact that the same family coordinated the simultaneous construction of two master-planned, themed landscapes, both designed to provide all the material and social structures for their inhabitants and, in so doing, create a particular kind of person—one producing members of the working class, and the other, members of the ruling class. As an added irony, 9th Street, formerly the mill worker's shopping district, is now generally considered by Duke students a de facto part of the Bubble, as it now is home to university-oriented restaurants, cafés, bars, and bookstores. This shift in use reflects the larger change in Durham's economic and cultural politics from an industrial to a service economy that bespeaks the formative role of the university in the life and landscape of the city.

Even more remarkable is the role the university's benefactors, the Duke family, had in the creation of the idea of the Carolina Piedmont as a region. As historian Allan Tullos documents in *Habits of Industry* (parts of which we read in the course), Duke Power, the hydroelectric concern that James B. Duke built from the proceeds of the family's tobacco empire, was the major force behind an advertising campaign in the 1920s (alongside the establishment of Duke University) promoting "the Piedmont Carolinas." Duke's publicity machine trumpeted the region as a source of "willing labor, unhampered by artificial limitations on output [read: unionization]; native born of old pioneer stock and not imbued by un-American ideas" (170). It was this labor force, composed of tenant farmers desperate for more than a subsistence existence, that created the fortune underwriting the Duke Endowment, setting into motion the changes that Duke students experience in the landscape today but can seldom name or describe. In creating Duke University, James B. Duke, as Tullos writes, "incorporated and absorbed the lives of thousands of anonymous Carolina Piedmont workers in Duke tobacco factories and textile mills and along the path of Duke power lines. From the mastery of the streams and rivers of the region's natural world to the education of preachers in Duke University's divinity school, Buck Duke sought his immortality through the transformation of the Carolina Piedmont" (166). From this perspective, the place and the region to which Duke students so often feel no connection whatsoever is intricately tied up with the history of the university not only in its material relationships but in the cultural politics of place formation itself.

If students come to see that the relationship between their education and their surroundings is complex and multimodal, through a range of conceptual resources and objects of study, from stone walls to archival documents, then they must design the kind of texts that can account for this variegation. Students were challenged in this course to design and produce multimodal essays, changing fonts and formatting, and moving between text and illustration, to grapple with visual evidence, historical and architectural scholarship, primary source research in the University Archives, and of course the folklore of the Durham Stories. Student writers rearranged the features of their texts, and the way their parts relate to each other, even as they rewrote their understanding of the places they inhabit and the way their parts relate to broader spaces. More is at stake here than just typographically reflecting the variety of media through which the process of place occurs. If, as John Trimbur argues in "Delivering the Message," the homogeneity and visual poverty of traditional academic writing design attempts to deny the materiality of academic cultural production, these more visually and structurally complex essays work to situate themselves at the intersection of academic and popular writing, where the discourse of town and gown meet. Could the restructuring of the page itself, the reconfiguration of this text so typical of discourse inside the Bubble that appears, but only appears, to be governed by a definite, static, and constant set of conventions, facilitate other reimaginations of the intersection between campus landscapes and other spaces and places?

More important, the writing changes, but does the place change? Many colleagues with whom I have discussed this course have asked me if I have developed a community service or service learning component. It is my belief that at Duke, this type of course is a necessary precursor to meaningful interaction. The Bubble metaphor often mediates acts of community service in such a way as to render any kind of reciprocity unlikely, if not impossible. In October 2003, for example, Duke students participated in a Habitat for Humanity "Blitz Build," with a twist: instead of sending students "out" into adjacent neighborhoods (the site for the house was, in fact, only three blocks from the celebrated stone wall), the house was constructed on the Duke campus and moved by truck to its permanent location at a cost of $8,000. Ostensibly, the reason for this expensive extra step was to raise Habitat's campus visibility. But student op-ed columnist Joost Bosland (writing in his regular feature tellingly titled "Inside the Bubble") was not the only one to ask, "What sort of message does this send to our neighbors? We show them that we are too afraid to work in their part of town. We show them that we are too afraid to ask donors to venture to the site where the house is actually needed."

Given the power of the dominant discourses of place among students, I wonder if adding a service component to a course like "Bull City and Beyond" would only reinforce the existing construction of the campus as the place of plenty, of potential, and the surrounding city as devoid of the resources to help itself, a petitioner in need of aid from Duke's benefactors. But I want to acknowledge that, in terms of rendering material aid to Durham residents, this course does not stage an intervention in community life.

Perhaps, however, we need to question whether "intervention" is something that must always and only occur beyond the university walls. To postulate that the only place in need of intervention is the town, and not the gown, might be another, trickier form of academic exceptionalism. Where this course intervenes is in the university, in the attenuated cosmopolitanism of its discourses of place that declares certain spaces uninteresting at best, dangerous at worst, without bothering to inquire as to what is actually going on in them. The form of the intervention is to render visible what is so often denied in metaphors like "the Bubble"— that is, the university's implication in local networks of culture, politics, and history. When I ask students to carry out archival research, it is not only to encourage them to acquire a fuller understanding of the texts and artifacts that have shaped their place; it is also to have them understand that the implication of the campus in local networks of meaning is so thorough as to result in material traces even in those most "academic" of academic sanctums, the archive. (The same is true but even more so at ETSU's Archives of Appalachia, perhaps the single most important source of archival information about the Appalachian region and an invaluable resource in the making of this book.) And when I ask students to reconfigure and redesign an academic text, it is so that they will carry forward from the first-year classroom into the rest of their educations an expanded sense not only of how their university campus connects to broader spaces but how the practices of academic writing themselves might be changed to better define and redefine those connections.

If students learn, for example, that Benjamin Newton Duke, brother of financial titan J. B. "Buck" Duke and point man for the Duke family's benevolence to the Methodist seminary that became their eponymous university, was also the owner of textile producer Erwin Mills and the builder of West Durham, they can no longer deny the connection their own presence in Durham has to the lives and the collective history of the workers they tend to disregard and the landscape both workers and students have so profoundly shaped. What they do with the knowledge of that connection, what political, ethical, or critical imperatives they derive from that knowledge, is up to them, but they can no longer willfully disregard the place their education has in the social construction of the region. Moreover, by researching local, regional, and institutional history in university libraries, archives, and special collections as well as in direct observation of the place and its people, students can come to understand that the resources of the very university that tacitly or explicitly encourages their isolation from the local scene can provide the basis for the creation of new understandings of and arguments about the interrelationship of campus and community. Finally, by designing a series of essay assignments that are cumulative and recursive, I require students to experiment with form in ways that mirror the intellectual experimentation they are engaged in. Rather than a series of discrete and discontinuous essays, students create a variegated, elaborate, and multifaceted work that adapts academic strategies to more contingent representational tactics that have evolved in relation to the exigencies of their particular project.

This course represents just one possibility for the expression of a pedagogy that foregrounds the intricate web of literacies and landscapes that shape community life. This exercise would not be a descriptive one, however. Understanding the patterns of representation that construct this particular place forms an instrumental part of designing tactics for intervention in those processes of representation. Students and teachers can collaboratively reconstruct not only the relative authority of different kinds of texts, and their geographical, political, and material relationships to the site of the community, but also the genre conventions, physical and logistical requirements, and standards of evaluation involved in the multiplicity of genres of cultural production being carried out in the community. Then this knowledge can be put to use to create public texts that intervene in the conflicts and struggles that shape local public discourse and characterize local public life.

How could the instructor make resources from the more rarefied discourses of "high" literature and cultural critique available that would challenge or augment the constructions of these matters in vernacular texts by linking them to broader perspectives, to other places? And then how might a student design a text or set of texts that would use this knowledge of the geographical distribution and variety of forms and content of representations to stage an intervention? What would the instructor have to learn in order to effectively guide, respond to, and evaluate the work of her students in these interventions? And how, then, could the instructor, equipped with the knowledge of local conflicts and issues and the forms these debates take, use that knowledge to reposition and redefine her own research and writing so as to shape local public discourses more effectively?

I leave these tactics in interrogatory forms because I do not wish to issue edicts or commend strategies for adaptation to anyplace, and because this project does not end, but begins, with the conclusion of this chapter. These questions must be answered, or at least pursued, in response to the problems and priorities of institutions and communities in particular places. I have tried here to construct a research and writing methodology to enact this place-centered investigation of the forms and issues that create connections between the often-supposed parochial interests of regional communities with broad patterns of conflict and struggle. For this methodology to be truly transformative, however, this project must be taken up on a broader scale: changing communities, perhaps, but as a necessary first step, changing the academy, drawing academic practice more fully into the public life of communities and regions in vital and vernacular ways.

Epilogue: There's Something about Mary (Reprise)
Mrs. Edwards and Me

In the interest of full disclosure, I feel I need to explore the irony that I owe my own upbringing, the relative prosperity of my family that underwrites my education, to many of the social forces that I have just suggested undermine, in some ways, ETSU's commitment to the town of Johnson City and the southern Appalachian region. Am I biting the hand that has fed me? Or trying to wish my own nostalgic, idealized version of the region into existence?

My dad was hired by ETSU as an assistant professor of physics back in 1965, a newly minted Ph.D. from Clemson University, part of the wave of faculty hiring that accompanied the coming-of-age of the baby boom generation, the wave that propelled ETSU in its movement away from its normal school roots to become a full-fledged university in 1963. (I have augmented my memory here and there with reference to Frank Williams's history of ETSU, *A University's Story*.)

That normal school history did have certain benefits for faculty, however, that proved to be quite formative for me. ETSU still played host, during my childhood, to a laboratory school for its teacher-trainees, though by the time I attended it, it had ceased to serve much of its experimental function; in fact, when the college became a university, the school changed its name from the Training School to the University School. While the student teachers took their training in the city and county schools about as much as they did in my school, the University School—grades one through twelve, all in one building located across the street from my dad's office in the science building—stayed on as a kind of unspoken fringe benefit for faculty. I am just speculating, but I recall few staff kids in my elementary classes; brothers Harry and Troy Jenkins leap to mind, but only because they were for years the only African American students in all of University School, all twelve grades, close to 600 students. In fact the school did not enroll any African American students at all until 1965.

Admission to the school was available almost exclusively to the children of university employees—a lengthy waiting list controlled admission to the few available slots. Because there was no bus service, I am guessing that attendance was particularly convenient for faculty kids, more so than staff kids, because their mothers, at least in my early youth, were mostly housewives, and their fathers had a flexible-enough workday to be able to arrange transportation. Maybe other social factors—the homogeneity of the white-middle-class student body, with everybody's parents' doing the same work, holding the same degrees, and earning an income within a few grand of each other—created barriers for working-class kids, kept them from wanting to be and their parents from wanting them at University School. I know from experience the school had a reputation for elitism.

Not that I noticed, or really had much opportunity to notice. I was probably in third or fourth grade before I even began to understand that there were adults who did not work for universities, kids whose dads were not called "Dr. So-and-so." My school world and my home world reinforced this myopia; the world can seem an awfully stable place when your parents still live in the house they brought you to from the maternity ward, the house they built just before your birth. The neighborhood I grew up in (the aforementioned "Scholar Holler," officially "Seminole Woods," just south of campus) was made up almost entirely of young faculty, all brought in to help ETSU expand into a modern research university. To the left was another physics professor, to the right an English professor, across the street a chemistry prof and next to him my dad's physics department chair. And kids were everywhere: with the adults all roughly the same age, a whole generation of young people played kick-the-can and football and four-square in the streets spring, summer, and fall, and in the winter, when we would get our occasional snow, those same streets, climbing Tennessee hillsides, made ideal sledding courses. The network of cul-de-sacs winding up toward a low ridge carried no through traffic; they seemed to us primarily for our use, cars being an occasional inconvenience. A band of forest created a natural border up at the top of Scholar Holler as well as a setting for adventuring, sometimes even over the ridge into Forest Hills, seemingly a different world but in fact another neighborhood predominantly of young faculty, a mirror image of Seminole Woods.

Though it seemed exotic to visit their habitat on a Saturday expedition (not to mention transgressive, Forest Hills being well beyond the range of a parent's call), we would see the Forest Hills kids back at University School on Monday. The neighborhood allegiances were among the few subcultural divisions in our student body, and bred no real animosity; we had the usual cliques and popularity contests, though not so much jock culture as we had no football team (I always attributed this to our small size, until I realized that rural, single-A high schools up in the mountains were able to field perfectly good squads). In a setting where most kids had at least one Ph.D. parent, discipline problems were relatively rare and high academic achievement carried with it little of the stigma it can where a greater range and variety of backgrounds and abilities are present. University School kids tended to assume we were better and smarter than our city and county school counterparts.

It was idyllic, and I am grateful, make no mistake—though I may never know what else was going on there, what hurtful domestic situations escaped neighborly scrutiny. Nor can I assess or atone for the invisible cost to the women of the neighborhood who, without knowing it, might have done more or different things with their lives than the traditional values of the neighborhood offered; I will never meet the people of color or the queer couples or any of the other people who never settled in our neighborhood because they could not fit in. Too, I know the peace and prosperity of a neighborhood like mine was bought, in our capitalist culture, only at the cost of deprivation of others invisible to us in our middle-class enclave. And it is not as if my father didn't work hard to get where he is, or to stay there, the son of a hardworking salesman whose almost mystical belief in higher education belied his own roots in the small farms of working poor whites in eastern North Carolina. And my mother not only worked hard in our home to provide for our family's needs, but went to work as a teacher's aide helping special needs children when I was in sixth grade. She became a middle-school teacher in the city school system, forging working commitments in my family to elementary and secondary public education.

Still, I wonder. I wonder whether I would be here now, working on a book at the age of thirty-eight, if I had ever known much about other worlds. But the university was literally where I grew up, where I lived, especially if you consider Seminole Woods a kind of annex to campus. I have had access to a research library, laboratories, playing fields literally all my life. When I got tired or bored in elementary school, I would play sick and go over to my dad's office across the street. He would dig through the department film library and find something about Mars or the Apollo missions and ensconce me in an empty classroom to watch.

Maybe, then, my call for increased connection and interrelation between academic and local cultures is an expression of some yearning or regret on my part. I recognize that despite my relatively low pay and the current cruelties of the academic job market, I enjoy a life of privilege, safety, and comfort; my cultural capital keeps me from having to work in dangerous or mind-numbing conditions. Maybe my rhetorical theories of region are a little self-serving, allowing me to parlay my skills into a connection to place that is not really there.

But I hope not, and here's why: even as hermetically sealed from the rest of the world as my life might seem, other local landscapes and cultures still located and shaped me, shaped us University School kids, shaped the life of "Scholar Holler," and not just in name only. And this fact is part of what makes me believe and insist throughout this study that local cultures are more complex and convoluted than they are ever given credit for—that even in the almost preternaturally uniform surroundings in which I grew up, Appalachian cultures and histories, legacies of conflict and struggle, found ways to touch and to transform me—even to suggest to me that that academic subculture I grew up in is a part of, not apart from, the Appalachian regional culture that surrounds it. The problem is that the relationship is not one of unity exclusively but also of conflict.

As that huge band of faculty kids roamed through Scholar Holler, Mrs. Edwards kept an eye on all of us, for years (I interviewed her on July 15, 1997, about her background and these experiences). Mrs. Edwards became a part of my family's daily life right before I was born. Mrs. Edwards was the cleaning woman retained by a good many of the faculty wives of Seminole Woods—at one point she spent a half day each at ten different homes; she recalls that at one point she looked after twenty-seven children (child care was a de facto part of her responsibilities)—2.7 kids per household, which seems almost a parody of the nuclear family ideology of the neighborhood.

Mrs. Edwards's life cut a curious swath across the white-middle-class-brick-ranch landscape of Seminole Woods. I may not have been aware of the uniformity of my surroundings, my school, my neighborhood as a kid, but I was quite aware of her difference. Once, as my brother and I, him about eight, me maybe five, played in the backyard, we ran up to the door and discovered a black snake coiled tightly around the handle. He must have been absorbing the warmth. For two little boys in a neighborhood like this one, the snake was an event. We ran babbling to Mrs. Edwards, who was the only adult home at the time. Impassive, she went to the garage for a hoe, came out to the back door and knocked the snake loose with the handle, then with a rapid motion of the blade—chopchop-chopchopchop!—hacked the snake into collops and calmly walked away. My brother and I stood there watching the pieces of snake twitch, absolutely amazed.

Mrs. Edwards was different. She was from the Country—out by the river, not far from that crazy little town where they hanged the elephant. She smoked. She was (eventually) divorced. She always brought her lunch to our house (which somehow struck me as odd), and she always offered to share. She called a Coca-Cola a "dope." She somehow managed to be

Mary Ella Edwards (1916–2000).
Photograph 1984 courtesy of
Janet Powell.

deferential to us—always apologizing for interrupting *The Price Is Right*
with the vacuum—and yet firmly in command. Even though I knew
almost nothing about her, about her past, about her present, for that
matter, I was aware from early on that Mrs. Edwards represented a different life, a different set of skills—yet she was also an integral part of the
landscape of my home and upbringing. I was too young at the time to
think about, much less call, the difference in the social location of this
adult and the others in my life "class," and even now it seems there is
more to it than that. My relationship with Mrs. Edwards, her presence in
that neighborhood, was an identifiable moment of place happening, of
the tensions and pleasures of difference—material, cultural, social, historical—taking a particular form on a specific landscape.

In this neighborhood of 2.7 children per household, Mrs. Edwards
(born Mary Deadrick, in 1919; died 28 January 2000) was herself one of
thirteen children, nine boys and four girls, born and raised on the banks
of the Nolichuckey River between Jonesborough and Erwin, Tennessee.
Her father liked to say that he had him a baseball team. But he didn't have
it long: he died of spinal meningitis in 1931; his wife died, choked to death
by a goiter, the next year. By this time five of the children had married and
moved away, but an older set of twins, brothers Bruce and Byrd, thirteen-

year-old Mary, and five younger children stayed on and worked the family farm.

Bruce and Byrd were polar opposites in a household as marked by conflict and struggle as the landscape of my youth was by unity and harmony. Bruce was capricious and cruel: "He was mean to us," Mrs. Edwards told me, "as a dog . . . he would beat us up—me and Esther—he would beat us up, and just hit us with anything he could find, and he was ill-natured and high tempered. . . . Bruce was evil and hateful and he just beat us up over nothing." Byrd, however, inherited his responsibilities gracefully: "Byrd was different altogether, and he wouldn't hit us nor whup us. We always felt by him like a daddy, like he was our daddy. Cause he never whip us, we knowed to mind, just snap his fingers we knowed to mind him, just like that you know. We knowed to mind what Byrd said." The twin brothers, one good and one evil, couldn't share power and authority in the house forever:

so they got into it over Bruce beating us younguns up one time. And Byrd told him if he couldn't beat that just to get his clothes and get out of there. He was not going to stand by and have us kids beat up, you know. And, so, they got in a fight and fought about it, and of course the double-bladed axe was down at the woodpile, stuck in a block of wood, and they fought off down that way and Bruce grabbed the axe, he was going to chop Byrd's head off and so we took the axe, me and Esther got the axe, and took it in the house so Bruce couldn't get ahold of it 'cause we was afraid he would kill Byrd, you know, or something, and we took it in the house and they fought around there for a long time. And Byrd just finally told him to get out and go if he couldn't be good to us younguns, he wasn't going to have us mistreated. Just to get out and go and we'd get along better without him, so he did pack up and left.

[Bruce] went and stayed with one of my aunts for a long time and he finally went to Illinois, to one of our other aunts, and he stayed out there with them in Illinois for a long time . . . cause we had an aunt and uncle out there, and they had a service station, apartments and different things, so anyway he stayed with them a while and then he joined the service, and I guess it was about seven or eight year before we ever seen him again. Which we was glad 'cause of the way he was to us.

With the evil Bruce vanquished, their lives returned to a difficult, but at least not brutalizing, norm. Mrs. Edwards lived out what most people think of when they imagine "Appalachia": subsistence farming, growing corn and cane and watermelons, selling apple butter and molasses, extra milk and butter, keeping chickens and hogs and cows, gathering walnuts in the fall to buy the one pair of brogans each child would wear for the winter, riding in the wagon to the same church where she is buried today. All without benefit of running water and electricity.

I cannot imagine how my life must have looked to her, and when I asked all she would say is that "you uns was all good to mind and done what I told you." And yet the ironic fact is that the very work that brought her to Scholar Holler, into this liminal relationship to the insular university community, came at the cost of her own formal education. Mrs. Edwards began the domestic work that would provide most of her cash income for the rest of her life around the age of sixteen. She and her sister Esther would take in shirts for local bachelors, an enterprise that expanded into cleaning house and washing in homes all around the community, and eventually this cottage industry crowded out her opportunities for schooling.

> I had to stay out of school a day a week to do the washing cause there was so many of us I couldn't do it of an evening, you know, and I'd stay out one day a week and do the washing and I lacked two months of being through with the tenth grade. Finally I just told Byrd I was going to quit, cause I was getting behind so much with my work at home, and he said well, Mary, I guess you could, just quit if you want to, cause he said you're killing yourself with trying to work and going to school and everything and he said just stay here and you and me'll get along as best we can, so we made it.

Making it for Mrs. Edwards, for Byrd Deadrick and the children in his charge, was difficult but apparently not bitter. To some degree the community she lived in, like Scholar Holler, shared a common economic background; even of the people she first worked for, Mrs. Edwards says, "we was all just poor together." All through our talk she uses the first person plural without a clear reference to who else is involved: "we seen it rough, Doug." And our conversation is punctuated with references to collective effort: "we all stuck together," "we had to stay together to make a living." Yet I also know—from the story of Bruce and Byrd—that life was not only an economic struggle but sometimes a violent, physical struggle as well. Surely those who escaped bodily injuries felt and continue to feel the injuries of class, of gender, of what came to be called underdevelopment—even if they did not have this vocabulary to describe it. Mary and Esther had to take the double-bladed ax from Bruce. And this history of struggle, in the person of Mrs. Edwards, entered that seemingly seamless academic community in Scholar Holler, and my brother and I watched her kill a black snake and were amazed.

How that happened is a complex history as well. As a child Mrs. Edwards probably did not go to Johnson City more than once a year at the most. Now in the (unincorporated) community of Lamar where Mrs. Edwards lives, only a mile or two from the house she grew up in, most folks keep a garden and maybe a little livestock but go to Johnson City or Erwin or Jonesborough, all within about ten miles, to work for their primary income. Mrs. Edwards was not exempt from these historical patterns. The preacher at her church, a man named Cameron for whom she kept house, moved to Johnson City to take a new congregation that included my family's next-door neighbors, including a colleague of my dad's in the physics department. I am speculating, but one can surmise that the expansion of faculty and students at the growing university created new demands on community institutions, including churches, that created patterns of local migration. Mrs. Edwards continued to keep house for Preacher Cameron, and when these young, relatively affluent junior faculty couples sought domestic help, Mrs. Edwards came highly recommended. Soon she was presiding over that brood of twenty-seven faculty kids roaming the slopes of Scholar Holler, and her son Butch became an employee of ETSU's physical plant. In one generation Mrs. Edwards saw her and her family's livelihood, the focus of their daily life, shift from subsistence farming to performing crucial if unrecognized and undercompensated support for the expansion of higher education. My family, like all of them, I suppose, paid Mrs. Edwards cash—no benefits, no pension, no health insurance, no minimum wage.

When I ask her about the changes that refocused her and her community's lives on the city that they once visited annually, maybe, changes that drew first the professional classes (Preacher Cameron), then the working classes (Mrs. Edwards, and then Butch) into the broader service of the university, she shakes her head. The woman who can remember the details of incidents and conversations from 1931 says, "I really don't know what to tell you, Doug, 'cause I can't remember that far back."

Even (perhaps especially) for those who have experienced it firsthand, then, there is not a language for the changes and conflicts that have characterized regional life this century. Our vocabulary of regional life is very effective for telling the kinds of stories that confirm, sometimes sensationally, deeply rooted images of humble subsistence farming and bitter memories of the violence of patriarchy, the nostalgic and horrific renditions of a static, ahistorical regionalism that some moments of Mrs. Edwards's stories might seem to confirm. Try to describe a region undergoing constant transformations, shifting patterns of population and employment, of class and culture, of politics and power, and vocabulary and imagination fail us as much as Mrs. Edwards's memory.

Regional life, far from inert, is rife with connections—be they conflicts, confrontation, or cooperation—moments that dramatize important struggles for justice, faceless and routine defeats, daring or modest experiments in new forms of social organization. But the connections are there. They could underwrite powerful solidarities across the tensions that animate the public lives of regions. Mrs. Edwards and I have common causes, deep bonds of affection that could also sponsor rational alliances. But they are obscured by a culture that separates, categorizes, that has labeled the complex set of skills that thirteen-year-old Mary Deadrick used to survive a childhood marked by poverty and domestic abuse "illiteracy," that views the landscape that has transformed dramatically over the course of one lifetime as uneventful, and isolated, that sees the place where she has experienced happiness, love, and perseverance despite the obstacles posed by her gender and social class as a "place without hope." We need new names for the experiences of people like Mrs. Edwards, largely invisible, but nonetheless crucial, on the edges of the American university, histories that connect her memories and her experiences to the broader contours of American public life, that understand the vexed relationships between Mrs. Edwards and me, between the university and the community, between the city and the country, the region and the nation and the globe. I hope in this book I have drawn a few such maps, but also offered some insights into how such maps could be drawn, and how to teach others to do so as well.

Appendix
Durham Stories

In the spring semesters of 2003 and 2004, my students in Writing 20, Academic Writing (section 01, spring 2003, and sections 01 and 24, spring 2004), collected narratives about Durham from their fellow Duke University students. Students distributed by email the following prompt to three other students:

> Please briefly relate in writing a story about Durham: the city itself, the people who live there, its government, landscape, institutions, etc. This story may be something from your personal experience, or something you have heard from someone else. Include, at the beginning of the story, your race, gender, age, and hometown.

Contributors were also sent the following release statement (the version below is from Spring 2004):

> By responding to this email, you give your consent for your response to be collected and published as a part of a larger project; to be studied and discussed by Writing 20, sections 01 and 24; and to be used as a part of essays by the students and the instructor of that class which may be published at some future time. However, your name will be removed from your response prior to any of these activities and will never be made public.

The narratives were collected by the students and sent to me; I compiled them into a single document in random order, numbered them, and distributed the collection to the class for use in the research and writing projects. The texts of the Durham Stories cited in this book are included here, unchanged except for formatting and font. Subsequent to the publication of this book, the complete text of the Durham Stories will be donated to the University Archives of Duke University.

Durham Stories, 2003

31. White male, age 19, Charlotte, North Carolina
The Roads of Durham

One of the first things I learned when I came to Duke was that it really wasnt the best idea to bring a car to school. The roads in the area are confusing as hell and the neighborhoods around Duke have uncomfortably high crime rates. This combination led to an interesting experience of mine.

It was only about 3 weeks into fall semester when three guys and myself went out to buy beer for a party. As was the norm for the first few weeks, I was lost almost immediately. Soon we were no where close to anything that seemed familiar or the least bit comforting. After about 20 minutes of driving around aimlessly in the ghettos somewhere around east campus we decided to bag it and ask for directions. So we went into some food mart at a gas station and bought the beer (which was ridiculously expensive: $15 for an 18 of nattie ... thats a *expletive* crime if you ask me).

When we asked the clerk for directions, there was no response. We asked again, slowly, and still nothing. The worker was either mute or lacking the ability to speak english. ... vive la difference. So anyways, we hopped back in the car for more aimless driving, but there was one problem: my car's alternator was (messed) up and the car began to die. I was like, "well this is great guys, we are all going to be robbed, beaten, and murdered."

In the end, my car was able to suck it up and we made it back to East Campus—a true diamond in the rough. Anyways . . . the night was terrible and i had to get my car towed (not the only towing of my first semester—thank you very much DUKE TRANSPORTATION).

Durham Stories, 2004

3. Chinese male, age 23, Singapore

It was a hot and sultry evening in the summer, and I was with a group of friends tucking into dinner at Toreros along Main Street. The food was splendid, fabulous in fact. The servings were huge. Our servers laughed at our jokes and taught us a bit of Mexican, even as we ordered our regular dishes. The atmosphere was great and I was surprised to see so many young adults dining at this fine establishment. Mind you, it was summer: college students were on vacation. I wondered where the crowd came from. I guessed most of them were well-educated, had just entered the job market, taking up positions in the RTP or at the university.

We settled our bill and walked towards the parking lot next to Fish-mongers. The sky had turned crestfallen, with shades of dark blue popping out of nowhere. There was a distinct breeze and it started to drizzle. We made a mad dash for the car. Just as one of my friends opened the door, a black African-American male came up towards him, pushed his shoulder and asked for money. My friend refused and immediately went into the car. The guy did not back off, but became more aggressive, accosting him in an unforgiving manner. I thought to myself—if the black dude pulls out a gun, I will race across to disarm him. As fortune would have it, we pulled away safely, leaving him cursing us with bated breath.

It was an intriguing experience because nothing happened. Yet, the potential for something dreadful to occur was very real, and thus the incident remains etched across my mind. Beyond the university lie so many unknowns lurking, ready to pounce on you if you let your guard down all but a minute.

47. White female, age 20, Gainesville, Florida

While Duke is the epitome of order and structure; impressive and imposing and looming under Gothic architecture, Durham wildly flails about itself, unsure and despondent. My first year at Duke I ventured into the streets off of East campus quite frequently, searching in vain for refinement and social spots as an escape from the cold stone of Duke. Durham is a maze, either because of streets that loop and twist and curve either so suddenly and unexpectedly one is caught off guard and simultaneously, because old warehouses and poorly marked streets run into each other, forming a chaotic stretch of what is deemed "downtown." Coming from a college town myself, I was quite shocked to find myself regulated to weekends after weekends spent at Duke, hoping for movies on the quad or a fun party on West Campus. Durham has taught me what lies within it's shady streets are of trivial concern to Duke students, and that as privileged inhabitants of the Duke world, life outside Duke does not exist. I know little about Durham because Durham is portrayed to me as scary and dangerous. While this naïve and limited knowledge is partly my own fault—a fault due to my own biased expectations, it is still a product of Durham itself. I have learned to adjust and appreciate Durham however. The nooks and crannies that once seemed dark and ominous hold treasures of restaurants and shops, where refined society and college style meet and mingle. Durham has not changed, but my expectations have, and that for now, is enough.

55. Korean male, age 18, Paramus, New Jersey

Before coming to Duke, I never really gave the city of Durham any much thought. I guess you can say that even after living here for about five months, I still haven't given Durham any much thought. It might just be me, but living on Duke campus doesn't necessarily mean that you're living in Durham, North Carolina. Duke and Durham seem like two separate entities. Duke is its own town in its self. The stone walls that encircle East Campus seem to echo the separation of city and university in a physical sense. I think that there is such a separation from town and university because honestly, Durham does not have that much to offer the University Students. The nearby 9th street is not nearly enough to entice the hundreds of university students to patronize. It is a just a string of a couple of eateries, a book store, and a tattoo parlor. Granted, at times 9th street can be a nice place to hang out on a weekend night, but it does not fulfill many peoples weekend requirement of fun.

56. White female, age 18, Frederick, Maryland

Six of us hurried across the fields by East Campus in the direction of 9th Street. The late September weather encouraged jackets at night, none of which us girls were wearing because they would cover our carefully picked outfits. A laughing and loud group, we passed by Whole Foods and the Cycle Shop with purses and boys in tow. Our group had become incohesive and we were walking and chatting in twos staggered down the block. I was walking with Mark and we could see our friends ahead stop to speak to a dark figure in the unlit parking area across from Cosmic. As I approached I could see he was a middle-aged black man in worn clothes arguing with two of my friends. He just wanted a little money for food. I have encountered many situations similar to this in New York and Washington and have always walked by without acknowledgement. This is not because I believe they will take my money and buy drugs or alcohol. I simply feel that there are places where people can go to seek help and that by handing them money it is only prolonging there willingness to remain panhandlers. This particular gentleman was not leaving us alone and we were all beginning to get uncomfortable. The guys we were with told us to keep walking. They said they would handle it. Although I didn't think anything would happen, it still made me nervous to leave them with this man in an unlit area. Halfway down Main Street they caught up with us. Mark said they had given him a couple dollars so that he would leave them alone. Everyone had been in a party mood and it was hard to just shake it off and go dance it up knowing that this man was still on the street begging for money. Less than a block from East Campus—full of students pursuing an excellent education, many from wealthy families and comfortable homes—was a man with nothing. I have so much more than this man, yet I did not want to help him. Is it the job of people more fortunate than others to hand out dollar charity? Or is it that man's responsibility to take care of himself and pursue a life off the street? On that September evening, I had decided that is was not my responsibility.

Appendix

Works Cited

Anderson, Benedict. *Imagined Communities: Reflections on the Origin and Spread of Nationalism.* Rev. ed. London: Verso, 1991.

Anderson, Jean Bradley. *Durham County: A History of Durham County, North Carolina.* Durham, N.C.: Duke University Press, 1990.

Anderson, Larry. *Benton MacKaye: Conservationist, Planner, and Creator of the Appalachian Trail.* Baltimore: Johns Hopkins University Press, 2002.

Anglin, Mary. "AIDS in Appalachia: Medical Pathologies and the Problem of Identity." *Journal of Appalachian Studies* 3:2 (1997): 171–88.

Apocalypse Now. Dir. Francis Ford Coppola. Paramount, 1979.

Appalachian Trail Guide to Tennessee-North Carolina. 10th ed. Harpers Ferry, W.Va.: Appalachian Trail Conference, 1992.

Arthur, Paul. "Let Us Now Praise Famous Yokels: *Dadetown* and Other Retreats." *Cineaste* 23:1 (1997): 30–33.

"August 17, 1988: 'I Sometimes Tell People I Was Born in a Cotton Patch.'" *Foxfire* 22 (Fall 1988): 123–49.

Bakthin, Mikhail. "Forms of Time and Chronotope in the Novel." In *The Dialogic Imagination,* ed. Michael Holquist, 84–258. Austin: University of Texas Press, 1981.

Batteau, Allen. *The Invention of Appalachia.* Tucson: University of Arizona Press, 1990.

Benedict, Pinckney. "The Wrecking Yard." In *The Wrecking Yard and Other Stories,* 19–39. New York: Plume, 1995.

Billings, Dwight, Gurney Norman, and Katherine Ledford, eds. *Confronting Appalachian Stereotypes: Back Talk from an American Region.* Foreword by Ronald Eller. Lexington: University of Kentucky Press, 1999.

Billings, Dwight, Mary Beth Pudup, and Altina Waller, eds. *Appalachia in the Making: The Mountain South in the Nineteenth Century.* Chapel Hill: University of North Carolina Press, 1995.

Bishop, Elizabeth. *The Complete Poems: 1927–1979.* New York: Farrar, Straus, and Giroux, 1979.

Blee, Kathleen, and Dwight Billings. "Where 'Bloodshed is a Pastime': Mountain Feuds and Appalachian Stereotyping." In *Confronting Appalachian Stereotypes: Back Talk from an American Region,* ed. Dwight Billings, Gurney Norman, and Katherine Ledford, 119–37. Lexington: University Press of Kentucky, 1999.

Blue Velvet. Dir. David Lynch. De Laurentis Entertainment Group, 1986.

Blum, Louise. "Tenured, Lesbian, and a Mother in God's Country." *Chronicle of Higher Education* 49:6 (4 October 2002). <http://chronicle.com/free/v49/i06/06b01101.htm> (accessed 8 October 2005).

Bosland, Joost. "Travesty for Humanity." *The Chronicle Online,* 7 October 2003. <http://www.chronicle.duke.edu/vnews/display.v/ART/2003/10/07/3f82a789d5b9e?in_archive=1> (accessed 8 October 2005).

Boyer, Ernest. *Scholarship Reconsidered: Priorities of the Professoriate.* Princeton: Carnegie Foundation for the Advancement of Teaching, 1990.

Bragg, Alice Faye. "Appalachian Residents Know This Is Home." *Charlestown Gazette,* 7 April 1995, 3D.

Brodhead, Richard. *Cultures of Letters: Scenes of Reading and Writing in Nineteenth-Century America.* Chicago: University of Chicago Press, 1993.

Brown, Angela K. "Elephant's Hanging Haunts Town of Erwin." *Johnson City Press*, 8 November 1999, 1+.

Browne, Robert A. *The Appalachian Trail: History, Humanity, and Ecology.* Stafford, Va.: Northwoods Press, 1980.

Bullard, Robert. *Dumping in Dixie: Race, Class, and Environmental Quality.* Boulder: Westview Press, 1990.

Burton, Thomas. "The Hanging of Mary, a Circus Elephant." *Tennessee Folklore Society Bulletin* 38:1 (March 1971): 1–8.

Butler, Robert James. "The American Quest for Pure Movement in Dos Passos' *U.S.A.*" *Twentieth Century Literature* 30:1 (Spring 1984): 80–99.

Calhoun, Craig. "Cosmopolitanism Is Not Enough: Local Democracy in a Global Context. Paper presented at Conference on Local Democracy and Globalization, University of North Carolina, Chapel Hill, March 2001.

Calvino, Italo. *Invisible Cities.* Trans. William Weaver. San Diego: Harcourt Brace, 1974.

Cape Fear. Dir. Martin Scorsese. Universal, 1992.

Carson, Jo. "Good Questions." In *Bloodroot: Reflections on Place by Appalachian Women Writers*, ed. Joyce Dyer, 72–79. Lexington: University Press of Kentucky, 1998.

———. *Stories I Ain't Told Nobody Yet.* New York: Theater Communications Group, 1989.

"Carter County Deputies Made 113 Arrests in August." *Johnson City Press-Chronicle*, 12 September 1985, 7.

Coen, Ethan. "True Stories." *Harper's*, July 1997, 34–35.

Cook, Pam. "Scorsese's Masquerade." *Sight and Sound*, April 1992, 14–15.

Couto, Richard. *Making Democracy Work Better: Mediating Structures, Social Capital, and the Democratic Prospect.* Chapel Hill: University of North Carolina Press, 1999.

Cresswell, Tim. *In Place/Out of Place: Geography, Ideology, and Transgression.* Minneapolis: University of Minnesota Press, 1996.

Cunningham, Rodger. *Apples on the Flood: Minority Discourse and Appalachia.* Knoxville: University of Tennessee Press, 1987.

Dainotto, Roberto. *Place in Literature: Regions, Cultures, Communities.* Ithaca: Cornell University Press, 2000.

Davis, Janet. *The Circus Age: American Culture and Society under the Big Top.* Chapel Hill: University of North Carolina Press, 2002.

de Certeau, Michel. *The Practice of Everyday Life.* Trans. Steven Rendall. Berkeley: University of California Press, 1984.

Deliverance. Dir. John Boorman. Warner Brothers, 1972.

Dos Passos, John. *The 42nd Parallel.* 1930. Rpt., Boston: Houghton-Mifflin, 1960.

———. *The Big Money.* 1933. Rpt., New York: Signet, 1969.

———. "Harlan: Working under the Gun." *New Republic*, 2 December 1931, 62–67.

———. *1919.* 1932. Rpt., New York: Signet, 1969.

Dunbar, Roxanne. "Bloody Footprints." In *White Trash: Race and Class in America*, ed. Matt Wray and Annalee Newitz, 73–88. New York: Routledge, 1997.

Dunn, Durwood. *Cades Cove: The Life and Death of a Southern Appalachian Community, 1818–1937.* Knoxville: University of Tennessee Press, 1988.

Edwards, Mary Ella. Interview by the author. 15 July 1997.

The Electric Valley. Dir. Ross Spears. James Agee Film Project, 1984.

"Elephant Graveyard." *Roadside America.* <http://www.roadsideamerica.com/pet/eleph .html> (accessed 14 January 2006).

"Elephant Hanging Basis for Cusack Screenplay." *Johnson City Press*, 22 April 1999, 3.

Works Cited

"Elephant Hanging, Erwin TN, 1916." Vertical File. Archives of Appalachia, East Tennessee State University, Johnson City.

Eller, Ronald. *Miners, Millhands, and Mountaineers: Industrialization of the Appalachian South, 1880–1930.* Knoxville: University of Tennessee Press, 1982.

Ellin, Nan. *Postmodern Urbanism.* Cambridge, Mass.: Blackwell, 1996.

Emblidge, David. *The Appalachian Trail Reader.* New York: Oxford University Press, 1996.

Entrikin, J. Nicholas. *The Betweenness of Place: Towards a Geography of Modernity.* Baltimore: Johns Hopkins University Press, 1991.

Fargo. Dir. Ethan Coen. Gramercy, 1996.

"Fargo (1996)." *Internet Movie Database.* <http://us.imdb.com/Title?Fargo+(1996)> (accessed 13 April 1998).

Fichtelberg, Joseph. "The Picaros of John Dos Passos." *Twentieth Century Literature* 34:4 (Winter 88): 434–52.

Foresta, Ronald. "Transformation of the Appalachian Trail." *Geographical Review* 77:1 (January 1987): 76–85.

Foucault, Michel. "Of Other Spaces." Trans. Jay Miskowiec. *diacritics* 16:1 (Spring 1986): 22–27.

Fox, John, Jr. *The Trail of the Lonesome Pine.* 1908. Rpt., Lexington: University Press of Kentucky, 1984.

Frampton, Kenneth. "Toward a Critical Regionalism: Six Points for an Architecture of Resistance." In *The Anti-Aesthetic: Essays on Postmodern Culture*, ed. Hal Foster, 16–30. Seattle: Bay Press, 1983.

Freire, Paulo. *Letters to Christina: Reflections on My Life and Work.* Trans. Donaldo Macedo. New York: Routledge, 1996.

——. *Pedagogy of the Oppressed.* New York: Continuum, 1970. Rpt., 1995.

Garreau, Joel. *Edge City: Life on the New Frontier.* New York: Doubleday, 1991.

Giroux, Henry A. "*Pulp Fiction* and the Culture of Violence." *Harvard Educational Review* 65:2 (Summer 1995): 299–314.

Granger, George L. Letter to the Editor. *Johnson City Press*, 21 February 1992. Courtesy of the University Archives, East Tennessee State University, Johnson City.

Greenblatt, Stephen. *Marvelous Possessions: The Wonder of the New World.* Chicago: University of Chicago Press, 1991.

Gröning, Karl, and Martin Saller. *Elephants: A Natural and Cultural History.* Cologne: Könemann, 1998.

Grossberg, Lawrence. "Bringing It All Back Home: Pedagogy and Cultural Studies." In *Between Borders: Pedagogy and the Politics of Cultural Studies*, ed. Henry Giroux and Peter MacClaren, 1–25. New York: Routledge, 1994.

Guttenberg, Albert Z. *The Language of Planning: Essays on the Origins and Ends of American Planning Thought.* Foreword by Lewis Hopkins. Urbana: University of Illinois Press, 1993.

Harley, J. B. "Maps, Knowledge, and Power." In *The Iconography of Landscape: Essays on the Symbolic Representation, Design and Use of Past Environments*, ed. Denis Cosgrove and Stephen Daniels, 277–312. Cambridge: Cambridge University Press, 1988.

Harvey, David. "From Space to Place and Back Again: Reflections on the Condition of Postmodernity." In *Mapping the Futures: Local Cultures, Global Change*, ed. John Bird, Barry Curtis, Tim Putnam, George Robertson, and Lisa Tickner, 3–29. New York: Routledge, 1993.

Hayden, Dolores. *The Power of Place: Urban Landscapes as Public History.* Cambridge, Mass.: MIT Press, 1995.

Heath, Stephen. "Narrative Space." In *Narrative, Apparatus, Ideology: A Film Theory Reader*, ed. Philip Rosen, 379–420. New York: Columbia University Press, 1986.

Herbst, Jurgen. *And Sadly Teach: Teacher Education and Professionalization in American Culture*. Madison: University of Wisconsin Press, 1989.

"The History of the Tennessee Trash Ad." *Trash-Free Tennessee Sounds Good to Me*. <http://www.state.tn.us/trash/history.html> (accessed 19 December 2000).

hooks, bell. *Reel to Real: Race, Sex, and Class at the Movies*. New York: Routledge, 1996.

———. *Teaching to Transgress: Education as the Practice of Freedom*. New York: Routledge, 1994.

Hopkins, Jeff. "A Mapping of Cinematic Places: Icons, Ideology, and the Power of (Mis)representation." In *Place, Power, Situation and Spectacle: A Geography of Film*, ed. Stuart C. Aitken and Leo E. Zonn, 47–65. Lanham, Md.: Rowman and Littlefield, 1994.

Houk, Robert. "Campbell Resolution Withdrawn in State Senate." *Johnson City Press*, 19 March 1992, 1+.

———. "Resolution Seeks Campbell on List." *Johnson City Press*, 22 February 1998, 1+.

———. "Threat 'Baloney,' Whitson Says." *Johnson City Press*, 17 March 1992, 3.

Hsiung, David. *Two Worlds in the Tennessee Mountains: Exploring the Origins of Appalachian Stereotypes*. Lexington: University of Kentucky Press, 1997.

Imbrogno, Douglas. "The Who, What, Why, When and Where of Appalachia." *Charlestown Gazette-Mail*, 26 March 1995. E1+.

Jackson, John Brinckerhoff. *Discovering the Vernacular Landscape*. New Haven: Yale University Press, 1984.

Jameson, Frederic. *The Geopolitical Aesthetic: Cinema and Space in the World System*. Introd. Colin MacCabe. Bloomington: Indiana University Press, 1992.

Kirby, Jack Temple. *The Countercultural South*. Athens: University of Georgia Press, 1995.

LeCroy, Anne. Letter to the Editor. *Johnson City Press*, 26 April 1992. Courtesy of the University Archives, East Tennessee State University, Johnson City.

Lee, Tom. *The Tennessee-Virginia Tri-Cities: Urbanization in Appalachia, 1900–1950*. Knoxville: University of Tennessee Press, 2005.

Lewiecki-Wilson, Cynthia, and Jeff Sommers. "Professing at the Fault Lines: Composing at Open Admissions Institutions." *CCC* 50:3 (February 1999): 438–62.

Lewis, J. O. *Johnson City, Tennessee*. 1909. Rpt., Johnson City, Tenn.: Overmountain Press, 1989.

Limerick, Patricia Nelson. "Region and Reason." In *All Over the Place: Rethinking American Regions*, ed. Edward Ayers, Patricia Nelson Limerick, Stephen Nissinbaum, and Peter S. Onuf, 83–104. Baltimore: Johns Hopkins University Press, 1996.

Lippard, Lucy. *The Lure of the Local: Senses of Place in a Multicentered Society*. New York: New Press, 1997.

Lipsitz, George. *Time Passages: Collective Memory and American Popular Culture*. Minneapolis: University of Minnesota Press, 1990.

Logan, David G. Letter to the Editor. *Johnson City Press*, 21 February 1992. Courtesy of the University Archives, East Tennessee State University, Johnson City.

Lutz, Tom. "Cosmopolitan Vistas: Willa Cather, Hamlin Garland, and the Literary Value of Regionalism." In *To Recover a Continent*, ed. Robert Sayre, 86–106. Madison: University of Wisconsin Press, 1998.

MacDonald, Gerald. "Third Cinema and the Third World." In *Place, Power, Situation and Spectacle: A Geography of Film*, ed. Stuart C. Aitken and Leo E. Zonn, 27–45. Lanham, Md.: Rowman and Littlefield, 1994.

Works Cited

MacKaye, Benton. "An Appalachian Trail: A Project in Regional Planning." *Journal of the American Institute of Architects* 9 (October 1921): 325–30.

——. *The New Exploration: A Philosophy of Regional Planning.* 1928. Rpt., Urbana: University of Illinois Press, 1962.

Marx, Karl. "The Eighteenth Brumaire of Louis Bonaparte." 1852. Rpt. in *The Marx-Engels Reader*, 2nd ed., ed. Robert C. Tucker, 594–617. New York: Norton, 1978.

——. "Manifesto of the Communist Party." 1883. Rpt. in *The Marx-Engels Reader*, 2nd ed., ed. Robert C. Tucker, 469–500. New York: Norton, 1978.

"Massengill Monument." Pamphlet. N.p.: Massengill-DeFriece Foundation, n.d.

Matewan. Dir. John Sayles. Cinecom, 1986.

McAfee, Cindy. "Hanging of 'Big Mary' Maps Erwin." *Kingsport Times-News*, 14 August 1982, 1+.

McDonald, Michael, and John Muldowny. *TVA and the Dispossessed: The Resettlement of Population in the Norris Dam Area.* Knoxville: University of Tennessee Press, 1982.

McNair, James. "Mount Rumpke's Owners Squeezed for Space." *Cincinnati Enquirer*, 26 September 2002. <http://www.enquirer.com/editions/2002/09/26/loc_mount_rumpke_owners.html> (accessed 13 June 2003).

Medium Cool. Dir. Haskell Wexler. Paramount, 1969.

Melton, R. H. "N.Y. Mayor's Trash Talk Riles Virginia." *Washington Post*, 15 January 1999, A1+.

Miller, Susan. *Textual Carnivals: The Politics of Postmodernism.* Carbondale: Southern Illinois University Press, 1991.

Morgan, Arthur. *The Making of the TVA.* Buffalo: Prometheus, 1974.

Mortensen, Peter. "Going Public." *CCC* 50:2 (December 1998): 182–205.

——. "Representations of Literacy and Region: Narrating 'Another America.' " In *Pedagogy in the Age of Politics: Reading and Writing (in) the Academy*, ed. Patricia Sullivan and Donna Qualley, 100–120. Urbana, Ill.: NCTE, 1994.

Mumford, Lewis. "The Regional Framework of Civilization." *The Lewis Mumford Reader*, ed. David Miller, 207–16. New York: Pantheon, 1986.

" 'Murderous Mary' Focus of Show." *Johnson City Press*, 25 May 1993, 3.

Myers, Norma. "A Guide to the Bumpass Cove-Embreeville Collection." Courtesy of the Archives of Appalachia, East Tennessee State University, Johnson City.

Nell. Dir. Michael Apted. 20th Century Fox, 1994.

Nelson, Cary, Paula Treichler, and Lawrence Grossberg. "Cultural Studies: An Introduction." In *Cultural Studies*, ed. Lawrence Grossberg, Cary Nelson, and Paula Treichler, 1–16. New York: Routledge, 1992.

Nesmith, Jeff. "It's All Garbage, and a Few Majors Control It." *Dayton Daily News*, 4 April 1999, 13A.

O'Connor, Flannery. "A Good Man Is Hard to Find." In *The Complete Stories*, 117–33. New York: Noonday, 1971.

Ohmann, Richard. *Politics of Letters.* Middletown, Conn.: Wesleyan University Press, 1987.

Olson, Ted. "This Mighty River of Earth": Reclaiming James Still's Appalachian Masterpiece." *Journal of Appalachian Studies* 1:1 (Fall 1995): 87–98.

"Our Students." *East Tennessee State University*, 2001. <http://www.etsu.edu/sacs/pr/students.htm> (accessed 11 August 2003).

"Parks and Recreation." *Johnson City, TN.* <http://www.johnsoncitytn.org/ParksRecreation/?BISKIT=3789151226> (accessed 14 January 2006).

Parsons, Kermit. "Collaborative Genius: The Regional Planning Association of America." *Journal of the American Planning Association of America* 60:4 (Autumn 1994): 462–82.

Penrose, Jan, and Peter Jackson. "Conclusion: Identity and the Politics of Difference." In *Constructions of Race, Place, and Nation*, ed. Peter Jackson and Jan Penrose, 202–9. Minneapolis: University of Minnesota Press, 1994.

Pizer, Donald. *Dos Passos' U.S.A.: A Critical Study*. Charlottesville: University Press of Virginia, 1988.

——. *Twentieth-Century American Literary Naturalism: An Interpretation*. Carbondale: Southern Illinois University Press, 1982.

Potteiger, Matthew, and Jamie Purinton. *Landscape Narratives: Design Practices for Telling Stories*. New York: Wiley, 1998.

Powers, Gregg, and John Thompson. "Body Parts Found in Boone Lake." *Johnson City Press*, 13 October 2002. <http:// johnsoncitypress.com/printstory.asp?SectionID=DETAIL&ID=16100> (accessed 5 June 2003).

Pratt, Mary Louise. "Arts of the Contact Zone." *Profession 92* (1992). Rpt. in *Ways of Reading*, eds. Anthony Petrosky and David Bartholomae, 442–60. Boston: Bedford/St. Martin's Press, 1993.

Price, Charles Edwin. *The Day They Hung the Elephant*. Johnson City, Tenn.: Overmountain Press, 1992.

Pudup, Mary Beth, Dwight Billings, and Altina Waller, eds., *Appalachia in the Making: The Mountain South in the Nineteenth Century*. Chapel Hill: University of North Carolina Press, 1995.

Pulp Fiction. Dir. Quentin Tarantino. Miramax, 1994.

Rathje, William, and Cullen Murphy. *Rubbish! The Archeology of Garbage*. New York: Harper Collins, 1992.

Reichert Powell, Douglas. "Voices from the South: Mapping Appalachia." *Southern Exposure: A Journal of Politics and Culture* 24:3 (Fall 1996): 47–51.

——. "You Can't Get There from Here: An Appalachian Trail." *Historical Geography* 26 (1998): 129–50.

Reid, Herbert, and Betsy Taylor. "Appalachia as a Global Region: Toward Critical Regionalism and Civic Professionalism." *Journal of Appalachian Studies* 8:1 (Spring 2002): 9–32.

Relph, Edward. *Place and Placelessness*. London: Pion, 1976.

Ryan, Michael, and Douglas Kellner. *Camera Politica: The Politics and Ideology of Contemporary Hollywood Film*. Bloomington: Indiana University Press, 1988.

Said, Edward. *Culture and Imperialism*. New York: Knopf, 1993.

Salstrom, Paul. *Appalachia's Path to Dependency: Rethinking a Region's Economic History*. Lexington: University Press of Kentucky, 1994.

Sanders, Linda. "Bumpass Cove: One year Down, but More Fighting to Go." *Johnson City Press-Chronicle*, 27 July 1980, 3.

Saylor, Melissa. "Five Arrested after Probe at City Park." *Johnson City Press*, 18 May 2002, 1+.

——. "Residents Concerned about Buffalo Patrons." *Johnson City Press*, 12 May 2002, 1+.

Schroeder, Joan Vannorsdall. "The Day They Hanged Mary the Elephant." *Blue Ridge Country*, June 1997, 18–21.

Shapiro, Henry. *Appalachia on Our Minds*. Chapel Hill: University of North Carolina Press, 1978.

Simo, Melanie. *Forest and Garden: Traces of Wilderness in a Modernizing Land, 1897–1949*. Charlottesville: University of Virginia Press, 2003.

Smiley, Jane. *Moo*. New York: Alfred A. Knopf, 1995.

Spann, Edward. *Designing Modern America: The Regional Planning Association of America and Its Members*. Columbus: Ohio University Press, 1996.

Works Cited

"Sparks World-Famous Shows." Advertisement. *Johnson City Staff*, 12 September 1916, 4.

Spradlin, Alyssa. "Area Authorities Investigating Two Separate Homicides." *Johnson City Press*, 22 April 2002. <http://johnsoncitypress.com/default.asp?SectionID=DETAIL&ID=10402> (accessed 14 January 2006).

——. "Sheriff: Lake Death Looks 'Ritualistic.' " *Johnson City Press*, 14 October 2002. <http://johnsoncitypress.com/PrintStory.asp?SectionID=DETAIL&ID=16129> (accessed 5 June 2003).

Stahl, Ray. *Greater Johnson City: A Pictorial History*. 3rd ed. Norfolk, Va.: Donning, 1992.

Stanley, Tal. "Changing Places: Reading Justice from McDowell." *Journal of Appalachian Studies* 2:1 (Spring 96): 69–78.

Steinbeck, John. *The Grapes of Wrath*. 1939. Rpt., New York: Viking Penguin, 1976.

Stevens, Wallace. *The Collected Poems*. 1954. Rpt., New York: Vintage, 1990.

Still, James. *River of Earth*. 1940. Rpt., Lexington: University Press of Kentucky. 1978.

Sutter, Paul. " 'A Retreat from Profit': Colonization, the Appalachian Trail, and the Social Roots of Benton MacKaye's Wilderness Advocacy." *Environmental History* 4:4 (1999): 553–577.

"Tennessee Trash Lyrics." *Trash-Free Tennessee Sounds Good to Me*. <http://www.state.tn.us/trash/lyrics.htm> (accessed 19 December 2000).

Thompson, John. "The Case of the Bodies in the Lake." *Johnson City Press*, 20 October 2002. <http://johnsoncitypress.com/PrintStory.asp?SectionID=DETAIL&ID=16362> (accessed 5 June 2003).

Thompson, John, and Jim Wozniak. "Body Parts May belong to Georgia Pair." *Johnson City Press*, 16 October 2002. <http://johnsoncitypress.com/PrintStory.asp?SectionID=DETAIL&ID=16190 (accessed 5 June 2003).

Toth, Emily. "Ms. Mentor: What to Do When You've Been Exiled to the Provinces." *Chronicle of Higher Education Career Network*, 29 January 1999. <http://Chronicle.com/jobs/v45/i22/4522mentor.htm> (accessed 6 February 1999).

Trimbur, John. "Delivering the Message: Typography and the Materiality of Writing." In *Rhetoric and Composition as Intellectual Work*, ed. Gary Olson, 188–202. Carbondale: Southern Illinois University Press, 2002.

——. "Literacy and the Discourse of Crisis." In *The Politics of Writing Instruction: Postsecondary*, ed. Allan Bullock and John Trimbur, 277–96. Portsmouth, N.H.: Boynton/Cook, 1991.

Tullos, Allen. *Habits of Industry: White Culture and the Transformation of the Carolina Piedmont*. Chapel Hill: University of North Carolina Press, 1989.

Twin Peaks. Produced by Mark Frost and David Lynch. ABC. 1990–92.

Turner, Martha Billips. "A Vision of Change: Appalachia in James Still's River of Earth." *Southern Literary Journal* 24:2 (Spring 1992): 11–25.

Verghese, Abraham. *My Own Country: A Doctor's Story of a Town and Its People in the Age of AIDS*. New York: Simon and Schuster, 1994.

Watkins, Floyd. *In Time and Place: Some Origins of American Fiction*. Athens: University of Georgia Press, 1977.

Watson, James. "Architect Presents Master Plan for Winged Deer Park." *Johnson City Press*, 6 May 2001, 1+.

Watson, Sam. "Move to Overhaul Selection Process Tabled by Regents." *Johnson City Press*, 20 March 1992, 1+.

Weston, Alan. "Campbell Question Clouding ETSU Search." *Kingsport Times-News*, 5 March 1992, 1.

Wharton, Annabel. "Gender, Architecture, and Institutional Self-Presentation: The Case of Duke University." In *The Place of Thought in Writing*, ed. Van E. Hillard and JuliAnna Smith, 317–45. Needham Heights, Mass.: Simon and Schuster Custom Publishing, 1996.

Whisnant, David. *All That Is Native and Fine: The Politics of Culture in an American Region*. Chapel Hill: University of North Carolina Press, 1983.

———. *Modernizing the Mountaineer: People, Power and Planning in Appalachia*. Rev. ed. Knoxville: University of Tennessee Press, 1994.

Williams, Frank B., Jr. *A University's Story: 1911–1980*. Johnson City: East Tennessee State University Press, 1991.

Williams, John Alexander. *Appalachia: A History*. Chapel Hill: University of North Carolina Press, 2002.

Williams, Raymond. *The Country and the City*. New York: Oxford University Press, 1973.

———. *Keywords: A Vocabulary of Culture and Society*. Rev. ed. New York: Oxford University Press, 1983.

Williamson, J. W. *Hillbillyland: What the Movies Did to the Mountains and What the Mountains Did to the Movies*. Chapel Hill: University of North Carolina Press, 1995.

Wilson, Alexander. *The Culture of Nature: North American Landscape from Disney to the Exxon Valdese*. Cambridge, Mass.: Blackwell, 1992.

Wilson, Darlene. "The Felicitous Convergence of Mythmaking and Capital Accumulation: John Fox Jr. and the Formation of An(Other) Almost-White American Underclass." *Journal of Appalachian Studies* 1:1 (Fall 1995): 5–44.

Wilson, Roxy. Scrapbook. Bumpass Cove-Embreeville Collection (6:3). Archives of Appalachia, East Tennessee State University, Johnson City.

Wozniak, Jim. "Body Parts ID'd; Indictment to Be Sought." *Johnson City Press*, 18 October 2002. <http://johnsoncitypress.com/PrintStory.asp?SectionID=DETAIL&ID=16275> (accessed 5 June 2003).

———. "Emma Hawk Enters Not Guilty Plea." *Johnson City Press* 15 April 2003. <http://johnsoncitypress.com/PrintStory.asp?SectionID=DETAIL&ID=22108> (accessed 5 June 2003).

———. "Ex-wife of Willis Claims He Thinks She Can Clear Him." *Johnson City Press*, 5 March 2003. <http://johnsoncitypress.com/PrintStory.asp?SectionID=DETAIL &ID=21176> (accessed 5 June 2003).

———. "Iris Glen Still Has Friends, Foes." *Johnson City Press*, 26 November 1995, 1+.

———. "Keystone Votes Give Boost in Carter's Win." *Johnson City Press*, 29 April 1993, 1+.

———. "Pro-Status Quo Forces to Control Panel." *Johnson City Press*, 28 April 1993, 1+.

———. "Willis' Case Delayed Again in New York." *Johnson City Press*, 25 May 2003. <http://johnsoncitypress.com/PrintStory.asp?SectionID=DETAIL&ID=23449> (accessed 5 June 2003).

Wray, Matt, and Annalee Newitz, eds. *White Trash: Race and Class in America*. New York: Routledge, 1997.

Wrobel, David, and Michael Steiner, eds. *Many Wests: Place, Culture, and Regional Identity*. Lawrence: University Press of Kansas, 1997.

Index

Index

19, 34–35, 171; theoretical components of, 19–26, 36; history of, 21–22; and architecture, 21–22, 25, 26, 148; and planning, 22–24, 25, 26, 30–31, 58, 60, 148; cultural scholarship, function of, 25; overview of, 28–31; and pedagogy, 31, 93, 94, 98–99, 185–86, 195–96, 214–15; process of creation of text on, 36–39; and naming of new constructed space, 69–70; and "waste spaces," 83; and grass-roots activism, 98; and Willis murder case, 104, 121–23, 146; and films, 104–5, 144–46; and regional fiction, 152, 153–54, 171, 177–79; and representations of place, 171; and historical perspective on conflict, 177; as cultural critique and cultural production, 191–92. *See also* Dumps and dumping; Films; Parks; Universities and colleges; specific authors and novels

Cronenberg, David, 142

Crumley, Joe, 122

"Crying Indian" character, 81–82

The Culture of Nature (Wilson), 44

Cunningham, Rodger, 109

CUNY system, 200

Cuoto, Richard, 95

Cusack, Dick, 12

Cusack, Joan, 12

Cusack, John, 12

Dadetown, 142–43

Dainotto, Roberto, 13, 14, 106

Damascus, Va., 64

Darabont, Frank, 117

Davis, Janet, 16

Dayton, Ohio, 40

Dayton Daily News, 84

Deadrick, Bruce and Byrd, 231–33

Deadrick, Mary. *See* Edwards, Mary Ella

De Certeau, Michel, 22, 23, 24, 47, 55, 56, 58, 170

Decreation versus recreation, 70, 72, 75, 80–81

Deliverance: illiteracy in, 97; rape in, 105, 108, 109, 110, 111, 115, 123; allusions to, in popular culture, 105–6; landscape

narrative structure of, 106; visual vocabulary of, 106, 108–9; compared with *Apocalypse Now*, 106–8; hillbilly characters in, 108–10, 123; spoken language in, 109, 110; albinism in, 109, 114–15; compared with *Cape Fear*, 111, 112, 113, 114–15, 116; compared with *Fargo*, 132, 134; accent in, 143

Democracy, 25, 71

De Niro, Robert, 110

Dern, Laura, 101

Determinism, ideological, 42–43

Dollywood, 45, 46

Dos Passos, John: displacement and movement in *U.S.A.* by, 30, 155–63, 168–71, 174; national epics by, 150, 153, 154, 178; and labor unrest in Appalachia, 154–56; and Appalachia, 154–56, 172; family in *U.S.A.* by, 160, 161–62, 182; compared with Steinbeck, 166, 167, 168, 169, 171; completion of *U.S.A.* by, 172; compared with Still's *River of Earth*, 173, 176; theme of *U.S.A.* by, 176; critique of material relationships among different places in, 178; *U.S.A.* compared with Carson's *Stories I Ain't Told Nobody Yet*, 179, 180; *U.S.A.* compared with Smiley's *Moo*, 197

Dreiser, Theodore, 154

Drug use and drug trade, 77–78, 131

Duke, Benjamin Newton, 215, 221, 224

Duke, James Buchanan "Buck," 5–6, 221–22, 224

Duke, Washington, 220

Duke Endowment, 221

Duke Power, 221–22

Duke University: faculty of, 215; as research university, 215; wall surrounding, 215, 220; sexual assault charges against lacrosse team of, 215–16; students of, 215–16, 222–23, 237–40; aerial photograph of, 216; writing instruction at, 216–24, 237–40; and *Durham Stories*, 217–21, 237–40; Bubble metaphor for, 219, 220, 222, 223; landscape of, 219–21; establishment of, 221–22; divinity school of, 222;

Archives of, 222, 223; and Habitat for Humanity project, 222–23

Higher education. *See* Universities and colleges; specific institutions of higher learning

Highlander Center, 94–95

Hillbilly characters in films, 105–10, 111, 114, 123

Hindman Settlement School, 172

Historical Geography, 37

Historical theme parks, 44–45

HIV. *See* AIDS

Holmes, Marie, 123

Homeless people, 78

Homophobia, 52–55, 77, 110, 115

Homosexuality. *See* Gay men; Lesbians

hooks, bell, 119–20, 129, 177

Hopkins, Jeff, 120–21

Hopkins, Lewis, 25

Hopper, Dennis, 123

Hot Springs, N.C., 64

Howells, William Dean, 176

Hsiung, David, 79–80

Hudson (Bill) and Associates, 81

Hunter, Holly, 123

Hurricane Katrina, 3–4

Identity politics, 177

Ideological determinism, 42–43

Illiteracy, 105–10, 116, 117

I'll Take My Stand, 149

Imbrogno, Douglas, 37–38

India, 51

Indonesia, 44

Invisible Cities (Calvino), 33–34, 38, 45, 57, 65

Iris Glen Environmental Center (dump), 90–92, 96, 98

Jackson, Andrew, 87, 155

Jackson, John Brinckerhoff, 69, 140

Jackson, Peter, 122

Jackson, Samuel L., 127, 128

Jameson, Frederic, 140–42

Java, 51–52

Jefferson, Thomas, 87

Jenkins, Harry and Troy, 227

Johnson, Andrew, 87

Johnson City, Tenn.: maps of environs of, 2, 27, 39, 47, 50; and "Murderous

Mary" (circus elephant), 11, 15; Verghese's memoir on, 28, 51–55, 68; parks in, 29, 70–81; dumps and dumping in, 29, 82–83, 90–96, 98; and Carson's *Stories I Ain't Told Nobody Yet*, 30, 31, 147–48, 153–54, 179–85; as Powell's hometown, 40, 50, 68, 82, 87, 204, 210, 227–35; AIDS project in, 52, 53; gay bar in, 52–53; economic power in, 68; location of, 68; population of, 68; railroad in, 68, 78; downtown in, 68–69; and suburban sprawl of North Johnson City, 68–69, 71, 72, 78–79; Buffalo Mountain Park in, 70, 71–72, 75–81, 103; Winged Deer Park in, 71–75, 78, 79–81, 101, 103–4, 122, 123, 124, 130; log cabin in Winged Deer Park in, 72–73, 99; Massengill statue at Winged Deer Park in, 73–75; woodland turnouts near, 76–77, 80; and Bumpass Cove dump, 82–83, 92–96, 98; Citizens for Responsible Government (Carter Coalition) in, 91–92, 96; charter of, 96; weirdness in, 100–104; murders in, 101–4, 121–24, 130–31, 140, 146; Y-section of, 206; industry of, 206–7; roads in, 206–7; Scholar Holler/Seminole Woods in, 210, 228–35; Forest Hills in, 228–29; churches in, 234. *See also* East Tennessee State University

Johnson City Press, 12, 78, 90, 91

Johnson City Press Chronicle, 11

Johnson City Staff, 10, 11, 16

Jones, John A., 201

Journal of the American Institute of Architects, 58

Kampuchea, 44, 45

Kane, Irving, 81

Katrina, Hurricane, 3–4

Keep America Beautiful campaign, 81–82

Keitel, Harvey, 127

Kellner, Douglas, 115, 126

Kentuckians for the Commonwealth, 142

Kinch, C. B., 201

Kingsport Times-News, 11

Kirby, Jack Temple, 76

Media: on place forms, 29–30; on
Appalachia, 30; as social invention,
119–20, 125, 137, 143; and pedagogy of
place, 119–21, 130–31. *See also* Films
Medium Cool, 117–19
Mental bureacratism, 192–93
Miami University (Ohio), 8, 13, 14, 15
Midwest, 137–38, 143, 196–200
Miller, Henry, 111
Miller, Susan, 213–14
Mining. *See* Coal mining
Mitchum, Robert, 111
Modernism, 19
Moo (Smiley), 196–200
Morgan, Arthur, 48–49, 149
Morgan, Harcourt, 49
Morgan, J. P., 158
Morrissey, Kathleen, 6
Mortensen, Peter, 108, 193–95
Mount Rumpke, Ohio, 84
Movies. *See* Films; specific movies
Muldowny, John, 49
Mumford, Lewis, 23–24, 31, 58, 69, 99,
149, 150, 166
"Murderous Mary" (circus elephant),
hanging of, 8–18, 20, 21, 100
Murders: hanging of circus elephant
(Mary), 8–18, 12, 20, 21, 100; in
Johnson City, Tenn., 101–4, 121–24,
130–31, 140, 146; in films, 122–45
Museum: region as, 40, 41–45, 50; and
nationalism, 43; and colonialism, 43–
44, 46; as objectification of cultural
practice, 46; compared with maps, 50
My Own Country (Verghese), 28, 51–55,
68

Nance, Jack, 102
National Committee for the Defense of
Political Prisoners, 154–55
National Enquirer, 12
Nationalism, 43
National Parks Service, 62
Native Americans, 156, 157, 210
Native-as-innocent, 117
Native-as-savage, 117
Natural Born Killers, 123
Nell, 117, 132, 143

Nesmith, Jeff, 84
New Deal, 48–49
The New Exploration (MacKaye), 70
New Orleans, La., 3–4
New Regionalism, 46
New Republic, 155
New York City: 9/11 attack on, 3–4; gar-
bage from, dumped in Virginia, 85–
89, 96; in Dos Passos's *U.S.A.*, 169
9/11 attack, 3–4
Noble Savage image, 81–82
Nolte, Nick, 110
Normal schools, 208–9, 227. *See also*
Universities and colleges
North Carolina Central University, 215
Novels. *See* specific authors and titles

Ohio: migration from Appalachia to, 40,
156, 162; dumps and dumping in, 84
Ohmann, Richard, 209
Olmsted, Frederick Law, Sr., 70, 77
Olmsted Brothers, 215
Ontkean, Michael, 102
Otherness: of regionalism, 13, 14; of Ver-
ghese, 52; of exurban spaces, 105; and
cannibalism, 114; of albinism, 114–15

Padgett, Hilda, 14
Pakula, Alan, 142
Panhandlers, 217–18
The Parallax View, 142
Park, Steve, 133–34
Parks: in Johnson City, Tenn., 29; Great
Smoky Mountains National Park, 44;
historical theme parks, 44–45;
National Parks Service, 62; as recreational facilities, 67–68, 70, 72; Buffalo
Mountain Park (Johnson City, Tenn.),
70, 71–72, 75–81, 103; Olmsted on, 70,
77; as civic spaces, 70–71; Winged
Deer Park (Johnson City, Tenn.), 71–
75, 78, 79–81, 101, 103–4, 122, 123, 124,
130; log cabin in Winged Deer Park,
72–73, 99; Massengill statue at
Winged Deer Park, 73–75; woodland
turnouts as outlaw parks, 76–77, 80;
rules of, 77; illegal drug and alcohol
use in, 77–78; sexual behavior in, 77–

78; homeless people in, 78; police surveillance in, 78
Pastoral genre, 138
PCBs, 93
Pedagogy: critical regionalist pedagogy,
31, 93, 94, 98–99, 185–86, 195–96, 214–
15, 216–25; media's pedagogy of place,
119–21, 130–31; banking-model pedagogy, 124–25, 141, 145; problem-posing
approach to, 125, 141; Carson and literary pedagogy, 185; writing instruction
in universities and colleges, 189, 192,
195, 211–12, 213, 216–25; Freire on
mental bureacratism, 192–93; Freire
on space in education, 192–93, 200;
Freire on universities, 193, 214; and
part-time and non-tenure-track faculty, 211–12; community service or
service learning component of university courses, 222–23. *See also* Universities and colleges
Penates and Lares, 33–34, 38, 45, 65
Penrose, Jan, 122
Pentecostalism, 112–13
Phillips, Fred, 104
Piedmont Carolinas region, 5–6
Piper, Ruth, 14
Pizer, Donald, 155–56
Place: sense of, 14–15, 18–19, 34–35, 171;
betweenness of, 34; Entrikin on, 34;
and writers' creation of landscape,
34–36; as map, 40–42, 45–50; as ideas
about spaces constructed by people,
67; media's pedagogy of, 119–21, 130–
31; crisis and process of construction
of, 122; and visual arts, 152–53; and
displacement and movement in Dos
Passos's *U.S.A.*, 155–63, 168–69, 174;
and displacement and movement in
Steinbeck's *Grapes of Wrath*, 162–70,
174; and placelessness, 168; and critical
regionalism, 171; as multivocal, 177; in
Carson's *Stories I Ain't Told Nobody
Yet*, 183; and universities and colleges,
185, 187–92, 194–96; and colleges in
provincial places, 187–90, 196–200;
disconnection between academics
and, 190–91, 200, 201–4; and Freire on

space in education, 192–93, 200. *See
also* Landscape; Maps; Region
Planning. *See* Regional planning
Police, 78, 104
Pollard, Hoyt, 109
Polychlorinated biphenyls (PCBs), 93
Popper, Deborah, 6
Popper, Frank, 6
Populism, 208
Potteiger, Matthew, 89
Powers, Gregg, 101
The Practice of Everyday Life (de Cer-
teau), 22
Presnell, Harve, 135
Price, Charles Edwin, 16
Progressive Era, 30–31
Provincialism: and regionalism, 19–20;
and colleges in provincial places, 187–
90, 196–200
Public parks. *See* Parks
Public spaces, 70–71, 80–81, 151. *See also*
Parks
Pulp Fiction: and Willis murder case, 30,
105, 122, 123–24, 130–32; challenge of
violence in, 125; plot of, 125–30; com-
pared with *Fargo*, 134, 135, 136, 137, 138,
139, 141, 145
Purinton, Jamie, 89
Psycho, 123

Race: and hanging of "Murderous
Mary" (circus elephant), 18; in films,
114–15, 117, 129; white-supremacist
theories of, 151
Railroads: in Erwin, Tenn., 15–16; and
circus, 16; in Johnson City, Tenn., 68,
78; and company towns, 92
Raising Arizona, 123
Ransom, John Crowe, 149
Rape, 105, 108, 109, 110, 111, 115, 123, 215
Rathje, William, 84
Recreation versus decreation, 70, 72, 75,
80–81
Recycling, 91. *See also* Environmentalism
Redford, Robert, 117
Reevis, Steven, 137
Region: meaning of, 5–6; as description
of relationships and interactions, 10,

classifications of, 211, 212; prestige of faculty doing teaching versus research in, 211, 213; part-time and non-tenure-track faculty in, 211–12; community service or service learning component of courses of, 222–23. *See also* specific universities and colleges

University of Iowa, 89

University of Tennessee, 49

University of Virginia, 149

U.S.A. (Dos Passos): displacement and movement in, 30, 155–63, 168–71, 174; as national epic, 153, 154, 178; Appalachia in, 154, 155–56, 172; family in, 160, 161–62, 182; gender in, 161; compared with Steinbeck's *Grapes of Wrath*, 166, 167, 168, 169, 171; New York City in, 169; completion of, 172; compared with Still's *River of Earth*, 173, 176; theme of, 176; compared with Carson's *Stories I Ain't Told Nobody Yet*, 179, 180

Valley of the Tennessee, 48, 150

Vanderbilt University, 94, 98

Veblen, Thorstein, 158

Verghese, Abraham, 28, 51–55, 68, 89

Videodrome, 142

Violence. *See* Crimes; Murders; Rape

Virginia: dumps and dumping in, 85–89, 96; compared with Tennessee, 87; presidents and Founding Fathers from, 87

Visual arts, 152–53, 179, 184

Voight, Jon, 110

"Voyeur-god," 22, 47, 170

Walking rhetorics, 22, 24, 56, 58

Walls, Linda, 94

Walsh, Raoul, 123

Walters State Community College (Tenn.), 200

Washington, George, 87

Washington Post, 86

Waste industry. *See* Dumps and dumping

Waste Management Incorporated, 86, 90–91, 94

Waste Resources, 82, 92–93

Watkins, Floyd, 151

West (U.S.), 46, 136–37, 157, 169

West Durham, N.C., 215, 224

Western North Carolina Alliance, 142

Wexler, Haskell, 117, 118, 124

Whigs, 208

Whisnant, David, 22–23, 48, 49, 172

White Heat, 123

White-supremacist race theories, 151

"White trash" as label, 90, 91, 93

Whitman, Walt, 167

Whitson, Zane, 201

Williams, Frank, 227

Williams, John Alexander, 6, 44, 48, 51, 52

Williams, Raymond, 19, 21, 51, 138

Willis, Bruce, 126

Willis, Debra, 131

Willis, Howard Hawk, 102–4, 121–23, 130–31, 136, 137, 140, 146

Willis, Wilda, 123, 131

Wilson, Alexander, 44, 45, 71, 137

Wilson, Darlene, 151

Wilson, Roxy, 93, 94

Winged Deer Park (Johnson City, Tenn.): naming of, 71; compared with Buffalo Mountain Park, 71–72, 78, 79–81; log cabin in, 72–73, 99; Massengill statue at, 73–75; and Willis murder case, 101, 103–4, 122, 123, 124, 130

Witt, Allen, 208

Women. *See* Gender

Women's suffrage, 17

Wray, Matt, 112

"The Wrecking Yard" (Benedict), 87–89

Wright, Frank Lloyd, 166–67

Writing instruction, 189, 192, 195, 211–12, 213, 216–25. *See also* Pedagogy

Wrobel, David, 46

Wycherly, Margaret, 123

Young, Robert, Sr., 73, 75, 76